Toward Humanity and Justice

Dr. Kenneth Bancroft Clark, autographed: "To Woody, who still hopes. Kenneth Clark."
Courtesy of Kenneth B. Clark Archives.

Toward Humanity and Justice

The Writings of Kenneth B. Clark
Scholar of the 1954
Brown v. Board of Education Decision

Edited by Woody Klein

Foreword by John Hope Franklin

Westport, Connecticut
London

Library of Congress Cataloging-in-Publication Data

Clark, Kenneth Bancroft, 1914–
    Toward humanity and justice : the writings of Kenneth B. Clark, scholar of the Brown
  v. Board of Eduction decision / edited by Woody Klein ; foreword by John Hope Franklin.
    p. cm.
    Includes bibliographical references and index.
    ISBN 0-275-97509-6 (alk. paper)
    1. African Americans—Civil rights—History—20th century. 2. African Americans—
Social conditions—20th century. 3. African Americans—Legal status, laws, etc.—
History—20th century. 4. United States—Race relations.—5. Racism—United States—
History—20th century. 6. United States—Social conditions—1945– 7. Social sciences—
United States—History—20th century. I. Klein, Woody, 1929– II. Title.
E185.61.C623   2004
305.896'073—dc22   2003053672

British Library Cataloguing in Publication Data is available.

Library of Congress Catalog Card Number: 2003053672
ISBN: 0–275–97509–6 (alk. paper)

First published in 2004

Praeger Publishers, 88 Post Road West, Westport, CT 06881
An imprint of Greenwood Publishing Group, Inc.
www.praeger.com

Printed in the United States of America

The paper used in this book complies with the
Permanent Paper Standard issued by the National
Information Standards Organization (Z39.48–1984).

10 9 8 7 6 5 4 3 2 1

Herbert Hill and James E. Jones, Jr., *Race in America.* © 1993. Reprinted by permission of The University of Wisconsin Press.

Kenneth B. Clark, "Morale of the Negro on the Home Front: World Wars I and II," *The Journal of Negro Education* 12.3 (1943): 424–428. Reprinted by permission.

Kenneth B. Clark, "Desegregation: An Appraisal of the Evidence," *Journal of Social Issues* 9 (1953): 1–77. Reprinted by permission.

Edmond Cahn, "1955 *Annual Survey of American Law*: Part Five—'Legal Philosophy and Reform,' " *New York University Law Review* 30 (January 1955): 655–668. Reprinted by permission.

Edmond Cahn, "Jurisprudence," *New York University Law Review* 30 (January 1955): 150–169. Reprinted by permission.

Kenneth B. Clark, "The Desegregation Cases: Criticism of the Social Scientist's Role," *Villanova Law Review* 5.2 (Winter 1959–1960): 224–240. Reprinted by permission.

Eleanor Holmes Norton, "Perspective on Kenneth B. Clark," interview, June 4, 2002. Reprinted by permission.

Author interview with Charles B. Rangel. Reprinted by permission.

Extracts from a letter by Hugh B. Price, June 6, 2002. Reprinted by permission.

Extracts from a letter by Kweisi Mfume, July 1, 2002. Reprinted by permission.

Extracts from a letter by Clifford L. Alexander, Jr., June 26, 2002. Reprinted by permission.

Herbert Hill, "Kenneth Clark on White Unions and Black Workers." Reprinted by permission.

Franklin A. Thomas, comments to the author, July 3, 2002. Reprinted by permission.

Hilton B. Clark, "Afterword: An Academician and an Activist." Reprinted by permission.

Kenneth B. Clark, extracts: numerous written materials including unpublished addresses, white papers, letters, notes, personal observations, Metropolitan Applied Research Center (MARC) reports, transcripts from interviews, and memorandums. Reprinted by permission.

I believe that to be taken seriously, to be viable, and to be relevant, social science must dare to study the real problems of men and society, must use the real community, the market place, the arena of politics and power as its laboratories, and must confront and seek to understand the dynamics of social action and social change. The appropriate technology of serious and relevant social science would have as its prime goal helping society move *toward humanity and justice* with minimum irrationality, instability, and cruelty.

—Dr. Kenneth B. Clark, *Dark Ghetto*, 1965

To my friend, Kenneth Bancroft Clark,
who has inspired me all of my adult life.

Contents

Foreword: "The Last Integrationist"

I first met Kenneth Bancroft Clark more than forty years ago at Howard University, and we became friends almost immediately. My first impression of him was that he was quiet. When we began to work on the *Brown v. Board of Education* case, I found him to be *quite an individual*. He wrote beautifully, he spoke well, and he had a deep and abiding commitment to equality and justice. He was profoundly committed to the cause of integration. At the time, I worked in my own bailiwick with other historians on that case. In the early summer and fall of 1953, I went to New York every weekend to work on that case, and I frequently saw him there.

Historically, Ken's role in *Brown v. Board of Education* was very important. In fact, it turned out to be spectacular. He was quoted by the Court in its decision about the psychological studies he made of children in southern schools involving dolls, showing that segregated black children in public schools had an inferior self-image of themselves compared to white children. Scholars have cited that study as the key to the Court's finding that "separate but equal" was unconstitutional, and it earned Kenneth Clark a special place in history.

We had a lot in common. For one thing, there was Howard University. We also had ideals and convictions that we shared. The *New York Times* once referred to him as "The Last Integrationist." I resented that because I regard myself as the last integrationist! In all seriousness, however, we both believed that our society had to move forward, and the only way it could do so was through integration in all walks of life. We differed in one concept: He thought black colleges were dispensable, and I did not. I took the view that they play an important role in educating America about its own past. They set a standard for blacks and whites alike. But Kenneth was vehemently opposed to the concept of black separatism in any form, even on a temporary basis.

One of the things I most admired about Kenneth Clark was that he did not compromise his own fundamental values. He would always hold fast to his position. He was uncompromising in his beliefs—declaratory and absolutely no-nonsense. He was firm and unequivocal. Yet, at the same time, in his quiet, low-key way he would make his case, point by point, in a logical, rational manner that was often listened to beneath the din of other dissenters.

Through his public platforms and his writings, he helped transform the fight for equality and racial justice into a meaningful movement. He put his beliefs and writings as an intellectual into practical applications. The antipoverty agency Harlem Youth Opportunities Unlimited (HARYOU) is but one example. He played multiple roles in our society. An example was the founding in 1976 of his consulting firm, the Metropolitan Applied Research Center (MARC), which advised some of the Fortune 500 companies on equal employment practices. His programs had substance and were carried out in terms that everyone could understand. He was vigorous. While slight in build, he was a giant as a catalyst for change. I think the movement went forward in part because of his contributions. He had many contacts with both black and white leaders, all across the spectrum. He was respected by all.

My friend Kenneth was not the same after his beloved wife, Mamie Phipps Clark, who was also a psychologist, died in August 1983. He called me within an hour after her passing. The light kind of went out. He no longer had the enthusiasm he once had. But I never gave up on him, and I still talk to him on the telephone and occasionally visit with him at his home in Hastings-on-Hudson, New York. He has a great sense of humor and was a wonderful family man. My late wife and I saw him and Mamie regularly. We spent so many nights together talking. Those were delicious moments.

I believe the nation has made much progress in the past half century, and Kenneth Clark's contributions helped enormously. I don't compare him with anybody else in the civil rights movement. He is in a class by himself. He stands way up at the top. He was an important influence in my life, and I shall always be grateful for his friendship. He was a caring and compassionate man who understood those who differed with him and tried, through painstaking argument, intelligent conversation, and subtle persuasion, to win them over. He never lost hope, even when the movement was faced with some of its most difficult challenges in the 1960s. He remained steadfast and calm in the heat of the battle. Others came to seek his advice, and he had direct and honest exchanges with powerful public men like Robert F. Kennedy, along with friends like Sidney Poitier and James Baldwin, in his study in Hastings-on-Hudson, New York. Through sheer determination he tried to bridge the gap between whites and blacks during the most difficult and tense hours of civil rights marches in the South during the Kennedy and Johnson administrations. He talked with a variety of civil rights leaders during one crisis after another. He was prescient. As a psychologist, he was a scholar of human behavior and thus understood why individuals and groups acted the way they did.

Kenneth Clark was one of the four or five most influential people in my life. We are very good friends, and I happily accepted the privilege of introducing the highlights of his life's work in this important and incisive volume. I think it is vital that his writings are published for future generations. His words helped illuminate many critical issues and led to changes of major importance in the movement toward integration. His views need to be saved and remembered forever. They are his legacy. I hope that all people, black and white of all ages, for years to come will read his words that have stood the test of time. The wisdom contained herein is worth preserving through the ages.

John Hope Franklin
Duke University
Durham, North Carolina

Preface

Kenneth B. Clark has had a profound influence on my life for the past forty years. We first met in 1964 when he called me from his office in New York City at Harlem Youth Opportunities Unlimited (HARYOU), a federally supported antipoverty program, and asked to meet with me. At the time, I was covering the civil rights movement as a reporter on the *New York World-Telegram & Sun.* He told me he had been reading my articles and said he had a "good story" for me. I went to his office the next day and was greeted by a gentle, slightly built man with an inviting smile. He spoke quietly. However, it was not how he talked but what he said that lit a fire under me. He told me he wanted to publicly accuse Democratic Congressman Adam Clayton Powell, one of the most powerful members of Congress, of attempting to take over the $110 million federally sponsored antipoverty program in Harlem and use it as "pork" for his political cronies. Dr. Clark said Congressman Powell had sent "emissaries" from his office that threatened to block funds earmarked for the HARYOU project unless the congressman was allowed to name its executive director. As the project's creator and author, Dr. Clark was acting chairman of the board.

I was immediately taken with the idea of this academic intellectual challenging the integrity and political motives of a nationally known—and controversial—Congressman, but I also knew that Dr. Clark would be up against the entrenched Democratic Party, which then included New York Senator Robert F. Kennedy all the way up to President Lyndon B. Johnson. I mentioned this. He just smiled and said he had to speak because it was the right thing to do. After the story broke in my paper, it was reported as page-one news the next day in the *New York Times.*[1]

Before meeting Dr. Clark, I had spent a decade as an investigative reporter covering the slums of New York writing about people—mostly blacks and Puerto Ricans—trapped in appalling poverty in decaying buildings owned by absentee slumlords. I admired Dr. Clark for honestly believing that HARYOU could make a difference. As the weeks and months passed, however, it became clear that Adam Powell would prevail, so Dr. Clark eventually resigned from his post a few months later. That did not deter him in the slightest, however, from continuing to write and speak out.

In perspective, the breadth and depth of Dr. Clark's commitment to social justice are reflected in the compilation of his most significant writings and statements on the following pages. His observations, covering the period from 1939 to 1993, are extracted from his books, pamphlets, debates, formal addresses, interviews, Op Ed pieces, transcripts of radio and television interviews, oral histories, round table discussions, conversations, testimonies, and book reviews. His writings are followed at the end of each chapter by personal commentary from people in all walks of life who valued his contributions.

In researching his body of work during the past three years, I found many references to the U.S. Supreme Court's landmark 1954 *Brown v. Board of Education* decision, which catapulted him into the national spotlight. Dr. Clark had no idea at the time of how widely acclaimed his psychological studies of the damage to segregated black schoolchildren in the South— one of the key social science documents admitted by the Court—would become. His studies entailed the use of black and white dolls with black schoolchildren to discover the extent to which they had a negative perception of themselves as a result of being segregated from white children. Dr. Clark would eventually come to describe his role in *Brown* as "a high point in my career."[2] Indeed, he eventually became known in academic circles variously as "the scholar of the civil rights movement," "the doll man," and "the scholar of *Brown v. Board of Education*." There were a few critics—from the worlds of academia and politics—who challenged the validity of social science data as "evidence"—but despite that criticism, Dr. Clark's findings have been cited by other scholars and national leaders in every field for the past half century as the key building block on which the Court based its decision on *Brown*.

In the three years leading up to *Brown v. Board of Education*, Dr. Clark was asked by the National Association for the Advancement of Colored People (NAACP) to serve as its consultant to recruit other social scientists as expert witnesses in the appellate courts to buttress the case against segregation. He worked with a team of NAACP lawyers, headed by Thurgood Marshall, who would be named in 1967 by President Lyndon B. Johnson as the first black on the U.S. Supreme Court. Dr. Clark was responsible for summarizing the relevant psychological research up to that time and writing a report, "Appellant's Briefs—The Effects of Segregation and the Consequences of Desegregation: A Social Science Statement," signed by thirty-five social scientists and psychologists in 1952.

In 1953, Dr. Clark wrote another monograph article evaluating this "Social Science Statement." He later characterized this evaluation as "one of the major monographs that very few people know about but I consider one of the most important things that I wrote."[3] His best-known paper, which he wrote in 1950 and was entered into evidence, titled "The Effects of Prejudice and Discrimination on Personality Development," was cited in Footnote 11 by U.S. Supreme Court Chief Justice Earl Warren. This was the first time that psychological and sociological references were accepted by the Court, thus establishing social science data as a legitimate authority by the Court. Robert L. Carter, the NAACP attorney who argued the case together with Thurgood Marshall, summed up Dr. Clark's contribution in winning the case this way:

The Supreme Court explicitly relied on the views of these social scientists in its ruling. Kenneth Clark's help was thus critical to our success. . . . I have never wavered in the belief that the social science data supplied the essential ingredient needed for success in *Brown*. Without Kenneth's help that ingredient would never have been presented to the Supreme Court.[4]

Dr. Clark's 1950 study, in fact, contained words and concepts that Chief Justice Warren paraphrased in the most quoted section of *Brown*.[5] Kenneth Clark's rapid rise to prominence as an academic and activist—a seeming oxymoron—did not occur until his first book, *Prejudice and Your Child*, was published in 1955. In 1964, Dr. Clark produced a memorable 644-page report called *Youth in the Ghetto: A Study of the Consequences of Powerlessness and a Blueprint for Change*.[6] One year later, his widely acclaimed book *Dark Ghetto*, based on his lengthy 1964 study, became a prime textbook bluntly telling racial reality and elaborating the grotesqueness and pathology of America's worst dark ghetto—Harlem.

His rise to fame did not go to his head. Quite the contrary. The more he wrote and spoke, the more he realized that he was only on the periphery of the civil rights movement. He once stated:

In times of social crisis when effective action is demanded, it is easy to make speeches, write articles and advise others on what they should do. It is more difficult to translate ideas into a program of constructive action. It requires little personal courage to tell others that they should have courage. It is no dramatic act of bravery to tell others that they must insist upon their rights as citizens all the more when these rights are being threatened by those who would use violence. It takes no profound insight to recognize that the present chaotic pattern of race relations in certain regions of America demands a systematic program of human and democratic affirmation.[7]

On the thirtieth anniversary of *Brown*, Dr. Clark put the Court's finding in perspective when he wrote:

This was a momentous, historic decision, ranking, I believe, with such major democratic documents as the Magna Carta, the Bill of Rights, the Declaration of Independence, and, in its own most significant way, the Emancipation Proclamation. This document was a major statement of the importance of the significance of democracy, and it was a major statement of the way in which a society affects the most important aspects of being human, namely self-esteem of human beings.[8]

His work on *Brown* greatly enhanced his reputation, and as recently as 1989, one study referred to Dr. Clark as the "reigning academic" of the civil rights movement.[9] Moreover, Kenneth Clark became more than a social scientist acclaimed by academics and their students; he was called upon by national figures, including civil rights leaders and top government officials.

As important as his professional accomplishments were, however, those of us who were privileged to know and work with him knew there was one higher priority in his life—namely, Mamie Phipps Clark. As his wife, friend, colleague, and partner in professional life, she knew him better than anyone. She once said of him:

His first love is teaching. It always has been. He has given a great deal to his students, not only by teaching them how to think but also by impressing on them the possibilities of using their education to affect the society they live in. And, of course, his impact as a teacher has reached far beyond those who have actually been in a classroom with him. Most well known black people are not in the academic field—they're in the theatre or in sports or, increasingly, in politics—and so the renown and the great amount of respect Kenneth has achieved have been of a rather rare kind. And I think by achieving them he has given psychic sustenance to many blacks, whether or not they themselves have gone into teaching on the college level.[10]

After spending forty-five years working alongside her husband, Mamie Clark died in 1983 at the age of sixty-six. A year later, Dr. Clark paid tribute to her at the thirtieth anniversary dinner of the *Brown* decision:

I'd like to dedicate this sharing of ideas to my late wife, Dr. Mamie Phipps Clark, who was my collaborator, my supporter, and I've said more frequently since she left me what was a fact, namely that the research which was cited by the Supreme Court was initially her idea. I stole it from her while she was pregnant. And if that be sexism, so be it.[11]

Kenneth and Mamie Clark were arguably the most respected husband-and-wife team in the intellectual community, white or black. Her death profoundly affected him. His friends could clearly see that he was never the same again.

Kenneth Clark was arguably the best informed and most articulate observer of the civil rights struggle in the second half of the twentieth century, beginning in the 1950s and picking up momentum in the 1960s as the movement accelerated. He gained a rare perspective through his writings and his actions and was asked for his opinions by many foundations, organizations, government agencies, commissions, and of course, journalists. One civil rights historian stated in 1995: "In this new discourse, Clark—immigrant New Yorker and African-American social scientist—became a new Myrdal, an interpreter of the ghetto to the nation's conscience."[12] Gunnar Myrdal, once Clark's mentor, had written the introduction to *Dark Ghetto*. Clark was, indeed, seen as a national resource on race relations. He became known in some circles as "the icon of integration."[13] When "The 1968 Report of the National Advisory Commission on Civil Disorders"[14] was released—and it included Dr. Clark's testimony—its prime conclusion was stated: "This is our basic conclusion: Our nation is moving toward two societies, one black, one white—separate and unequal."[15]

It is clear from statements Dr. Clark made in his later years that he felt he did not accomplish what he set out to do. In 1993, at the age of seventy-nine, ailing and embittered, in one of his last public statements, he wrote,

My beloved wife is dead and my career is nearing an end. Reluctantly, I am forced to face the likely possibility that the United States will never rid itself of racism and reach true integration. I look back and I shudder at how naive we all were in our belief in the steady progress racial minorities would make through programs of litigation and education, and while I very much hope for the emergence of a revived civil rights movement with innovative programs and dedicated leaders, I am forced to recognize that my life has, in fact, been a series of glorious defeats.[16]

Despite this harsh self-appraisal, race relations remain at the heart of America's social conscience. In 1997, President Bill Clinton appointed a commission called "The President's Initiative on Race," chaired by Dr. John Hope Franklin. In 1998, this commission released its findings in a document titled *One America in the 21st Century: Forging a New Future*, which concluded: "The country still has much work to do if we are to become 'One America' respecting, even celebrating our differences. But embracing even more what we have in common."[17]

In 2003, yet another prestigious report on civil rights magnified its continuing importance on the national stage. Dr. Gary Orfield, Professor of Education and Social Policy at Harvard University and the John F. Kennedy School of Government, and founding codirector of The Civil Rights Project, released a report that said, in part,

The nation's civil rights goals have not been accomplished. The country has been going backward toward greater segregation in all parts of the country for more than a decade. Since the end of the Civil Rights era, there has been no significant leadership towards the goal of creating a successfully integrated society built on integrated schools and neighborhoods.[18]

I believe that Kenneth Clark's legacy as the scholar of the civil rights movement is assured. It is my hope and expectation that, for generations to come, his name will be revered by historians, scholars, writers, journalists—indeed, anyone who cares about race relations in America. He will, I hope, be seen in time as one of the giants in the field, and his works will be read in every college classroom in America and beyond. Nonetheless, I wish to make it clear to the reader that in the course of my research I found and specifically included—in the interests of objectivity—criticism of Dr. Clark's work by both academic and legal scholars, as well as Dr. Clark's replies.

Kenneth Clark once revealed a special insight into himself when he was approaching his sixtieth birthday (July 24, 1974) that still holds true today: "If I were my own most severe critic," he wrote,

the point I would make against Kenneth Clark is that he really is uncompromising in his belief that human beings should not be characterized on the basis of arbitrary things such as skin color and treated differently. Any form of differential treatment of human beings on arbitrary grounds is unacceptable to his concept of basic humanity and the requirement of dignity. Now, that is a far out position, but that is the position which I'll keep until I go to my grave.[19]

I am deeply indebted to a great many people for their help in the researching, editing, and publishing of this volume. I thank Hilton B. Clark for making Dr. Kenneth B. Clark's archives available to me. I owe a debt of gratitude to Russia Hughes, a longtime colleague of Dr. Clark's, for providing a detailed bibliography of Dr. Clark's works; to Thelma Shiboski, for her research and copy editing, and evaluating the original manuscript; to Marta Campbell, head of Collection Management at the Westport Public Library, for her untiring efforts to successfully locate valuable books and periodicals and for her personal commitment to this project; to Rachel Rice, Westport Inter-Library Loan Department, for her perseverance in obtaining books, documents, and periodicals from all parts of the country; and to Maxine Bleiweis, Westport Librarian, for permitting her reference librarians—Carole Braunschweig, Kathy Breidenbach, Debbie Celia, Beth Dominianni, Margie Freilich-Den, Janie Rhein, and Sylvia Schulman—to respond to my requests for information on a timely basis. In addition, I wish to thank Miggs Burroughs, a nationally known artist and designer, for his attractive book jacket.

Also, my gratitude to my Greenwood Publishing Group acquisition editors, Jim Sabin and Jim Lance; to Susan Baker, director, Westchester Book Services, for overseeing the production of this project; to Production Editor John Donohue, of Westchester Book Services, for his thorough professionalism and commitment to excellence; to Susan Badger, copy editor, for her extraordinary attention to detail; and to my Greenwood Publishing Group Senior Project Manager Emma Bailey, and to Greenwood professionals Margaret Mayberry, Leanne Small, Michelle Pini, and Carol Franson-Serra, for their ongoing support; to Albert Charles Lasher, my longtime friend and classmate at Columbia University's Graduate School of Journalism, for his sound advice in the research process; to the staffs of the Schomburg Center for Research in Black Culture, New York Public Library in Harlem; to the Manuscript Division, Library of Congress, in Washington, D.C.; to the Oral History Research Office in the Nicholas Murray Butler Library at Columbia University; to The Kenneth B. Clark Center at the University of Illinois–Chicago (UIC) campus, a research institution in UIC's Criminal Justice Department; and to each of the distinguished contributors cited in this book.

On a personal note, I wish to thank my late father, Albert M. Klein, for teaching me by example to reach out to people of all races, ethnic backgrounds, and religions; my mother, the late Fannie J. Klein, the first woman to be appointed Associate Professor at New York University Law School and who subsequently became assistant director of the New York University Law School's Institute of Judicial Administration, for whetting my appetite for the law; and the late Professor George F. Theriault, my adviser as a sociology major at Dartmouth College, who first introduced me to the works of Alexis de Tocqueville and Gunnar Myrdal.

My thanks also to my daughter, Wendy Klein, and my sister, Esther Willison, for their constant encouragement. And my profound gratitude to my wife, Audrey Lehman Klein, a freelance editorial consultant to the Greenwood Publishing Group, for her extraordinary patience, sound advice, and constructive suggestions in critiquing and obtaining permissions for my manuscript—as she has all of my previous journalistic endeavors over the past four decades. Without her as my partner, this book could not have been written.

Woody Klein
Westport, Connecticut

NOTES

1. The story was reported in "Threat on Fund Laid to Powell Men," *New York Times*, June 15, 1964, 1.

2. Kenneth B. Clark, "Education: My Way of Life," *Boys' Life* (November 1965): 12.

3. Dr. Clark made his comment about this monograph's importance in an address at the NAACP Legal Defense Fund dinner to commemorate the thirtieth anniversary of *Brown v. Board of Education*, May 17, 1984. His monograph, "Desegregation: An Appraisal of the Evidence," was published in the *Journal of Social Issues* 9 (1953): 1–77.

4. Contained in a letter from U.S. District Court Judge Robert L. Carter to the author dated May 14, 2002.

5. *Brown v. Board of Education of Topeka*, 1952–1955:

We conclude that in the field of public education the doctrine of "separate but equal" has no place. Separate education facilities are inherently unequal. Therefore, we hold that the plaintiffs and others similarly situated for whom the actions have been brought are, by reason of the segregation complained of, deprived of the equal protection of the laws guaranteed by the Fourteenth Amendment. This disposition makes unnecessary any discussion of whether such segregation also violates the Due Process Clause of the Fourteenth Amendment.

6. This study was the basis of a $110 million program, HARYOU, announced by President Kennedy and carried out by President Johnson as part of his War on Poverty initiative. It was an example of Dr. Clark applying his intellectual insights to social action.

7. Kenneth B. Clark, "The Crisis of American Democracy and the Negro" (address at the annual luncheon of the National Committee for Rural Schools, New York City, November 19, 1955).

8. Address by Clark at the NAACP Legal Defense Fund dinner, May 17, 1984.

9. Taylor Branch, *Parting the Waters: America in the King Years, 1954–1963* (New York: Simon & Schuster, 1988), 809.

10. Nat Hentoff, *The Nat Hentoff Reader* (Cambridge, MA: Da Capo Press, Perseus Books Group, 2001), 211–212.

11. Address by Clark at the NAACP Legal Defense Fund dinner, May 17, 1984.

12. Ben Keppel, *The Work of Democracy* (Cambridge, MA: Harvard University Press, 1995), 101.

13. David Maraniss, "Icon of Integration and the Durability of Racism," *Washington Post*, March 4, 1990, A22.

14. [Editor's note: President Lyndon B. Johnson established this commission on July 27, 1967. It was chaired by Otto Kerner, governor of Illinois, with New York Mayor John V. Lindsay as vice chairman. According to the report: "The summer of 1967 again brought racial disorders to American cities, and with them shock, fear, and bewilderment to the Nation. The worst came during a 2-week period in July, first in Newark, then in Detroit. Each set off a chain reaction in neighboring communities." The "Kerner Commission" issued its report on March 1, 1968. On page 1, the commission stated its main conclusion: "This is our basic conclusion: Our nation is moving toward two societies, one black, one white—separate and unequal."]

15. *Report of the National Advisory Commission on Civil Disorders* (Washington, DC: U.S. Government Printing Office, March 1, 1968), 1.

16. Kenneth B. Clark, "Racial Progress and Retreat: A Personal Memoir," in Herbert Hill and James E. Jones, Jr., eds., *Race in America: The Struggle for Equal-*

ity (Madison: University of Wisconsin Press, 1993), 18. See also Chapter 18 of this volume.

17. John Hope Franklin, Chairman, *One America in the 21st Century: Forging a New Future, the President's Initiative on Race*, The Advisory Board's Report to the President, Pre-Publication, September 18, 1998, i.

18. Gary Orfield, with Erika Frankenberg and Chungmei Lee, "A Multiracial Society with Segregated Schools: Are We Losing the Dream?" (study by the Civil Rights Project at Harvard University, 2003), 66. Dr. Gary Orfield, Professor of Education & Social Policy at Harvard University and the John F. Kennedy School of Government, is founding codirector of the Civil Rights Project.

19. Kitty Terjen, "On Kenneth Clark's 60th Birthday" (interview), *Southern Voice* 4.1 (October–November 1974): 31–32.

Introduction: *Brown v. Board of Education*— A Perspective

Paul Finkelman

In *Brown v. Board of Education of Topeka* (1954) the U.S. Supreme Court held that racial segregation in state-sponsored public schools violated the equal protection clause of the Fourteenth Amendment. In a separate companion case, *Bolling v. Sharpe* (347 U.S. 497, 1954), the Court held that the Fifth Amendment barred the creation of segregated schools in the District of Columbia and other federal jurisdictions. At the time of the decision, seventeen southern states and the District of Columbia required that all public schools be racially segregated. A few Northern and Western states, including Kansas, left the issue of segregation up to individual school districts. While most schools in Kansas were integrated in 1954, Topeka's were not.

Racial segregation in Southern public schools began during Reconstruction. Before the Civil War, all of the Northern states provided some public education for blacks, although some either allowed or required segregation in their public schools. This contrasted with the antebellum South, where public education was virtually nonexistent for free blacks. In 1860, for example, there were over 94,000 school-age, free black children in the fifteen slave states, but only about 2,600 were in any sort of school. This contrasts with Northern states like Ohio and Pennsylvania, where over 5,600 and over 7,500 black children, respectively, attended schools. In 1860 in the slave state of Virginia, only 41 of 22,081 free black children were in school, while New York, with a slightly smaller free black population, had 5,964 children in school. After the Civil War some Northern states prohibited segregated schools, while others allowed them to develop in a de facto manner—such segregation was not required by law but instead emerged through custom, housing patterns, and countless decisions by school boards and local governments. Nevertheless, throughout the North some schools were always integrated.

Both before and after the Civil War more than 95 percent of all blacks lived in the South. It was there that racial segregation became a way of life and the central institution for the overwhelming majority of African Americans. During Reconstruction for the first time public schooling became generally available in the South for both blacks and whites. There were some attempts at integration, but these generally failed because whites refused to attend school with blacks. When Reconstruction ended, the South rapidly became a thoroughly segregated society. Southern states mandated that blacks and whites attend separate schools, ride on separate railroad cars, use separate public drinking fountains, and in every other way, be separated. Oklahoma segregated its phone booths in the early twentieth century, Florida provided separate depositories for schoolbooks, and New Orleans segregated its red light district. Virtually every public facility and institution in the South was segregated, including hospitals, cemeteries, and asylums for the blind. In *Plessy v. Ferguson* (163 U.S. 537, 1896), the Supreme Court upheld segregation in railroad cars, asserting that segregated facilities would be constitutional if they were "equal." This became known as the "separate but equal" doctrine. In reality, *Plessy* did not so much create new law. Rather, it confirmed and constitutionalized what had already begun in the South. By 1910, that region of the country was entirely segregated.

In 1909 W.E.B. Du Bois, Joel and Arthur Spingarn, Morefield Story, Jane Addams, and a host of other black and white reformers organized what became the National Association for the Advancement of Colored People (NAACP). This was the nation's first true civil rights organization. Fittingly, many of its early members were the descendants of abolitionists. The NAACP was dedicated to fighting segregation. As early as 1915, in *Guinn v. United States* (238 U.S. 347, 1915), the organization spearheaded a successful legal assault on an Oklahoma statute that effectively disfranchised most black voters in the state. The NAACP continued to fight against discriminatory statutes in voting and housing in the 1920s and 1930s and defended blacks accused of crimes where race seemed to be a significant factor in the prosecution.

The main goal of the NAACP was to somehow mount a legal assault on segregation itself. In the 1930s and 1940s the NAACP successfully forced the formal integration of law schools and other professional schools at segregated universities in Mississippi, Maryland, Oklahoma, and Texas. These victories were based on the fact either that the state had no comparable school for blacks or that the school the state did provide was so vastly inferior to the white school that the Supreme Court easily found that the "equal" part of "separate but equal" was not met. In this period the NAACP also had forced some states to equalize public school funding and to pay black teachers on the same scale as white teachers. These victories chipped away at inequality but in fact did not challenge segregation itself. Indeed, these "equalization" suits all reinforced the idea that segregated schools were permissible as long as they were equal. Such suits had to be brought in each district or state and could only be won if there were massive factual proof of the lack of equality. A suit might lead to a few blacks attending a state law school, or one school district providing better education for blacks, but they could not affect the system of segregation itself. Thus, throughout the South, public education remained segregated—and for blacks, terribly unequal.

By the 1950s the NAACP was ready to challenge segregation directly. *Brown v. Board of Education* developed from challenges to segregation in South Carolina, Virginia, Delaware, and Kansas. A companion case came from the District of Columbia. All the cases challenged school segregation itself. The attorneys in these cases argued that segregation per se was unconstitutional even if the schools were "equal."

In fact, of course, the schools in these cases were not equal. The case from Clarendon County, South Carolina, demonstrates the fundamental failure of the separate but equal doctrine. In the 1949–1950 school year the average annual expenditure for white students in Clarendon County totaled $179, but for blacks it was only $43. The county's 6,531 black students attended school in sixty-one buildings valued at $194,575. Many of the black schools lacked indoor plumbing or heating. There were twelve buildings valued at $673,850 for the 2,375 white students in the county. These buildings were newer, in better repair, and had superior facilities. Teachers in the black schools received, on average, about two-thirds of the salary of the teachers in the white schools. In this very rural county, the white students had free school buses, while the blacks did not. Initially blacks in Clarendon County sued to create equal schools, but eventually the plaintiffs changed their demand and sought an end to segregation itself. In the case, *Briggs v. Elliott* (1950), the U.S. district court in South Carolina ordered equal funding of black schools but refused to mandate racial integration of the schools.

In Delaware, Virginia, Kansas, and the District of Columbia, other cases emerged in the early 1950s that challenged the legality of racially segregated schools. The Court consolidated these cases into what became known as *Brown v. Board of Education*, named after the lead plaintiff in the Kansas case, Oliver Brown. Mr. Brown had filed the suit against the Topeka Board of Education on behalf of his seven-year-old daughter, Linda, who each morning had to travel one hour and twenty minutes to her segregated school. To reach the school bus she had to walk six blocks and cross a dangerous railroad track. The school was twenty-one blocks from her home, but there was a school only seven blocks away, which her white friends could attend. They did not have to ride a bus or face dangerous crossings to reach their school. Oliver Brown demanded the same treatment for his daughter.

In these cases the NAACP used a variety of techniques to argue that segregation was per se unconstitutional. Part of this argument was based on the psychological studies of Dr. Kenneth B. Clark. In 1950 Dr. Clark had prepared a report for the Mid-Century White House Conference on Children and Youth called "The Effects of Prejudice and Discrimination on Personality Development." This study, and Dr. Clark's testimony as an expert witness, eventually helped convince the Supreme Court that segregation was damaging to children. The Court cited Dr. Clark in its opinion along with a number of other social scientists.

The Court initially heard arguments in *Brown* in 1952, but the justices did not decide the case that year. Political divisions on the Court ran deep, and the weak leadership of Chief Justice Fred Vinson made a decisive ruling unlikely. Over the summer the justices debated the case and then scheduled reargument in the case for 1953. Chief Justice Vinson died before the new arguments began. His replacement, Earl Warren, was a skilled politician who had been the most popular governor in the history of California. His leadership helped unify the Court. Warren believed that segregation was fundamentally wrong, and he successfully persuaded the other eight justices to support a single, unanimous opinion to end segregation. This was an important accomplishment, since one southerner on the Court, Stanley Reed, was prepared to dissent, and the irascible Felix Frankfurter, while agreeing with the outcome, was contemplating a concurring opinion. Warren himself wrote the opinion of the Court and convinced all the other justices to sign on to it. He wanted the Court to speak with one voice on this momentous issue. In his opinion, Warren avoided castigating the South for its unfair treatment of blacks, yet at the same time he emphatically asserted that segregation was "inherently" unequal and could never be made equal.

Warren noted that the question before the Court was simple: "Was segregated education unconstitutional?" In the first half of his opinion, Warren did not answer that question, and he gave no hint of the decision the Court would make. Reading the opinion in a courtroom packed with news reporters, he simply explained the facts of the cases before him and the history of the American doctrine of "separate but equal." Warren acknowledged that the history of the law regarding segregation was inconclusive. He noted that the debates over the Fourteenth Amendment did not discuss issues such as schools. Furthermore, he noted that in the 1860s schools were relatively unimportant to society, but by 1954 they had become a central institution for the nation. Thus, Warren concluded:

In approaching this problem, we cannot turn the clock back to 1868 when the amendment was adopted, or even to 1896 when *Plessy* v. *Ferguson* was written.

We must consider public education in the light of its full development and its present place in American life throughout the Nation.

In reading his opinion Warren inserted the word "unanimously" when spelling out what the Court had concluded. The decision surprised almost everyone in the audience. While many expected the Court to strike down segregation, few expected it would be unanimous. This result vastly enhanced the prestige of the decision and of the new Chief Justice.

Warren stressed the importance of education to a democratic society, claiming that education is "perhaps the most important function of state and local governments." He emphasized that "[i]t is the very foundation of good citizenship." Warren then restated the original question before the Court and provided an answer: "Does segregation of children in the public schools solely on the basis of race . . . deprive the children of the minority group of equal educational opportunity?" His answer: "We believe that it does."

Warren supported his analysis with references to research performed by sociologists, psychologists, and medical doctors on the damage to children caused by mandatory segregation. Finally, Warren concluded by saying that "in the field of education the doctrine of 'separate but equal' has no place. Separate educational facilities are inherently unequal." Warren followed this simple but impressive statement about equality and fundamental justice with a single paragraph of carefully written conciliatory language. Warren declared that segregation was unconstitutional but that the decision would have no immediate effect on the parties involved. Instead, the Court would hear reargument in the case the following year to consider how to implement its decision.

In April 1955 the Court heard four days of arguments on how to end school segregation. In what is popularly known as *Brown II* (1955), the Court refused to order an immediate end to segregation. Instead the Supreme Court turned the implementation of desegregation over to the federal district courts in the South. The district courts were ordered to monitor the desegregation process. In an unfortunate use of language, Warren told the judges to act "with all deliberate speed." This ambiguous phrase allowed many southern school districts to avoid desegregation for years. Linda Brown did not attend an integrated school until 1955, when she had reached junior high school. None of the children of the twenty plaintiffs in the Clarendon County case ever attended integrated schools.

Brown helped launch the modern civil rights movement and led to other court decisions that struck down all forms of legalized racial discrimination. Nevertheless, despite its importance, *Brown* was never wholly successful. More than thirty years after the decision, Linda Brown was back in court, suing to desegregate the Topeka schools. While no longer segregated by law, housing patterns, economics, and other social factors had left most of the city's schools divided along racial lines.

PART I

The Roots of Racism

Gunnar Myrdal

Kenneth Clark is desperately anxious that the ugly facts of life in the Negro ghetto become really known to the ruling white majority. Among these facts of life, one most difficult to convey is how it feels to be enclosed in segregation.

He speaks the language of reason and points to the immense waste, not only in human happiness but in productivity. . . . Even leaving aside the moral issue of justice and the more perfect realization of the American ideals of liberty and equality of opportunity, and speaking in cold financial terms, eradicating the rural and urban slums and giving the youth there an education for productive employment are probably the most profitable investments that can be made in America today.

But Clark is tired of the false objectivity, the "balanced view" of many of his liberal white friends on the other side of the horribly tangible plate glass, which is philosophically made possible by the inherited Anglo-Saxon naiveté and lack of clarity regarding the value problem. Therefore, he also speaks with passion but with honesty and, in the end, a belief in the possibility of integration as a one-way process. In the demand for true objectivity he must, indeed, demand human empathy and even compassion on the part of as many as possible of those who can read, think, and feel in free, prosperous, white America. He asks that they recognize that large reforms, far beyond the formal enactment of civil rights, have become necessary and urgent. He can press for these huge reforms with the better con-

science as, without waiting for them, he threw himself first into the
constructive, healing work in the HARYOU [Harlem Youth Activities
Unlimited] activity in Harlem.[1]

NOTE

1. [*Editor's Note*: From the foreword by Gunnar Myrdal to Kenneth B. Clark's
Dark Ghetto: Dilemmas of Social Power (New York: Harper & Row, 1965), ix–
xi.]

CHAPTER 1

Prejudice Through Generations

Before parents can offer their children solid protection against the potential ravages of the racist disease, they themselves must have a firm core of human values and a strong social morality. These characteristics guide parents' perspective and actions in their relations with other human beings. It is not enough that parents put ideals into words. Children seem to be more sensitive to social and psychological realities than to mere words. They won't believe what their parents say about minority status unless the parents themselves believe it and act on it. If parents are unsure, escapist, defensive, ambivalent, and full of conflict, their feelings will be communicated to their children. (Clark, "How to Protect Children against Prejudice," *Child Study* 26 [1951]: 4–5.)

Race prejudice damages the children of the dominant group as well as children of the minority group against which the prejudice is directed. As minority-group children learn about the inferior status to which they are assigned—as they observe the fact that they are almost always kept apart from the dominant group, who are treated with more respect by society as a whole—these children may react with deep feelings of inferiority and a sense of humiliation. They lose some of their self-esteem; they become doubtful about their personal worth. Like all other human beings, they need a sense of personal dignity; but almost nowhere do they find their dignity as human beings respected. Under these conditions it is inevitable that the minority-group child is thrown into a conflict that affects not only his attitudes toward himself but also his attitudes toward his group. "Am I and my group worthy of no more respect than we get?" he asks. And thus the seeds of self-hatred and of rejection of his own group are sown.

The children of the dominant group who are required to adopt the prejudices of their society are taught to gain status at the expense of the status of others. They are not expected, when comparing themselves with members of a minority group, to evaluate themselves in terms of the basic standards of personal ability and achievement.

Children who are being taught race prejudice at the same time and by the same persons and institutions that teach them the moral, religious, and democratic principles of the brotherhood of man and the importance of justice and fair play are likely to become confused. It is clear to children of average intelligence and higher that there is a contradiction between adults' race prejudice and their moral teachings. When this contradiction is imposed upon children, it may become a personal problem that demands personal attempts at solution. Some may try to solve the problem by intensifying their hostility toward the minority group. Others may react with feelings of guilt, which are not necessarily reflected in more humane attitudes toward the minority group. (Clark, address before the National Urban League at the National Conference of Social Work, Chicago, IL, June 30, 1953.)

One of the most characteristic and impressive things about the American people is their dedication to their children. Ours is indeed a "child-centered" society. Almost no sacrifice is too great for parents to make if it will benefit their children. Parents will work, scheme, attend church, buy life and endowment insurance, move from country to city, from city to suburbs, from one neighborhood to another, from south to north, from east to west—all for the welfare of their children. (Clark, *Prejudice and Your Child* [Boston: Beacon Press, 1955], 3.)

When white American parents demand that a school board maintain separate schools for white and Negro children, and when some of these parents encourage their children to refuse to attend a school to which Negro students have been recently admitted, they do so not only as an expression of their own racial feelings but also in the belief that they are protecting their children. If these parents understood that, far from protecting their children, acts of this type distort and damage the core of their children's personalities, they would not act this way. If they understood that the opportunity for a child to meet and know other children of different races, religions, and cultures is beneficial and not detrimental; that it contributes to social competence and confidence; that it increases a child's chances for personal and moral stability—then they would demand, in the name of their children, non-segregated public education. (Clark, *Prejudice and Your Child* [Boston: Beacon Press, 1955], 4.)

As the Negro observes the society in which he lives, he associates whiteness with superior advantage, achievement, progress, and power, all of which are essential to successful competition in the American culture. The degree of whiteness that the individual Negro prefers may be considered an indication of the intensity of his anxiety and of his need to compensate for what he considers the deficiencies of his own skin color. The various terms prevalent among Negroes to describe different shades of skin color indicate the degree of emotionality involved in the skin-color conflict. (Clark, *Prejudice and Your Child* [Boston: Beacon Press, 1955], 49.)

It is almost 10 years to the day since the United States Supreme Court handed down one of its historic decisions, a decision which has had a great impact and probably will have an even greater impact upon American society than the Civil War itself. In the 10 years, many things have happened. The reactions to decisions have been varied; at least insofar as race is concerned the actual changes in the organization of schools have probably not been too great; but the great change wrought by the *Brown* decision has been in the morale of the Negro in the United States and that change is reflected in what has been called the Negro Revolution.

There have been, during these 10 years, discussions concerning what the role of the social scientists actually was in the *Brown* decisions; what did they say; what effect did they have, if any, on the decision. Now obviously I cannot answer that last question but it is important to review in summary fashion what was said 10 years ago on this specific point—namely, the effect of segregation on personality development of American children and what developments within these last 10 years require modification, extension, elaboration of what was said a decade ago.

My source for the first part is the Social Science Brief which a number of us prepared and presented to the lawyers, who in turn presented it to the Supreme Court many years ago. At that time, we started out by defining precisely—or as precisely as possible—what we believed was meant by the term, segregation. It is as follows: For purposes of the present statement, segregation refers to that restriction of opportunities for different types of associations between the members of one racial, religious, national or geographic origin or linguistic group, and those of other groups which results from, or is supported by the action of any official body or agency representing some branch of government.

At that time we stated:

We are not here concerned with such segregation as arises from the free movements of individuals which are neither enforced nor supported by official bodies, nor with the segregation of criminals or of individuals with communicable diseases which aims at the protecting of society from those who might seek to harm it. Where the action takes place in a social milieu, in which the groups involved do not enjoy equal social status, the group that is of lesser social status will be referred to as the segregated group.

(Clark, "Effect of Segregation and Integration on Children's Personality" [address given at the Michigan State University Symposium on School Integration, East Lansing, MI, 1964].)

In the ghetto, the meaning of the illegitimate child is not ultimate disgrace. There is not the demand for abortion or for the surrender of the child that one finds in more privileged communities. In the middle class, the disgrace of illegitimacy is tied to personal and family aspirations. In lower-class families, on the other hand, the girl loses only some of her already limited options by having an illegitimate child; she is not going to make a "better marriage" or improve her economic and social status either way. On the contrary, a child is a symbol of the fact that she is a woman, and she may gain from having something of her own. Nor is the boy who fathers an illegitimate child going to lose, for where is he going? The path to any higher status seems closed to him in any case. (Clark, *Dark Ghetto: Dilemmas of Social Power* [New York: Harper & Row, 1965], 72.)

To a Negro, every white person is in a sense, a symbol of his own oppression. (Clark, *Dark Ghetto: Dilemmas of Social Power* [New York: Harper & Row, 1965], 238.)

Many Negroes live sporadically in a world of fantasy, and fantasy takes different forms at different ages. In childhood the delusion is a simple one— the child may pretend that he is really white. When Negro children as young as three years old are shown white- and Negro-appearing dolls and are asked to color pictures of children to look like themselves, many of them tend to reject the dark-skinned dolls as "dirty" and "bad" or to color the picture of themselves a light color or a bizarre shade like purple. But the fantasy is not complete, for when asked to identify which doll is like themselves, some Negro children, particularly in the north, will refuse, burst into tears, and run away. By the age of seven most Negro children have accepted the reality that they are, after all, dark-skinned. But the stigma remains; they have been forced to recognize themselves as inferior. Few if any Negroes ever fully lose that sense of shame and self-hatred. (Clark, *Dark Ghetto: Dilemmas of Social Power* [New York: Harper & Row, 1965], 64–65.)

When I was a student at Columbia in 1937, [Professor] Otto Klineberg argued that the peculiar quality of the American race problem was that slavery occurred in the New World within the framework of a Christian ideology. This imposed upon the slave traders and slaveholders, the necessity for a kind of rationalization, which would make slavery consistent with Christianity. The new gimmick which slavery in the New World added was to impose upon the slave the idea of sub-human status. (Clark, "On De Facto Segregation and Parish Education" [address before the United Presbyterian Church, New York, April 1965].)

The moral schizophrenia of America is reflected most clearly in the status of Negroes, starting with slavery and continuing to the contemporary ghettos, which blight the powerful and affluent cities of our nation. One cannot, therefore, discuss the dilemmas of the contemporary American Negro without at the same time becoming involved in an analysis of the historical and psychological fabric of American life. This is a thesis reflecting the bias of a social psychologist—a bias which might be rejected by more sophisticated historians, political and economic theorists, or tougher-minded social critics. I base my thesis on the psychological premise that the values, attitudes, and behavior of individual human beings and groups of human beings are determined by the complex socialization process that normal human beings are modifiable and are determined by their environment and culture, and not by any inherent, genetic, or racial determinants.

Let us now be specific. A basic dilemma of America is whether the Negro should be accepted and taken seriously as a human being and permitted the rights and privileges accorded other human beings in our political system. America has endured slave rebellions, developed an underground railroad, fought one of the most bloody wars in human history, and is now undergoing a series of urban ghetto implosions in the attempt to resolve this persistent bedeviling question. The Negro's part of this basic dilemma is whether to persist in his insistence upon his unqualified rights as a human being without regard to the risks or consequences—or whether to accommodate to the resistances by subtle or flagrant forms of withdrawal from the fray. American Negroes historically have sought many ways to deal with this dilemma—their general acceptance of slavery; the many psychological adjustments to subjugation and deflection of aggressive reactions; the varieties of back-to-Africa movements; the cults and fads, and the recent series of riots in our ghettos.

The gnawing doubts of white Americans as to their status and worth as human beings—the deep feelings of inferiority growing out of actual inferior status in the land of their origin in Europe—impelled American whites to develop and enforce social and institutional arrangements designed to inflict upon Negroes an inferior status. The demanding status needs of whites were powerful enough to counteract the logic, the morality, and the powerful political ethic of the egalitarian and democratic rhetoric, which is also an important American reality. (Clark, "The Present Dilemma of the Negro" [address given at the annual meeting of the Southern Regional Council, Atlanta, GA, November 2, 1967], 2–4.)

To the Negro child the most serious injury seems to be in the concept of self-worth related directly to skin color itself. Because school is a central activity at this age, his sense of inferiority is revealed most acutely in his lack of confidence in himself as a student, lack of motivation to learn, and in problems of behavior—a gradual withdrawal or a growing rebellion. (Clark, quoted in Peter I. Rose, ed., *The Study of Society: An Integrated Anthology* [New York: Random House, 1967], 500.)

The problems of American racism and the persistent ambivalence of American whites are part of the larger, difficult, and profound problems of the human predicament. To understand these problems we must try to understand the deep and awesome need of human beings to pretend, to strut, to bombast, to inflict cruelty upon others, to assert an omnipotence, to claim virtues, and to arrogate unto themselves power—all in a desperate struggle to disguise a gnawing sense of personal futility, to compensate for the intolerable possibility of inner emptiness, to reduce the burden of guilt, and to postpone the ultimate confrontation of the meaning, substance, value and worth of one's own being. (Clark, "American Racism and the Human Predicament" [address given at Carnegie-Mellon University, Pittsburgh, PA, April 3, 1968], 2–4.)

Perhaps the first civil rights struggle in the New World centered around an educational debate: Should the African slaves be taught to read and converted to Christianity? One could speculate with a detached bemusement that those who argued successfully that at least some should be taught used the rationale that the slave would be more docile if he learned to read the Bible. Probably those who took the opposite side undoubtedly justified their position on the grounds that ignorance was important for the maintenance of slavery within the context of a Christian society. The argument that the African was subhuman, or not quite human, would be weakened, if not destroyed, if the African were converted to Christianity and if it were demonstrated that the slave could be taught to read and to write. They predicted accurately that if the slaves were educated, pressures for the abolition of slavery as a dehumanizing form of relationship among men would build up and become irresistible once the slave demonstrated his capacity for education. It is much more difficult to subjugate human beings with impunity—or to justify that subjugation—once they are released from the more fundamental bonds of ignorance. (Clark, "Education: The Basis of Freedom" [address, Sol Feinstone Lecture, Syracuse University, 1971].)

The consequences of powerlessness among groups of people in American society is nowhere more evident than among neglected and abandoned children. They are the most powerless human beings in our society. Except for the child service agencies upon which they are totally dependent, they have no dynamic lobby or organization or procedure to protect and advocate their human rights. For dark-skinned children, even these agencies provide little hope, because they inevitably reflect the racial biases of the larger society and reserve the right to select the children who they will serve. This leaves minority group children abandoned children—children who suffer even more severely from the problems of poverty, low status and rejection than do the adult groups with whom they identify; children virtually without hope for permanent and successful adoption. They become sentenced to institutions which fail them with little prospect for escape. (Clark, introduction to "Why Some Choose Not to Adopt through Agencies," MARC Monograph no. 1, April 1972, 13–14.)

The problem of the persistent, at times massive, and cumulative academic retardation of Negro children, compared with the norms of white and other more privileged children, has been a consistent part of the total pattern of American racial history. One of the earliest controversies on the nature of the African slave who had been brought to the New World was whether he was capable of learning to read—or, indeed, whether he should be taught to read, even if capable of learning. The need to see Negro slaves as somewhat less than human, if not subhuman, seemed basic to the discussions concerning the level of their intelligence, and determined the policies and practices which governed the amount and quality of education provided for them and their children. Upon this background the academic retardation of Negro children developed and persists to the present. (Clark, "The Educationally Deprived: The Potential for Change," Metropolitan Applied Research Center, New York, NY, 1972.)

It is ironic that even as Thomas Jefferson expressed this democratic premise as the basis for the founding of this new nation, his own predicament as a slaveholder and as an apologist for the continuation of slavery in the United States was a symptom of the schizophrenia which continues to afflict the American social and political system. (Clark, "The American Revolution: Democratic Politics and Popular Reform" [address given at the Bicentennial of the United States of America, 1776–1976, American Enterprise Institute for Public Policy Research Distinguished Lecture Series, Washington, DC, 1976].)

As the person who directed the HARYOU [Harlem Youth Opportunities Unlimited] Research project, I cannot plead ignorance of the fact that children were victims of physical punishment in the New York City public schools. After publishing the verbatim comments of these teachers, I, like many others, remained silent and permitted this evil to persist. (Clark, introduction to "Corporal Punishment and School Suspensions: A Case Study," MARC Monograph no. 2, November 1974, 1–2.)

Black children or any other group of children can't develop pride by just saying they have it, by singing a song about it, by saying I'm black and beautiful or I'm white and superior. (Clark, quoted in Christopher Lasch, "American Life in an Age of Diminishing Expectations," in *The Culture of Narcissism* [New York: W.W. Norton, 1978], 144.)

The symptoms of lower-class society afflict the dark ghettos of America: low aspiration, poor education, family instability, illegitimacy, unemployment, crime, drug addictions and alcoholism, frequent illness and early death. But because the Negroes begin with the primary affliction of inferior racial status, the burdens of despair and hatred are more pervasive. (Clark, quoted in Leslie W. Dunbar, ed., *Minority Report: What Has Happened to Blacks, Hispanics, American Indians, & Other Minorities in the Eighties* [New York: Pantheon Books, 1984], 76.)

The most pressing victims of persistent injustice in America are black children. Poor and black children are being abused. They are the victims of poverty, homelessness, and inferior schools. Furthermore, they are destined to live under conditions that internalize deep feelings of inferiority. Their reactions to this feeling of inferiority are expressed in a number of ways, from anti-social to self-destructive, and many varied ways between. As a result, our society is spending more money on correctional institutions than on the quality of education that would prepare these human beings for a productive adulthood. It appears that more funds are being allocated for jails than for school and educational training. These abused children are left with a marked deficiency in academic achievement. (Clark, "The Abuses of Black Children" [address given at the 25th Anniversary Award Dinner of CTE, Inc., Stamford, CT, December 10, 1990], 3.)

COMMENTARY

Marian Wright Edelman

Dr. Clark's early research on how black children internalized negative connotations of blackness was both groundbreaking and heartbreaking. His findings put American society to shame. Dr. Clark was also one of the first scholars to warn white parents that racial prejudice and the destructive cycles of fear, hatred, and guilt connected with it were having a psychological impact on their own children, too. His focus on prejudice's effect on children was a powerful wake-up call that got American adults' attention, and his challenge to all adults to do something about it—if they truly wanted to raise their own children to be humane and stable adults in a civilized democracy—helped change American history.

Eleanor Holmes Norton

I think of Ken as a friend with a glorious wit, on the one hand, and on the other hand, I regard him as one of the most important public intellectuals of the twentieth century. He set the pace. Think of what Kenneth Clark wrote and what has happened since. He is the godfather of all the children's organizations—all who are today trying to put children first. Children were not at the top of our nation's list when Kenneth Clark was trying to place them there. Ken put children on the map.

Paul Robeson, Jr.

In *Prejudice and Your Child* (1955), Dr. Clark notes: "Over and above the political, economic, sociological, and international implications of racial prejudice, their major significance is that they place *unnecessary* [italics mine] burdens upon human beings, sometimes even distorting and damaging the individual personality" (p. 37). My experiences as a child in the United States and abroad established the manner in which I have carried these burdens, both as a child and as an adult. Dr. Clark notes that "[a]s minority-group children learn about the inferior status to which they are assigned—as they observe the fact that they are almost always kept apart from the dominant group, who are treated with more respect by society as a whole— these children may react with deep feelings of inferiority and a sense of humiliation" (p. 64).

I recall that my parents and my maternal grandmother helped me develop a strong and secure sense of personal achievement and ambition. I remember a comfortable identification as a black child with a racial pride that endured both in America and abroad. However, even with these reinforcements, I found coping with U.S. racism a burdensome task, sapping a great deal of energy. I was taught that I was as good as any white child and that I should feel and behave accordingly at all times. I was also taught that blacks as a people were equal in every way to whites and that racial prejudice was based on ignorance. As Dr. Clark points out, it is necessary to understand the causes and effects of prejudice, discrimination, and segregation "in order to become actively involved in the struggle to eradicate these symptoms of social maladjustment" (p. 13). Even so, I found it difficult to manage the anger that welled up in response to racial slights. I grew up with a clear sense of identity as an African American.

In retrospect, I believe that living abroad as a young child made it possible for me to internalize these attitudes. The virulent strain of racism, which existed then, and still persists now in the United States, would have foreclosed my ability to develop this powerful resource for easing the burden of prejudice. On the other hand, the very strength of this resource magnified the rage I felt when I encountered racial prejudice, especially the institutional kind. The unfairness of it, the power of it, and its hypocritical double standard imposed an especially heavy unnecessary burden. A lighter but nevertheless frustrating burden was imposed on me by the legion of well-meaning, nonracist whites who insisted that I should "be like" them in order to be accepted by white society. They were almost always incapable of understanding my total lack of a desire to assimilate or to behave in a "white" manner.

These two familiar burdens of race prejudice were removed from my shoulder entirely and for the first time when I spent two years attending an all-Russian school. There I encountered both a total lack of racial prejudice and a complete absence of any pressure to be anyone but myself. My schoolmates and the teachers accepted me fully for what I was and who I was. Years later, I realized that this experience had permanently removed an important but partially concealed racial burden from my shoulders. I call it "the black man's burden." Never again would I automatically distrust white people before I had reason to do so. My personal experience had taught me that this wasn't necessary. Without such personal experience, a black child cannot shed this unnecessary and constraining burden of automatic, universal distrust.

NOTE

1. [*Editor's Note*: Dr. Kenneth B. Clark prepared a report for the Mid-Century White House Conference on Children and Youth in 1950 called "The Effects of Prejudice and Discrimination on Personality Development" (see Appendix 2, this volume). The U.S. Supreme Court cited his report in Footnote 11 in its landmark May 17, 1954, *Brown v. Board of Education* decision, which ruled that laws requiring or permitting racial segregation of public education were unconstitutional. This report was revised and later published in 1955 by Beacon Press under the title *Prejudice and Your Child*.]

CHAPTER 2

The Pathology of Racism

The ghetto, as I studied it, is ambivalence; it is conflict. It is hope, it is despair, it is aspiration for mobility and it is apathy and stagnation. It is courage and it is defeatism; it is cooperation and it is concern, and it is also suspiciousness, competitiveness and rejection—rejection of others and rejection of self. It is a surge toward integration and assimilation in the larger context of American life, and it is increasing alienation and isolation. It is Martin Luther King and it is Malcolm X. It is timidity and it is withdrawal further within the protective walls of segregation. And we see all of these in the children who we have been studying in the past year. Often, more often than not, we see all of these conflicts and opposites and contradictions within the same individuals. Given the fact of objective deterioration and physical ugliness that characterizes so much of our Northern urban ghettos, the chances for the dominance of psychological negatives in its products seem to me increased. In fact, the pathological characteristics of the ghetto community determine its atmosphere, and tend to perpetuate themselves through cumulative deterioration and isolation. (Clark, "Effects of Segregation and Integration," address at Symposium on School Integration, Michigan State University, May 8, 1964.)

"Ghetto" was the name for the Jewish quarter in sixteenth-century Venice. Later, it came to mean any section of a city to which Jews were confined. America has contributed to the concept of the ghetto, the restriction of persons to a special area and the limiting of their freedom of choice on the basis of skin color. The dark ghetto's invisible walls have been erected by the white society, by those who have power, both to confine those who have no power and to perpetuate their powerlessness. The dark ghettos are social, political, educational, and—above all—economic colonies. Their inhabitants are subject peoples, victims of the greed, cruelty, insensitivity, guilt, and fear of their masters.

The ghetto is ferment, paradox, conflict, and a dilemma. Yet within its pervasive pathology exists a surprising human resilience. The ghetto is hope, it is despair, it is churches and bars. It is aspiration for change, and it is apathy. It is vibrancy, it is stagnation. It is courage, and it is defeatism. It is cooperation and concern, and it is suspicion, competitiveness, and rejection. It is the surge toward assimilation, and it is alienation and withdrawal within the protective walls of the ghetto.

The pathologies of the ghetto community perpetuate themselves through cumulative ugliness, deterioration, and isolation and strengthen the Negro's sense of worthlessness, giving testimony to his impotence. Yet the ghetto is not totally isolated. The mass media—radio, television, moving pictures, magazines, and the press—penetrate, indeed, invade the ghetto in continuous and inevitable communication, largely one-way, and project the values and aspirations, the manners and the style of the larger white-dominated society. (Clark, *Dark Ghetto: Dilemmas of Social Power* [New York: Harper & Row, 1965], 11–12.)

To a Negro, every white person is in a sense, a symbol of his own oppression. (Clark, *Dark Ghetto: Dilemmas of Social Power* [New York: Harper & Row, 1965], 238.)

Any kind of racism is a constriction of the mind. ("Q. & A. with Dr. Kenneth B. Clark," *This Week Magazine* [New York], June 9, 1969, 2.)

A sensitive minority of American youth—college students and ghetto casualties—are urgently trying to tell us that equivocation in the face of flagrant or subtle social injustices is no longer tolerable. A positive sense of their own being and human worth is eroded by a cloying, spiritually empty affluence and by remediable deprivation. Drugs and cults and romantic escapes into hedonism and even justifiable and random rage will not be enough to ease their unrest. Their anguished and at times seemingly incoherent cries have the basic coherence of insisting that the demands for colleges that are adaptive and the demands for cities worthy of the grandeur of man are basically the same.

The major charge that must now be made against American colleges and universities is that they have not fulfilled their responsibility and obligation to develop and train human beings with a morally relevant and socially responsible intelligence. They have operated as if it were possible for a detached, amoral intelligence to be adaptive. (Clark, *Pathos of Power* [New York: Harper & Row, 1974], 49.)

Racism has many distinguishing characteristics, but none among them is more deeply necessary to the racist psychology than self-deception. The black nationalist who tells himself that he is "together" and proud—but who fears to face whites in competition in the classroom or the job; the black "militant" leader who exploits the frustrations of his own people in cynical alliance with segregationists; the white segregationist who justifies his rejection of other human beings, citing alleged evidence of Negro inferiority; the white liberal who defends his double standard support of black separatism on benevolent grounds; the white public official who recommends benign neglect of the poor and the despairing—all these share in a dangerous fantasy that leads to self-destruction of the spirit, and corrupts and subverts a free society. This pattern of fantasies is the core of the contemporary American dilemma. (Clark, "Beyond the Dilemma" [address to the Academy of Religion and Mental Health, New York, April 29, 1970].)

Institutionalized patterns of segregation and discrimination plant prejudice in the minds of Americans. . . . The pioneer spirit still permeates the culture of America. Intense racial and other intergroup cleavages appear to be a necessary correlate. . . . This can be understood if it is recognized that security may be obtained not only objectively, through the manipulation and exploitation of the material environment for man's benefit, but also subjectively through the subjugation and humiliation of other human beings.

In society, it can become fashionable to dislike some group of people for various reasons: "Everyone else dislikes Jews and Negroes. I can't be different. I must dislike them, too. If I don't, my friends will reduce me somewhat to the status of these disliked people." In time, these ideas and attitudes become ingrained in the individual, accepted as a normal, natural way of life, and become more and more intense in motivational value. They become an aspect of life style, enmeshed in status, privileges, and personal aspirations.

One cannot completely understand the dynamics of intergroup cleavages without taking into account the nature of the reaction patterns in each group resulting from the cleavage. It appears that there are certain general pattern effects of these pathological cleavages, which reinforce and rigidify the already existing disturbances. The inherent humiliation of the Negro's status in American life—a humiliation quite often repressed but no less intensely felt—gives rise to latent feelings of insecurity and inadequacy. (Clark, quoted in "A Psychologist Looks at Discrimination Patterns," *mba Magazine* 6.4 [January 1972]: 33–34.)

There are specific modern examples of the link between class and race in American society. For instance, in the debates related to school desegregation in northern cities, the resistance to any realistic and effective desegregation of public schools is almost always expressed in terms of the fear of losing middle-class whites if black children are "bused" into "their schools." All white children are perceived to be "middle-class" and should be protected from contamination by low-class black children. (Clark, "The Declining Significance of Race," symposium address under the sponsorship of the Afro-American Studies Program, University of Pennsylvania, March 1979.)

In many respects, American racism is unique. Unlike British colonial racism which not only permitted, but trained non-whites to enter the upper and governing class in many of the former colonies, American racism was and remains, for the most part, "democratic" in that all blacks were perceived and treated alike. In American racism, class and race tended to be used and reacted to interchangeably. Traditionally, American whites tended to react to a person of color as if he were automatically lower class. This was and continues to be generally true without regard to distinctions among individual blacks in terms of education, economic status, and other generally accepted class symbols. Racial stereotypes were applied to all blacks.

One of the chief advantages of American racism for American whites—particularly those of the lower classes—is that it reinforces the important American myth of classlessness among whites by relegating all nonwhites to an inferior class. By defining all blacks as inferior, America keeps alive the companion myth of white superiority. It would be most difficult for American whites to give up racism because in doing so they would have to face the fact that there are significant class distinctions among whites and that most whites are not successful. (Clark, "Sophisticated Racism," in Joseph R. Washington, Jr., ed., *The Declining Significance of Race? A Dialogue among Black and White Social Scientists* [New York: Pantheon Books, 1979], 100–101.)

If you look at the history of various immigrant groups, you'll see they were fleeing oppression and really believed that the United States had streets paved with gold. The only things they really found were blacks constantly below everybody else. They had conflicting ethnic rivalries. But one thing white immigrants could do in America was to believe they were moving upward because the blacks were always there, down below. (Clark, quoted in Studs Terkel, *RACE: How Blacks & Whites Think & Feel about the American Obsession* [New York: The New Press, 1992], 334–335.)

COMMENTARY

Cornel West

Kenneth Clark is a towering figure among twentieth-century intellectuals. His *Dark Ghetto* (1965) remains a classic, and his exemplary work in the struggle for freedom is a great inspiration to us all.

CHAPTER 3

Morality, Ethics, and Racism

It is probably not enough to believe that racial prejudices, discrimination and segregation are morally wrong. In order to become actively involved in the struggle to eradicate these symptoms of social maladjustment and save our children from their harmful effects, it is necessary to know why they are wrong. Responsible citizens must understand clearly what negative racial attitudes are, how they affect our society, and the ways in which they are communicated to our children. When the effects of these forms of prejudice on personalities of children are clearly understood, then the efforts to immunize our children from their virulence will be made effective. (Clark, *Prejudice and Your Child* [Boston: Beacon Press, 1955], 18.)

The cause of the Negro could be lost were not our heritage inconsistent with continued oppression. (Clark, "A Struggle for Complete Human Dignity," *The Christian Register* [Boston: Christian Universalist Association] [July 1956]: 37.)

Undoubtedly a pattern of personality difficulties results when any human beings are placed in an unjust and unreasonable social situation. Although specific aspects of this pattern do not hold for every child in a rejected minority group, and although a range of individual differences among members of such a group is as wide as among other peoples, the evidence suggests that all these children are in some ways unnecessarily harmed by discrimination against them. Gnawing feelings of inferiority, generalized aggressiveness, withdrawn and submissive behavior, hypersensitivity about the self damage the foundations for a healthy personality structure.

There are some very real problems which are involved in the question of adequate treatment of personality difficulties of minority group peoples.

These problems, however, should neither be magnified nor minimized in terms of the factor of race alone. To do so would clearly present still another obstacle in the pattern of the mental health of a substantial group of the American people.

There is no evidence that these problems are either insurmountable or that they are resolved by insisting that only Negroes be assigned to Negro therapists and whites only to white therapists. Our nine years of experience at Northside Center [in Harlem] shows that granting equal competence, skill, insight, empathy, and overall social maturity among therapists, there is no problem in the assignment of white patients to Negro therapists and Negro patients to white therapists. While the problem of race is often raised in these situations, it is handled as an integral part of the therapeutic situation. When so handled by a therapist whose own values and clarity in this area make this possible for him, this problem facilitates rather than interferes with effective psychotherapy. (Clark, "Racial Factors and Effective Psychotherapy," draft White Paper, Clark Archives, Hastings-on-Hudson, NY, 1957.)

I testified to that when the United States Supreme Court was hearing the school desegregation case, and when the court ruled in 1954 that segregation was wrong, it cited some of our research findings and testimony. It was a high point in my career. (Clark, "Education: My Way of Life," *Boys' Life* [November 1965]: 12.)

The emotional ill health of the dark ghetto is a continuum ranging from the anxious but "normal" individual to the criminally psychotic. The harmful effects of American racism on personality development and psychological balance are unmistakable. Still, it is one thing to show that prejudice damages individuals and another to show that the emotional illness of a particular individual has been caused by prejudice and its social consequences. The link between the phenomenon of the dark ghetto and individual destructiveness and withdrawal seems clear in many cases; in others the relationship is less sharply drawn. The evidence concerning the nature and extent of individual psychoses and neuroses in the ghetto is far less available and not easy to interpret. There are comparatively few Negro or white psychiatrists in the ghettos; and psychotherapy has not had the vogue among Negroes that it has in white middle- and upper-class urban communities in large part because the middle class is the central group in the white community and it is not in the Negro community. Individual psychotherapy tends either to be restricted to those sufficiently and destructively ill enough to require the intervention of society—and here it is largely custodial in nature—or to those less seriously damaged who have the funds and the inclination to seek help for themselves. It would be, in fact, surprising to find many Negro patients receiving extensive voluntary personal treatment, though the number doubtless will rise as Negroes move into more high-status jobs, thereby gaining both the money to pay the high cost of prolonged therapy and the psychological orientation to accept it. (Clark, *Dark Ghetto: Dilemmas of Social Power* [New York: Harper & Row, 1965], 82–83.)

The problems of American domestic morality are not peculiar to America. American moral domestic problems loom large not only because they are important but also because America is a democracy with a tradition of discussing its problems and seeking to resolve them in the direction of democracy. This fact seems important to keep in mind in order to counteract understandable tendencies at times to despair and pessimism in reacting to American equivocation and seeming moral hypocrisy. Problems of racial injustice, economic inequities, and unsolved urban problems are very real and pressing in contemporary America. The slowness, indecision, and lack of commitment to place our financial, technological, governmental, and intellectual power to the task of resolving these problems with equity and justice, and in terms of the primary goals of social stability and national survival, are irritating to those of us who believe that the rational and intellectual powers of man can find constructive and humane solutions to social problems. We are disturbed when we see repeatedly the blockage of the constructive approach to these problems by primitive and irrational prejudices and passions.

The problems of personal morality are the most difficult and confused problems to talk about. These problems exist in a tangle of inner doubts, conscience, family, interpersonal, national and international conflict and chaos. These problems highlight in all of their terror the depths and dimensions of human aloneness and belongingness. It is in that ultimate of all confrontations—the confrontation of oneself—that one then understands the ease with which man succumbs to a variety of escapes from his responsibilities as an ethical being. (Clark, "Some Moral Problems of Our Times" [commencement address, The Stockbridge School, Interlaken, MA, June 11, 1967].)

I think a number of other observers of the human predicament have said that so far we have not seemed to have found some way of having people live full, meaningful, constructive lives without having other human beings upon whom to look down for one pretext or another. Apparently the German people needed Jews to make them feel superior. And whites apparently need Negroes to make them feel superior. And I suppose one of the worst things that could happen as long as our educational system does not solve the problem of giving human beings a sense of what it really means to be human, is for us not to have scapegoats, not to have someone to consider inferior to us. (Clark, guest on *What's Happening to America?* hosted by Edwin Newman, NBC Television, July 12, 1968.)

It is of psychological significance that the present impatience of the Negro and his unwillingness to accept any argument for the postponement of any of his rights as an American citizen reflects, among other things, the tremendous progress which has been made in race relations in America within the past twenty years. These real gains have whetted the Negro's appetite for the fruits of full equality as an American citizen without reservation, compromise, or postponement. (Clark, "The New Negro in the North," in Mathew A. Ahmann, ed., *The New Negro* [Notre Dame, IN: Fides Publishers, 1961], 38–39.)

As a social psychologist, I am concerned with problems of social change. But I could not in good conscience encourage young people interested in psychology to go into this field. It is one fraught with a tremendous amount of frustration, a pervading sense of futility. (Clark, in Mary Harrington Hall, "A Conversation with Kenneth B. Clark," *Psychology Today* 2.1 [1968]: 21.)

Racism in any form is dangerous, but particularly, as is now true among many whites and Negroes, when it is intellectually supported. Such supporters often fail to follow the implication of their rhetoric to its logical conclusion—that if segregation and separatism are desirable and good as a phase, and as a means, they are even more to be desired as ends in themselves. All the implications of the *Brown* decision and all the social science arguments in its support point to the inherent dangers of racism. (Clark, introduction to Louis Friedman, ed., *The History-Making Decision That Sparked the Civil Rights Revolution in the United States. Argument: The Complete Oral Argument before the Supreme Court in Brown v. Board of Education of Topeka, 1952–1955* [New York: Chelsea House Publishers, 1969], 1.)

Essentially, psychology is that science and perspective which is basic in systematic attempts to understand the nature of man. Psychology is the arrogance inherent in the human intellect, whereby man validates his claim to uniqueness by his ability to ask questions and his insistence upon demanding or creating answers. And through psychology man may become aware—or block his awareness—of the anxieties and fears and frustrations inherent in the possibility that his questions and his answers may not always reflect the compelling realities of his existence.

Psychology is the convergence of the totality of ideas through which man seeks to deify himself, justify his uniqueness, his sacredness—and which at the same time mocks and taunts him and drives him to seek a variety of ways of resolving his conflicts and affirming his being. It is the core of the social sciences—history, economics, political science, sociology, too, the significance of both biological and physical sciences, must be understood in terms of the manifestations of the awesome complexity and pathos of the human brain and its insatiable quest for understanding of the perceivable and conceivable environment and for the use of these misunderstandings as instruments for control—and as attempts to reduce threats to human life and to enhance the comfort, the creativity and the positive substance of human existence.

Psychology also can be viewed as the unifying, the cohesive factor which gives meaning to the humanities. Psychology is at the core of religion in the struggle for moral understanding; it is central to the struggle of philosophy for rational understanding and control. It is inextricably a part of the struggle of literature to probe and grasp and communicate the many dimensions of human motivation, both in their frailties and their grandeur. In poetry and the arts psychology is implicit in the experiments in communicating those aspects of human feelings and experience that are difficult to translate into mere words. To the extent that the humanities have their origin in man's inner being, in his attempts to objectify the initially vague yearnings, fears, doubts, hopes, exultations, to that extent they share an inescapable involvement with psychology. (Clark, "Everyday Life and Social Identity" [address given at the Smithsonian Institution Annual Symposium, Washington, DC, November 17, 1971].)

About seven years ago I accepted an invitation to participate in a seminar on the ethical and moral problems of American society, which was sponsored by the Aspen Institute at Aspen, Colorado. Among the other invited guests were business executives, college presidents, judges, government officials, managing editors, professors and theologians. Each of the 20 participants was permitted an hour or so to present what he considered a significant moral problem confronting the American social system.

Although there was no conflict or controversy in these discussions, one of the presentations has had a profound, almost obsessive impact upon my own thoughts about the character and quality of American life. In a rather quiet voice a recently retired vice president of one of the largest corporations in America told the group that one of the persistent problems faced by his office was how to keep the accounting records of the corporation in such a way so that they would be accurate and would also *obscure* the fact that a regular operating expense was "payoffs" to municipal officials to enhance the ability of the company to install its product in new buildings throughout the United States. Casually this participant cited this as just another example of a prevailing functional immorality with which big business had to come to terms.

When none of the other participants raised a question about the ethical implications of this practice, I eventually asked why a powerful corporation did not bring this matter to local and federal law enforcement officials. My colleagues at this seminar on ethical problems in America clearly considered my question naïve. They reacted to my persistence in seeking an answer to this question as if I were an unrealistic child who did not understand the economic and political rules of the great American gamer. Now I was shocked not only by the disclosure but equally shocked at the fact that my fellow seminar participants were not shocked. They were realistic in not permitting an academic discussion of ethical and moral values to be confused by "minor" specific examples of generally accepted institutionalized immorality.

That incident has forced me to look for some common denominator to these critical issues which tend to dominate the rhetoric of American political campaigns and form the verbal core of the promise of those who seek to retain or attain political office.

What is the systematic problem—the fundamental problem of perspective, values and character—which seems to be inherent in the chronic crises which plague American society? Obviously the answer to this question is not to be found in deprivation and poverty of resources. On the contrary, America suffers from an affluence which makes it possible to squander resources with apparent impunity. America also does not suffer from inefficiency; rather it has made a verbal ritual of the worship of efficiency. (Clark, "The Paradoxical Problem of American Society," address, Seminar on Ethical and Moral Problems of American Society, Duke University, March 1972.)

In a pragmatic, efficiency-dominated society, it is difficult for an ethically sensitive person to be taken seriously in the making of "tough-minded, hard-headed" decisions. Promotions don't come easily to these individuals. They are not likely to survive the "realistic" screening process which selects candidates for office in a democratic system. American democracy, with its divergent and competing racial, ethnic and class groups, cannot afford to elect to high office individuals who genuinely and uncompromisingly place ideals and ethical values above personal advantages and "realistic" moral compromises. Shrewd politicians, realistic statesmen, subtle demagogues, smooth political advisors become indistinguishable among themselves—but are clearly distinguishable from the unreality [people] who not only believe in but act upon fundamental ethical principles. Indeed, the concern with honesty and human values becomes the sign that an individual is not practical enough to be entrusted with the responsibilities of making realistic political and economic decisions.

The virulence of this ethical and moral sickness which pervades the American society is indicated by the fact that the symptoms, flagrant or subtle, are accepted by sophisticated realists—the controllers, policy and decision makers of our society—as normative, competitive, and necessary for efficiency, affluence, and effectiveness. In short, they are interpreted as signs of health. Those who insist that they are signs of a severe social disease are to be dismissed as starry-eyed moralists, sentimentalists and understandably without influence or power. As a matter of fact, the few serious moral critics of our society do not have constituents. Intellectually and temperamentally they cannot appeal to the masses. They cannot build for themselves appeals for the same reasons they would be impotent politically. Neither can they expect support from radicals of the right or the left because they tend to be as much concerned with methods as they are with ends; they cannot accept moral ends through immoral means.

The moral schizophrenia pervasive in the American social, political and economic system appears to be no more curable by words than is personal schizophrenia curable by psychotherapeutic preachments. Political, religious, civil rights panaceas have been tried and found palliative at best and cruelly disillusioning at worst. The persistence, however, of that critical minority of human beings who insist upon being unrealistic, who for some presently unknown set of reasons continue to argue that human beings are somehow capable of the possibility of empathy, compassion and sensitivity even as cruelty and hostility and insensitivity seem dominant, seems essential for hope. (Clark, "Moral Schizophrenia of America" [address, Duke University, March 1972].)

Social morality is illusive and difficult to define. It involves not only man's intelligence but his feelings and his total being. It depends upon man's capacity to give and to receive love, to be kind and to be empathic. Love in its most concrete sense is a primary emotion essential to the preservation of the species. It is a positive and adaptive emotion, which involves an affinity and desire for closeness with another human being. Kindness may be viewed as the generalized expression of love, concern, and sensitivity in interpersonal relations, empathy as the ability to feel into and to identify with the needs of another human being. An empathic person shares another's concerns, joys, anguish, despair, frustrations, hopes, and aspirations as if they were his own. Empathy, unlike love, is not concrete and primary but requires the capacity for abstract thought. Empathy is not possible for a limited, defective, egocentric, or animalistic human organism. Without empathy, neither social morality nor responsibility, neither justice nor human society itself would be possible. In empathy, human intelligence, love, and kindness converge.

There are so-called tough-minded realists who contend that love, kindness, and empathy are mere disguises for more powerful and primitive egocentric and animalistic impulses in man. They contend that there is no stable basis for social morality, and that all morality is a thin pretensive [*sic*] veneer quick to disappear under stress, deprivation, or adversity. The debate between the advocates of man's moral capacity and obligations and those who contend that only egocentric power imperatives are important has dominated man's struggle to define the dimensions of his humanity from the awakening of human consciousness up to the Vietnam protests. (Clark, "Social Morality and Scientific Objectivity," in *Pathos of Power* [New York: Harper & Row, 1974], 37–38.)

In this nuclear and space age when the arrogance of man seems close to realization, it has become increasingly clear that superior human intelligence, narrowly defined as the ability to manipulate ideas and things, does not guarantee human survival. In fact, the intelligence measurable by psychologists is the gravest threat to the survival of the human species. The extinction of life on this earth can now be achieved through the effort of constricted, segmentalized, isolated genius. This is no longer a figment of the overactive imagination of science fiction writers, but the overriding anxiety of our times. Before this monster, his own creation, man seems paralyzed by a silently pervasive panic. (Clark, "Social Morality and Scientific Objectivity," in *Pathos of Power* [New York: Harper & Row, 1973], 33.)

Let us make no mistake here: racism is a disease. (Clark, quoted in *The American Revolution: Democratic Politics and Popular Education* [Washington, DC: American Enterprise Institute for Public Policy Research, 1974], 6.)

As a social psychologist, I am aware that institutions and bureaucracies do not change easily; and, for reasons at present not clearly understood but I believe inherently perverse, educational institutions seem particularly resistant to change. But they must change if they are to survive. (Clark, *Pathos of Power* [New York: Harper & Row, 1974], 45.)

How can today's young people deal with racism? One thing I'd suggest is that you take it on as a conscious constructive approach to rebellion and revolt, rather than one that's self-destructive. I was hoping that the so-called revolt of the youth and college students in the late 1960s and early 1970s would have had some sort of moral or ideological core, but in looking back on those years, it is my judgment that they reflected the amorality of America; they had no moral or ideological base. After the decision not to draft college students into the Vietnam War, the steam went out of the anti-war movement. I think it is possible for young people to try to save this nation, and to do it in what the psychologists call that inevitable "assertion" stage, but they must give it substance in terms of moral assertion, because here is where the adults are really vulnerable. Here is where the young can really pillory their elders. By standing up to them and saying, "Stop this damned double-talk. On the one hand, you tell me about the

American creed and Judaism and Christianity and all that, and on the other hand, you are a walking refutation of it." Say it to them and then know that it isn't enough to simply say it; act it. As long as you refuse to perpetuate their hypocrisy, the parents and adults who are implicated are going to view with alarm whatever you do. They can't view it with any more alarm if you do something constructive. (Clark, "At This Stage of My Life," *Journal of Current Social Issues* 12.3 [1975]: 28.)

As far as I know, no profound historian or social philosopher has yet argued that the essential determinant of civilization is that small number of human beings who persist, in the face of overwhelming odds, in demanding, fighting for, and, if necessary, giving their lives for justice and morality. This is probably too simple a point for erudite scholars to build or reinforce their reputations upon.

As I have watched the ongoing struggles for social, economic, and racial justice in the United States and throughout the world, I have come to the conclusion that the common element in every civilized society—that important difference between subtle or flagrant forms of barbarism among human beings and the continuing struggle for decency—is a critical minority of individuals who are compelled to argue that human beings are capable of functioning on a higher level of social responsibility. These persistent individuals insist that the prevailing definitions of what is realistic and of what the controllers of power mandate and defend are not acceptable in a just society. They challenge the existing norms of behavior. They demonstrate the contradictions between the verbal and the religious ideals of their society on the one hand and the rewarded day-to-day practices on the other. They are rarely, if ever, popular. They are frequently ridiculed or ignored or, at times, even sacrificed. (Clark, preface to William Worthy, *The Rape of Our Neighborhoods* [New York: William Morrow, 1976], 11–12.)

Moral and ethical concerns cannot be avoided in an objective study of human interaction. Any attempt to define social science objectivity in terms of a "balanced view" which seeks to evade or deny moral and human truths is transparent and neither objective or scientific. (Clark, foreword to Donald K. Cheek, *Assertive Black . . . Puzzled White* [San Luis Obispo, CA: Impact Publishers, 1976], vii–viii.)

I have come to the conclusion that so far as the Negro is concerned, the ethical aspect of American liberalism or the American Creed is primarily verbal. (Clark, quoted in Carol Polsgrave, *Divided Minds: Intellectuals and the Civil Rights Movement* [New York: W.W. Norton, 2001], 204–205.)

COMMENTARY

Lawrence Plotkin

Kenneth B. Clark was in the forefront of the civil rights movement for over fifty years. He was a scholar and activist who served as a model to a new generation of researchers. He fought for desegregation in education and housing as well as the demolition of stereotypes. The outstanding characteristic of his personality was his persistence. Clark never stopped fighting for the full participation of African Americans into American society. His special focus, however, was the lives of black children, especially their education. There were significant victories and some defeats, but Kenneth never stopped trying. Clark's research, publications, and public appearances painted a picture of the kind of world we will eventually reach. He also diagnosed the personal and institutional racism that had to be overcome. What always amazed me is that he rarely lost his temper. The anger he felt was always internalized.

CHAPTER 4

The Human Cost of Racism

[The Negro's] only defense is to meet every act of barbarity, illegality, cruelty and injustice toward an individual Negro with the fact that 100 more Negroes will present themselves in his place as potential victims. (Clark, quoted in *Negro Heritage Library: A Martin Luther King Treasury* [New York: Educational Heritage, Inc., and Harper & Row, 1964], 25.)

It is one measure of the depth and insidiousness of American racism that the nation ignores the rage of the rejected—until it explodes in Watts or Harlem. The wonder is that there have been so few riots, that Negroes generally are law-abiding in a world where the law itself has seemed an enemy.

It is not possible for even the most responsible Negro leaders to control the Negro masses once pent-up anger and total despair are unleashed by a thoughtless or brutal act. As long as institutionalized forms of American racism persist, violent eruptions will continue to occur in the Negro ghettos. When they do happen, the oversimplified term "police brutality" will be heard, but the relationship between police and residents of the ghetto is more complicated than that. Unquestionably, police brutality occurs. (Clark, "The Wonder Is There Have Been So Few Riots," *New York Times Magazine*, September 5, 1965, 28.)

Not only is the pathology of the ghetto self-perpetuating, but one kind of pathology breeds another. The child born in the ghetto is more likely to come into a world of broken homes and illegitimacy; and this family and social instability is conducive to delinquency, drug addiction, and criminal violence. Neither instability nor crime can be controlled by police vigilance or by reliance on the alleged deterring forces of legal punishment, for the individual crimes are to be understood more as symptoms of the contagious sickness of the community itself than as the result of inherent criminal or deliberate viciousness. (Clark, *Dark Ghetto: Dilemmas of Social Power* [New York: Harper & Row, 1965], 81.)

The city has failed its Negro youth. There are evidences of it all around us. They've failed in the apprenticeship program and most of all the city has consistently failed to stimulate the kids to help themselves. The city has its back against the wall now. It can't turn away. It's got to act—and act soon. The city doesn't have any choices left. Time is running out for this city. The people of Harlem and Bedford-Stuyvesant are tired of promises and nothing else from City Hall. (Clark, quoted in Barry Gottehrer and the staff of the *New York Herald-Tribune, New York City in Crisis* [New York: WCC Books, Pocket Books, and David McKay Company, 1965], 29.)

It ought to be quite clear to you in this morass of confusion that I understand the American racial problem and its future not in terms of ideals, not in terms of the Judaic-Christian heritage, not in terms of Supreme Court decisions, not in terms of legislation, and not in terms of very persuasive, extremely militant, civil rights speeches on the part of our chief executive, but in the hard, tough concept of power and its use in terms of changing a status system. We must now understand, because it has become increasingly clear in the light of our verbal, legislative, judicial, and executive victories that America's Negro minority has, in fact, historically been and is contemporaneously relegated to lower status—that is, to a powerless position in the society. Probably the most likely mass reactions to the emptiness, the despair, the frustration inherent in nontangible, nonconcrete victories, and the perpetuation of powerlessness are the stagnation, the emptiness, the withdrawal that you find so common in the Negro children in the ghetto who do not believe in anything, including their own posturing leaders, who accept their defeat, and as adolescents reveal this in the hypodermic needle or in a total rejection of everything. These are the signs of chronic powerlessness. (Clark, "Social Power and Social Change in Contemporary America" [address to the Foreign Affairs Scholars Program, the Department of State, the Agency for International Development, and the United State Information Agency, U.S. Department of State, Washington, DC, July 18, 1966].)

The cost to our society of educational inefficiency is intolerable. In attempting to calculate the cost of this widespread educational wastage one must include a substantial proportion of the present costs for the care of the delinquents and criminals, the actual costs of their destructive crimes and violence, the costs of the chronically dependent, and the costs of those who are chronically mentally and physically diseased or incapacitated. This staggering economic burden does not include the incalculable cost resulting from the wastage of human resources, their unfulfilled potential for constructive contributions to our society, and the loss of the producing and consuming power of a substantial proportion of our population which, if developed, would contribute significantly to the strength and stability of the economy. The American taxpayer, government, business and industry are required to pay an unbearably high price for a shoddy and inefficient product—the public school education of low income and minority group children. (Clark, "The Disadvantaged Poor: Education and Employment" [address before the Chamber of Commerce of the United States, Washington, DC, 1966], 175–176.)

I have spent most or all of my adult life trying to make clear that race and color are dangerous superstitions, that once human beings get caught up in this kind of myth, it can be extremely destructive. In the lifetime of nearly every one of us in this room we have seen in the German experience what I have thought was the ultimate manifestation of horror, cruelty, and barbarity inherent in a society deifying a destructive myth. Having lived through that it seems to me that reason and conscience and decency and justice would argue for fighting to the very last breath against human's deification of the myth of color and race.

But the reality is that America does deify the myth or at least it lives by it. It is now a reality, which I am sorry to see, and sorry to have to accept, that an increasing proportion of Negroes is in fact turning their backs on the desegregation-integration approach to living in American society. They are in fact saying that if race and color are so important to whites, let's make them doubly important to us. This is the only way that we will be able to save our children from the degradation which the white society would seek to impose upon them. I still deeply believe that this is a fallacy. This is wrong. But this is the reality of the Negro's demand for decentralization and community control of his schools, a demand he will extend to other areas of life. The Negro was defeated in the pursuit of the desegregation route, and he seems to have accepted the defeat with relative peace and calm. It is my prediction, however, that he will not permit himself to be defeated in the pursuit of the decentralization or the community control route. It is clear to me as a social analyst and observer that in the pursuit of racial control of those institutions which he believes affect the lives and destiny and the future of his children, he seems now prepared to die, prepared to demand that America stop the pretense of democracy. Take off the mask of affability, and portray the full extent of racial cruelty that might lie below the surface. (Clark, "The Myth of Race, the Inseparable Destiny" [address as a member, New York State Board of Regents Fifteenth

Annual Westchester Conference of Community Services, White Plains, NY, November 21, 1968].)

The worst thing about the ghetto is the involuntary imprisonment of its people. The fact that they do not have the opportunities of freedom of choice and movement which all other people who lived in one or another type of ghetto had. Given this involuntary confinement, pathologies develop. . . . What is horrible to me is the quiet acceptance of human destruction, which is the pervasive fact of the ghetto. When they fight back, you at least know that they're still human. (Clark, quoted in Jack Van Riper, "Our Ghettos Are Concentration Camps" (interview), *New York Sunday News*, December 29, 1968, 4–6.)

Why are we confronted with hundreds of thousands of ghetto young people who cannot be integrated easily into the business and industrial life of our time? The answers to the question "why" appear to me embarrassingly obvious:

First, these young people about whom we are concerned, at least verbally, have been, and their parents before them have been, systematically excluded from any other than menial roles in the economy of our society.

Second, these young people are the victims—the human casualties—of a criminally inferior public education system, a system which at times seems deliberately to provide these youngsters with an education, or a non-education that would make it impossible for them to compete with others in the business, industrial, or academic society. Without regard to intent, and without regard to the alibis provided by the controllers of the educational establishment, it remains a fact, that children of our inner cities receive a criminally inefficient segregated education in the schools they are required to attend. Schools attended by low-income and low-status children annually spawn thousands of functional illiterates, incapable of moving directly into the industrial and commercial society without compensatory educational or training programs.

Third, the answer to this question of human casualties is that the ghetto itself exists. The ghetto is an institutionalized, unfree form of racism. It demonstrates clearly that some are less privileged, less worthy, and are subjected to less freedom of movement and involvement in the society than others. (Clark, "No Gimmicks, Please, Whitey" [address at the National Conference on the Effective Utilization by Industry of the Hard-Core Unemployed, Chicago, March 20, 1968].)

Only through effective social action and visible social changes brought about primarily through the efforts of these people themselves—and hopefully supported by those more privileged people who still have the capacity for empathy—can we hope ever to remove the walls of the ghetto, can we hope to release its human hostages and to remove that ghetto which is created inside of each of us as long as the ghetto outside remains the symbol of man's inhumanity to man. Only when this is done will the necessity for the ghetto no longer exist within you; only when the ghetto is destroyed, can there be an affirmative answer to that most anguished expression of the human predicament: "Am I my brother's keeper." (Clark, "Social Dynamics of the Ghetto" [address given at the Third Annual National Vocational-Technical Teacher Education Seminar, Miami Beach, FL, October 20, 1969].)

American ghettos are in fact, racial prisons. They reflect, I think, the American version of concentration camps. With practically all the pathologies of concentration camps—with the exception of systematic destruction of the human beings involved in a concentrated time period. . . . Those who are confined to the degrading, dehumanizing inner-city slum necessarily respond to such paradox with frustration, despair, and a sense of hopelessness, which, in turn, takes the form of a hostility and aggression which immediately and most directly is directed toward self, and toward one's whole group; and an outer-directed hostility expressed in terms of acting-out.

Powerlessness is the essence of this predicament. The ghetto resident, with few exceptions, seems unable to mobilize and sustain efforts to change the conditions of his life. In this regard, it seems to me important to make some comment on the cult of the indigenous which has developed out of the Office of Equal Opportunity, the War on Poverty. The essence of the "maximum-feasible-participation" of the indigenous aspect of the Economic Opportunity Act is really to ask the victims of America's social and racial cruelty to assume the primary responsibility for overcoming the manifestations of this cruelty. My close observation of community action programs over the past three years has made perfectly clear to me that the victims of the ghetto are not in themselves able to overcome the burdens and problems of the ghetto. They are not at present able to mobilize and sustain the variety of talents, strategies, tactics, and programs which are essential to making a serious attack on solving problems of the ghettos.

Unfortunately, America does not have the excuse offered by the post–World War II German people when confronted with the horrors of Nazism—almost every German said he didn't know. America now knows, clearly, what it has done and what it is now doing to human beings by confining them in negative, dehumanizing, and destructive ghettos. It knows that it is systematically destroying human potential. This is a tremendous burden. America knows that it cannot continue to do this without paying an excessively high price. I think I hear the rebelling young people—white and black—in our society, on our campuses, asking through the cacophony of their rebellion (and it is, to me, fascinating that the white students who are rebelling, sometimes seemingly randomly and mindlessly, are from middle and upper-middle class white families) for some evidence that America is serious about human beings. I think until we give them this evidence—not only in terms of what we do in Vietnam, but in terms of what we do about our ghettos, we can expect them to keep flaunting, to keep mocking, to keep saying to us that we are doomed. Americans don't like to be doomed. They don't like to be pessimistic. In fact if we have any national characteristic, it is that we want to be optimistic. But we usually wait until the very last moment to act so as to sustain our optimism. My optimism is based on the fact that we do tend to play brinkmanship. I am optimistic because I think we are on the brink and that we will act constructively when it is clear to all of us that we are. (Clark, "The Racial Prisons of America's Ghettos" [address to the National Conference on Social Welfare, Chicago, IL, June 1, 1970].)

I think we are very concerned about violence perpetrated toward people whom we are concerned about—high status people who are the victims of violence really create a tremendous amount of concern in America. Lower status people, when they are the victims of violence, we are not that concerned. Now, whether this is peculiar to America I'm not prepared to say. But certainly America has been able to take a tremendous amount of violence perpetrated against Negroes, for example, or civil rights workers, abolitionists. (Clark, guest on *What's Happening to America?* hosted by Edwin Newman, NBC Television, July 12, 1968.)

Americans are concerned about outbursts of certain types of violence. Now, the American people did not seem to me to be overwhelmingly shocked at the series of bombings of Negro churches in the south. Disturbances, yes, but not great shock. Now, if these were reversed, if they were white churches being bombed by black power advocates they would not only be shocked but there would be revulsion and there would be commissions, and there would be law and order mandates. (Clark, guest on *What's Happening to America?* hosted by Edwin Newman, NBC Television, July 12, 1968.)

COMMENTARY

Roger Wilkins

There is a legal concept called judicial notice that loosely means that some facts are so clear from life experience that they do not have to be proved in court. Thus, a party to a lawsuit does not have to offer proof that things fall toward the earth and not toward the sky or that on a clear day that same sky is blue. In the years before 1954, the fact that segregation and the repression and humiliations that went with it damaged us was as clear to blacks as the law of gravity or the color of the sky. Yet the vast majority of whites—including judges, most academics, and major opinion makers—could not see that fact because they were blinded by their firm belief in black inferiority. They were impervious to the ideas that the behaviors they disliked in blacks were produced by the brutal economic and cultural abuses blacks had endured from before the beginning of the Republic. They were also blind to the fact that the brutalizers were also doing damage to themselves and to our country.

Kenneth Clark and his beloved wife and partner, Mamie Clark, did the intellectual work that helped shatter many of the blinders of racism. In their research into the psyches of black children, they demonstrated that economic deprivation and massive cultural assaults on their subjects diminished their senses of themselves and thus their capacities to function as full human beings. The work culminated in the brief by the social scientists that Kenneth Clark marshaled and edited for submission to the Supreme Court as it deliberated the issues in *Brown v. Board of Education*. While the Court explicitly relied on the social scientists' work concerning the damage to blacks, it ignored the other telling point—that inflicting racist damage on blacks did significant damage to whites as well.

People who do not accept the result of *Brown v. Board* or its implications have attacked Clark's work over the ensuing five decades, but the evidence supporting their conclusions has only continued to mount. Some of it was supplied by Kenneth Clark himself in his very important book *Dark Ghetto*. The insights in that work supplied much of the underpinning of the work of the Kerner [National Advisory Commission on Civil Disorders] Commission in 1968.[1]

In addition to his scholarly and civil rights activities Kenneth Clark is also a brilliant teacher and a loving mentor. Scores of both white and black activists (including this writer) benefited from Kenneth Clark's great intellectual and spiritual generosity. There is no question that he belongs in the front ranks of the greatest civil rights heroes of the twentieth century.

NOTE

1. See the Introduction, note 14 for a discussion of the commission.

CHAPTER 5

Prejudice, Psychology, and Mental Health

One cannot deal realistically with the problem of minority status and problems of mental health without attempting to understand the deep, insidious—even though accepted as norm—psychological and psychiatric problems of the dominant group—those who are the alleged beneficiaries of the injustices perpetrated upon the powerless victims of American racism. Even liberal Americans sometimes seek to explain American racial practices of segregation in terms of a desire to protect white children from the detriment of exposure to the pathology imposed upon Negro children. It is difficult for Americans—including professionals in the psychological and psychiatric disciplines—to accept the evidence and the paradox that white children are also psychologically damaged by American racial injustices which are maintained for their advantage. As American privileged white children grow up they are inevitably exposed to the glaring contradictions between what they are taught about the virtues of American democracy—the American creed of brotherhood, equality and justice on the one hand, and on the other hand, they see the Negro discriminated against, rejected, segregated, and humiliated.

The fanatic or violent bigot presents a complex psychiatric dilemma. As long as he stays within the narrow framework of fanatic racism he is generally regarded as only a normal person with extreme views. He is not within the context of American racism seen as a sick individual. Clues to the emotionally disturbed type of racism may be found in the intensity of the expressed prejudices—the irrationality of the hatreds and fears and the evidence that the individual seems fixated and rigid in his hostility and inability to control his violence. But these individuals are not treated as if they are emotionally ill because the milder forms of the disease of racism have infected so many others in our society—including our diagnosticians. (Clark, *Minority Status, Social Power and Some Problems of Psychotherapy* [Hanover, NH: University Press of New England, 1957], 14–16.)

Racial prejudices and their institutionalized forms distort and dehumanize human beings. The essence of the American dilemma is in the distortions and despair in the lives of the victims of the persistent prejudices and the immobilizing guilt, ambivalence and moral cynicism which dominate or make empty the lives of those who are required to acquiesce to injustices perpetrated upon others. The struggle for mental health is necessarily made more difficult with these inevitable burdens of a racist society. Under such circumstances it may well be necessary to settle for the norm of passive adjustment and the absence of pathology as the practical substitute for dynamic and creative health.

In a racist society, it is not only possible but quite likely that the majority of prejudiced individuals will be normal, adjusted, and conform to the attitudinal and situational demands of that society. The argument for the amelioration and eventual elimination of racial distinctions in American life must therefore be predicated upon more fundamental value considerations. Racism in American society is inconsistent with the Judaic-Christian and democratic ideology which is inherent in our history and culture. As long as any aspect of racism prevails, it will necessarily be in conflict with this ideology and this conflict will necessarily be involved in the socialization of individuals. And this conflict will be internalized by the individuals in that culture. In our society racism imposes upon individuals arbitrary, unnecessary and remediable feelings of inferiority, guilt, irrational fears and hatred, conflicts, anxieties, awkwardness and hostilities. These are patently inimical to personal creativity and effectiveness. These, therefore, make impossible personal and social mental health.

If this analysis is fundamentally correct, it becomes the obligation of psychologists to mobilize their training, their methods and their insights and demand that our society use whatever methods which are consistent with our democratic heritage to remove this unnecessary burden from the personalities of our citizens. At this junction of world history, this is an urgent matter of national public health. The techniques for the enforcement of public health imperatives must be used and intensified in this sphere of mental health. Our nation desperately needs to conserve, train and use constructively and creatively all of its available human resources if it is to increase its chances of survival. It cannot now afford any human wastage on the tragically irrelevant grounds of race or color. (Clark, "A Theoretical Approach to Problems of Mental Health and Prejudice" [address, The Samuel H. Flowerman Memorial Lectures, New York, December 8, 1961].)

The emotional ill health of the dark ghetto is a continuum ranging from the anxious but "normal" individual to the criminally psychotic. The harm-

ful effects of American racism on personality development and psychological balance are unmistakable. . . . Harlem has the highest rate of admission
to state mental hospitals of any area in New York City. . . . Three percent
of the total population of New York City lived in Central Harlem, which
ranked first in rates of admissions to state hospitals, contributing 6.5 percent of all New York City admissions.

In the absence of adequate and urgently needed research into the degree
of actual prevalence of emotional illness in Negro urban communities, one
can do little more than speculate. . . . The report on urban mental illness
based on a neighborhood study conducted in mid-Manhattan and reported
publicly in 1962 concluded that one in three in the area was, in some
degree, emotionally disturbed.

It is clear that facilities for treatment are inadequate. In Harlem, for
example, there are four services for emotionally disturbed children, two of
them public, and two private. According to data supplied by three of these
agencies, they serve 56 young people under 24. But if one in 10 of the
general population is emotionally disturbed, as the National Association
for Mental Health estimates, more than 12 times this number of young
people alone in Harlem need help, not counting the adults. (Clark, *Dark
Ghetto: Dilemmas of Social Power* [New York: Harper & Row, 1965],
82–84.)

In the past two centuries the physical and biological sciences have demonstrated the pragmatic successes of human intelligence in understanding
and controlling important aspects of the environment. Moreover, scientific
developments have also demonstrated that understanding tends to bring
with it a technology that defines progress. The merger of the technologies
of astronomy and physics, for example, produced the "space age," marked
by rapid transportation and instant worldwide communication. The technologies of the biological sciences that led to the control of diseases recently
have brought us to the threshold of genetic manipulation through recom-
binant DNA techniques, with vast implications for species modification.

The mere fact that a client or patient seeks the help of a psychologist
emphasizes that humans must interact and that understanding of the human mind is predicated on understanding this "interaction." Verbal and
behavioral forms of communication have long been used in attempts to
persuade, influence, educate, and otherwise control the behavior of others.
These methods of communication have included education, propaganda,
religion, political indoctrination, and psychotherapy. However, their effectiveness did not require precision. Rather, their effectiveness tended to
reinforce whatever explanations or dogmas were offered, and their acceptance enhanced the power of those who offered them.

Superior human intelligence made it possible for the physical sciences to
provide human beings with ultimate weapons of destruction. Superior hu-

man intelligence must now make it possible for the psychological sciences to prevent human beings from destroying themselves. The needed future-relevant psychological sciences and precise psycho technologies must seek to understand and control man's violent impulses and the capacity of human beings to rationalize cruelty and injustice. (Clark, quoted in "Psychology," in *Medical and Health Annual* [Chicago, IL: Encyclopedia Britannica, 1965], 296–297.)

In view of their status and psychological distance, the social worker's concern to "relate to" the "client" seems pathetic in its failure of elemental empathy. The stated or unstated goal of this type of "therapeutic" relationship must then become that of helping the client "adjust" to his life realities, i.e., to keep him from "acting out" his rebellion in antisocial or self-destructive ways. (Clark, quoted in Peter I. Rose, ed., *The Study of Society: An Integrated Anthology* [New York: Random House, 1967], 499–510.)

Our disease could be terminal. Race conflict in America is the most flagrant, visible form of dry rot in our country. (Clark, in Mary Harrington Hall, "A Conversation with Kenneth B. Clark," *Psychology Today* 2.1 [1968]: 4.)

Probably the overriding question confronting the human species in this the beginning of the nuclear age, is that which deals with the ability of man to make the necessary changes in his perspectives, allegiances and functional values which are essential for the survival of the human species. It is becoming increasingly clear to a relatively few number of social philosophers that whereas in the past, moral and ethical concerns could be considered abstractions peculiar to the concerns of religious men, theologians and philosophers, these issues have now become the critical and determinative factors of human survival. Man's respect for his fellow man, the ability to respect man for his humanity—the need to translate the words "decency," "justice," "equality," "compassion," "kindness" and "love" into functional realities—are now not only the imperatives for unity among men, but are the sheer determinants of the survival of human civilization. (Clark, "Respect for Man—The Unqualifiable Basis for Unity" [address before the Conference on National Unity, Sterling Forest Gardens, NY, November 19, 1969].)

Let us make no mistake here: racism is a disease. (Clark, "The American Revolution: Democratic Politics and Popular Reform" [address given at the Bicentennial of the United States of America, 1776–1976, American Enterprise Institute for Public Policy Research, Distinguished Lecture Series, Washington, DC, 1976], 6.)

I'm at the stage of my life where I'm not going around shouting and expressing rage. As a psychologist—I hate to use this word—I'm enjoying watching the irrationalities of my fellow human beings, including myself. I look upon my life as a series of glorious defeats. No, not despair. I am merely looking at what exists. (Clark, quoted in Studs Terkel, *Race: How Blacks & Whites Think & Feel about the American Obsession* [New York: The New Press, 1992], 338.)

COMMENTARY

Alvin F. Poussaint

Dr. Kenneth Clark is without peer; he is a role model and inspiration to young black scholars and professionals around the world. Widely recognized for his groundbreaking doll studies that provided major support for the 1954 Supreme Court desegregation decision, Dr. Clark, as a scholar and public intellectual, has effectively advanced the cause of social justice. Following his example, I—like many others in academia—became an activist on behalf of African Americans. Dr. Clark's historic contributions have given breath to America's promise of democracy; generations to come will be enriched by his legacy.

PART II

The Continuing Search for Social Justice

David Levering Lewis

There have been few twentieth-century American social scientists whose scholarship has been more ethically illuminating and socially productive. That we are now about to celebrate the half-century mark of the abolition of the pernicious national doctrine in law and custom of separate racial equality is due in great measure to Kenneth Clark's research, publications, and intellectually courageous example. His public service as thinker and activist has been a beacon for genuine democracy.

CHAPTER 6

Education: The Key to Freedom

No one can think for you. You must think for you. You must have the courage even to be wrong—and to correct one's errors when the evidence demands correction. Social progress and good human relations do not just happen. They are the products of the joint activity of people who maintain their adolescent idealism, critical intelligence and moral courage. They come from people who recognize and react to small injustices among individuals as well as large social problems. In short, one must have the courage not only to see that the Emperor is without clothes—but to say so as a necessary first step in clothing his nakedness. (Clark, commencement address, New Lincoln School, New York City, 1955.)

We must assume the risks that are required to make our colleges relevant to a civilization desperately in need of the critical and creative intelligence of committed human beings. We must do everything we can to control the greatest contemporary danger—the ravage of a soulless, valueless intelligence. (Clark, address, Association of College Admissions Counselors, Philadelphia, PA, October 7, 1963.)

The clash of the cultures in the classroom is essentially a class war, a socioeconomic and racial warfare being waged on the battleground of our schools, with middle-class and middle-class aspiring teachers provided with a powerful arsenal of half-truths, prejudices, and rationalizations, arrayed against hopelessly out-classed working-class youngsters. (Clark, "Clash of Cultures in the Classroom" [address to the Social Science Institute, Coppin State Teachers College, Baltimore, MD, March 15, 1963].)

Today, education is perhaps the most important function of state and local governments. Compulsory school attendance laws and the great expenditures for education both demonstrate our recognition of the importance of education to our democratic society. It is required in the performance of our most basic public responsibilities, even service in the armed forces. It is the very foundation of good citizenship. Today it is a principal instrument in awakening the child to cultural values, in preparing him for later professional training, and in helping him to adjust normally to his environment. In these days, it is doubtful that any child may reasonably be expected to succeed in life if he is denied the opportunity of an education. Such an opportunity, where the state has undertaken to provide it, is a right which must be made available to all on equal terms. (Clark, "Educational Stimulation of Racially Disadvantaged Children," in Harry Passow, ed., *Education in Depressed Areas* [New York: Teachers College Press, 1963], 142.)

Children who are treated as if they are uneducable invariably become uneducable. (Clark, *Dark Ghetto: Dilemmas of Social Power* [New York: Harper & Row, 1965], 128.)

As I get older, it becomes increasingly and embarrassingly clear to me, the greater the difficulty I have in making my ideas about the subject matter coherent. When I was younger, it seemed to me that things were much more clear. Solutions were easy. The gimmicks were there on the shelf just to be pulled out and used. As I reach this grand stage of being a grandfather, my son has much clearer ideas about this same society than I do. I do know that education is the most important process and function of a democratic society. And I do know that the most important factor in the educational process is the human being—the teacher and the student. (Clark, address to the National Committee in Support of Public Schools, Washington, DC, April 4, 1967.)

The hope for a realistic approach to saving public education in American cities seems to this observer to be found in a formula whereby it can be demonstrated to the public at large that the present level of public school inefficiency has reached an intolerable stage of public calamity. It must be demonstrated that minority group children are not the only victims of the monopolistic inefficiency of the present pattern of organization and functioning of our public schools.

It must be demonstrated that business and industry suffer intolerable financial burdens of double and triple taxation in seeking to maintain a stable economy in the face of the public school inefficiency which produces human casualties rather than constructive human beings.

It must be demonstrated that the cost in correctional, welfare, and health services are intolerably high in seeking to cope with consequences of educational inefficiency—that it would be more economical, even for an affluent society, to pay the price and meet the demands of efficient public education.

These must be understood and there must be the commitment to make the average American understand them if our public schools and our cities are to be effective. If we succeed in finding and developing . . . better alternatives to the present educational inefficiency, we will not only save countless Negro children from lives of despair and hopelessness—and thousands and thousands of white children from cynicism, moral emptiness, and social ineptness—but we will also demonstrate the validity of our democratic promises. (Clark, "Alternative Public Schools: A Response to America's Educational Emergency" [address to the National Conference on Equal Educational Opportunity in America's Cities, sponsored by the U.S. Commission on Civil Rights, Washington, DC, November 16, 1967], 215–216.)

I just don't think one can sit back and watch generation after generation of Negro youngsters be lost educationally while the society piddles around reorganizing its schools to meet the needs of the twentieth century. . . . One of the things that fascinates me is that American whites have been so damaged by racial segregation and racism that they cannot understand they are perpetuating the damage on their own children. (Clark, quoted in *Reading Newsreport* 5.1 [October 1970]: 12.)

Education and freedom are important protections of the frailties of man. They must be cherished and nourished and deepened for the ultimate good—the humanization of man. (Clark, "Education: The Basis of Freedom" [address, 1971 Sol Feinstone Lecture, Syracuse University, Syracuse, NY, 1971], 7.)

Although there are a variety of motivations, it is reasonable to believe that many American students revolted and sought mindlessly and self-destructively to destroy educational institutions because they found the moral and ethical sterility of these institutions intolerable. This is a deadly serious game. It is a game involving the search for the essence and the substance that determine the meaning of being human. It is a game that risks the tolerable limits of the human predicament.

As a social psychologist, I am aware that institutions and bureaucracies do not change easily; and, for reasons at present not clearly understood but I believe inherently perverse, educational institutions seem particularly resistant to change. But they must change if they are to survive. The fundamental structure, authority, and prestige patterns of higher educational institutions have been challenged irrevocably. Amid the babel of sometimes silly student protests, some probing questions have been asked by a critical minority of the present generation of students about the purposes, the function, and therefore, inevitably, the governance of our universities. They must be answered, not just in words or rationalization, but by demonstrations of increased efficiency and social programs. This dimension of social responsibility I believe to be the chief determinant of whether human intelligence and education are to be dangerously and incredibly destructive or whether intelligence and education will provide the means to build more just and rational societies worthy of man. (Clark, "Professor and Student: Moral Inconsistency and the Failure of Nerve," *The American Scholar* [1972], 156–164.)

The search for truth, while impotent without implementation and action, under girds every other strategy in behalf of constructive social change. (Clark, quoted in *The Idea of the University of Chicago: Selections from the Papers of the First Eight Chief Executives of the University of Chicago from 1891 to 1975* [Chicago: University of Chicago Press, 1976], 511.)

There was a disproportionate number of excellent black minds on the [Howard University in 1932] campus—men like Ralph Bunche, Franklin Frazier, Alain Locke, Charlie Houston, Abraham Harris, all giants in their field—because they were denied places on faculties of white universities. (Clark, quoted in Richard Kluger, *Simple Justice: The History of* Brown v. Board of Education *and Black America's Struggle for Equality* [New York: Alfred A. Knopf, 1976], 129.)

We now know that children who are not stimulated at home or in the community or in school will have low [IQ] scores. Their scores and, what is even more important, their day-to-day academic performance can be improved if they are provided with adequate stimulation in one or more of these areas. . . . If a child scores low on an intelligence test because he cannot read and then is not taught to read because he has a low score, then such a child is being imprisoned in an iron circle and becomes the victim of an educational self-fulfilling prophecy. (Clark, "The Problem of the IQ," unpublished manuscript, Clark Archives, Hastings-on-Hudson, NY, n.d.)

Urban public school systems have, for the most part, continually failed to educate the masses of their students for a constructive role in a complex industrialized society; they have produced hundreds of thousands of functional illiterates who are unable to compete with educationally more privileged youth on a single competitive standard, academically or vocationally. This persistent educational default has become a major dilemma for industry and at all levels of government. (Clark, "A Possible Reality: A Design for the Attainment of High Academic Achievement for the Students of

the Public Elementary and Junior High Schools of Washington, D.C."
[New York: Metropolitan Applied Research Center, 1972.])

Initially, the academic retardation of Negro children was explained in terms
of their inherent racial inferiority. The existence of segregated schools was
either supported by law or explained in terms of the existence of segregated
neighborhoods. More recently the racial inferiority or legal and custom
interpretations have given way to more subtle explanations and support
for continued inefficient education. Examples are theories of "cultural deprivation" and related beliefs that the culturally determined educational inferiority of Negro children will impair the ability of white children to learn
if they are taught in the same classes. It is assumed that because of their
background, Negro children and their parents are poorly motivated for
academic achievement and will not only be unable to compete with white
children but will also retard the white children.

In the years 1965 to 1967 another formidable and insidious barrier in
the way of the movement towards effective, desegregated public schools
has emerged in the form of the black power movement and its demands
for racial separatism. Some of the more vocal of the black power advocates
who have addressed themselves to the problems of education have explicitly
and implicitly argued for Negroes' control of "Negro Schools." Some have
asserted that there should be separate school districts organized to control
the schools in all-Negro residential areas; that there should be Negro
Boards of Education, Negro superintendents of schools, Negro faculty, and
Negro curricula and materials. These demands are clearly a rejection of the
goals of integrated education and a return to the pursuit of the myth of an
efficient "separate but equal," or the pathetic wish for a separate and superior racially organized system of education. (Clark, quoted in Beatrice
Gross and Ronald Gross, eds., *Radical School Reform* [New York: Simon
& Schuster, 1969], 116–118.)

Accountability means to hold those people who are responsible for providing services, hold them to account, hold them responsible for providing
those services; they must be held to respectable levels of performance in
the task for which they are being paid. The professional personnel of our
schools, teachers, principals, and other administrators, are being paid and
paid quite well by the taxpayers to teach children. If they do not teach the
children, the children will not learn. And if children do not learn, then
teachers and principals are not doing the job for which you as parents and
taxpayers are paying them. And it is awkward for me, a teacher—I've spent
all my adult life in education—an educator, as a member of the New York
State Board of Regents, to have to admit, to confess to you that we, as
educators, are responsible for the failure of our schools. The Board of Regents of the State of New York is accountable for the quality of education

provided for all of the children of the State of New York. And the Board
of Regents has not been held accountable for the low quality of education
for your children because you have not held them accountable. The Board
of Education of the City of New York is accountable for the quality of
education for your children. And you have permitted the Board of Education, through the succession of Boards of Education during the past ten
years, to permit the quality of education provided for your children to
decrease. (Clark, "Who Is Responsible for Educational Accountability?"
[address to a conference sponsored by The Coalition of Community Organizations on Educational Accountability, New York, August 7, 1971].)

The public schools in America's urban ghettos also reflect the oppressive
damage of racial exclusion. School segregation in the south had, for generations, been supported by law; in the north, segregation has been supported by community custom and indifference. It is assumed that children
should go to school where they live, and if they live in segregated neighborhoods, the schools are, as a matter of course, segregated. But the educational crisis in the ghettos is not primarily, and certainly not exclusively,
one of the inequitable racial balances in the schools. Equally serious is the
inferior quality of the education in those schools. Segregation and inferior
education reinforce each other. Some persons take the position that the first
must go before the second does; others, that the reverse is true. What is
clear is that the problem of education in the urban ghetto seems to be a
vicious cycle: If children go to school where they live and if most neighborhoods are racially segregated, then the schools are necessarily segregated, too. If Negroes move into a previously white community and whites
then move away or send their children to private or parochial schools, the
public schools will continue to be segregated. If the quality of education in
Negro schools is inferior to that in white schools, whites feel justified in
the fear that the presence of Negroes in their own school would lower its
standards. If they move their own children away and the school becomes
predominantly Negro, and therefore receives an inferior quality of education, the pattern begins all over again. The cycle of systematic neglect of
Negro children must be broken, but the powerlessness of the Negro communities and the fear and indifference of the white community have combined so far to keep the cycle intact. (Clark, *Dark Ghetto: Dilemmas of
Social Power* [New York: Harper & Row, 1965], 111–112.)

As I understand what the new breed of student rebels is saying beneath the
incoherence of their frustration and bravado, it is that they are no longer
able to accept the irrelevance, the isolation, the preoccupation with trivia,
the indifference and insensitivity to flagrant injustices which pass for academic objectivity and are offered as higher education. Beneath the din and
cacophony of the righteous indignation and police sirens with which they

are answered, I think I hear these students saying that they want, they demand, they are willing to sacrifice their own personal comfort and future for a morally relevant, personally fulfilling form of education.

I think they are trying to say that they are revolting against all institutions of higher education which define their functions within the limited and dehumanizing scope of vocational schools preparing students to take their place in white collar industrial and commercial factories and preparing them to adjust to the affluent stagnation of antiseptic and empty suburbs, while the inner city dies and strangles lower-status peoples in jungles of injustice and inhumanity. Perhaps they are saying that they can no longer endure colleges and universities which can pride themselves and accept the prestige and respect brought in terms of the number of insensitive Ph.D.'s and the numbers of uneducated physicians, engineers and wealthy leaders of industry which they produce. (Clark, "Learning from Students" [commencement address, Antioch College, June 22, 1968].)

The problem of Antioch's support of [its] Afro-American Institute and the controversy with the HEW [federal Department of Housing, Education, and Welfare] as to whether Antioch's support of this racially organized and exclusionary facility on its campus did or did not violate Title VI of the Civil Rights Act is to me a serious matter involving racial justice and dignity, and the role of the college and university in helping to free the human mind and body of primitive passions. . . . I have been, not only disturbed, but vigorously opposed to the college's decision to participate in any form of racial exclusion.

I opposed this for the same reasons that we fought together in the school segregation cases which led to the *Brown* decision. I continue to believe . . . that racial prejudice, discrimination and segregation are damaging to the human personality without regard to the racial rationalizations or excuses offered in support of such practices.

To exclude someone of one race or to admit that it would be appropriate to do so on the grounds that his background or experience are irrelevant, that they render him unable to achieve is precisely what white segregationists have been doing to blacks for centuries. Yet this seems to be the burden of rationalization at Antioch for a black separatist policy. Yet, it is whites who need a black studies program most of all.

I am convinced that Antioch has not only violated this sacred obligation by its approach to the Afro-American Studies Institute, and by permitting the existence of and financially supporting the racially exclusionary Unity House on its campus, Antioch has also tarnished its own glorious traditions of stubborn resistance to the fashionable. It was this history which made me profoundly proud to be identified with Antioch College.

In permitting a group of students to inflict their dogmatism and ideology on other students and on the total college community; and in being silent while some students intimidate, threaten, and in some cases physically assault the Negro students who disagree with them, the Administration at Antioch has not only defaulted in its responsibilities, but, I believe has made a mockery of its concern for the protection and development of human dignity without regard to cost. (Clark, letter of resignation from the Board of Trustees at Antioch College, May 16, 1969, Clark Archives, Hastings-on-Hudson, NY.)[1]

Any of the present anti-busing proposals, if enacted into law, will destroy . . . any ethical distinctions between the racism of the United States and South Africa. Traditionally, southern and northern communities have utilized the busing of children to public schools as a most effective method for maintaining racially segregated schools. This practice has continued up to recent years in spite of the *Brown* decision of 1954. Bus transportation has been an integral part of the American educational process—both public and private schools—since 1919. By that year the then 48 states of the Union had authorized public funds for school transportation.

While there is little systematic research evidence, it appears from general observation that the children's response to bus transportation to and from school is generally positive. There is at present no evidence to suggest that reasonable busing—within acceptable distances and time—is itself a negative experience or a rejection by the children themselves. (Clark, "Anti-busing . . . Racially Restrictive," *New York Times*, March 10, 1972, 1.)

I would agree completely that Negro colleges and white colleges be eliminated because the policy of education by race is inimical to education. But, in addition, there is the reality that the existence of Negro colleges is a manifestation of, a contribution to, the institution of racism. Double standards of accreditation. Double standards of meanings of degrees. Double standards of content. Invariably these double standards are in the direction of inferior standards for the Negro college, which again makes the college an institutionalized racist phenomenon. So when we say the elimination of Negro colleges, we mean the elimination of all of these contextual things which support and reinforce racism so that a Negro kid comes out of a college with obviously inadequate resources. He allegedly has an A.B—which is not an A.B. in terms of competitive function. (Clark, "Racism and American Education: A Dialogue and Agenda for Action," An Urban Affairs booklet [New York: Metropolitan Applied Research Center, 1970], 88.)

Our public schools are turning out each year hundreds of thousands, if not millions, of functional illiterates, youngsters who spend 12 years, if they do not drop out before, in educational institutions which seem to have abandoned the functions of education and operate primarily as custodial institutions. Such youngsters cannot take advantage of any form of higher education without an intensive preparatory program. The masses of our privileged children are also being subjected to a peculiar and insidious form of educational inferiority, morally and ethically handicapped by hot-house, isolated, racially homogeneous schools wherein they are being prepared for a nineteenth century rather than twentieth century world. (Clark, address given at the National Association of Student Administrators 49th Annual Conference, New York, April 11, 1967.)

The complicated problems of the Negro student in interracial colleges probably reflect the more fundamental problems of the goals and effectiveness of higher education in America. American colleges, which must deal now with the consequences of unequal and segregated education in primary and secondary schools, must accept much of the responsibility for reversing these consequences and preventing their continuance in future generations. It may well be, further, that American colleges and universities will have to find a formula whereby values, social sensitivity and a concern for social justice become an avowed part of the excitement of the intellectual quest. Until this is done, we will have to continue to settle for racial tokenism or a campus microcosm of America's racism on the part of our colleges and for the pretensive [*sic*] futility—the moral emptiness—of Negro and white graduates. Until such a formula is found, America's claims to democracy and the role of our colleges in providing the catalyst for the democratic society will continue to be contaminated by the irrelevance of race. (Clark, "The Negro Student in Northern Inter-Racial Colleges: An Overview," *The Black Student* 1 [1966]: 7.)

Frequently critics of educational technology have asserted that the use of computers contributes to the isolation and an individualistic competitive approach toward learning and academic achievement. It has also been stated that educational technology and the cost of computers will tend to result in a disparity between their availability in schools in higher income communities, and those in low-income communities. If these are true and not remedied, it would be a disturbing fact that educational technology would result in an increasing gap between the academic achievements of more privileged children and the educational performance of the less privileged. It is my belief, however, that these problems can be prevented and remedied. Educational technology needs not be either dehumanizing, or contribute to and increase educational inequality. On the contrary, with proper planning and concern, programs and software can be developed and used wherein educational technology will contribute toward a more solid, substantive, and human value-oriented approach to the goals of education.

Educational technology can involve cooperative, rather than competitive, learning among students. Programs can be developed in which academic achievement and personal self-esteem can be an important part of a total pattern of learning through the helping of others. Educational technology can facilitate a learning process which involves social sensitivity, empathy, and caring about others. . . . This approach to an extended and deepened view of educational and humanizing technology will essentially involve teachers in the socially interactive learning process. Under these circumstances, teachers will not only become more and more familiar with the vast possibilities of computers, but they will also be learning with their students. Together, they will contribute to the ingredients of humor, self-respect, and the respect for variability among other human beings. (Clark, "Humanizing Education through Technology" [address, Science Weekend Symposium APA Convention, New Orleans, August 11, 1989].)

If the Great Society is to be anything other than an effective political slogan, if the promises of the antipoverty program are to be anything other than another showcase of words, storing up for depressed people more cruel frustration in the future, if these things are to have any modicum of reality, the basic initial point of attack must be our educational system. (Clark, address delivered at a seminar on the Social and Economic Implications of Integration in the Public Schools, Manpower Policy and Program, U.S. Department of Labor, Washington, DC, November 12, 1964.)

Probably one of the most important educational responsibilities facing America today is to build into the curriculum at all levels sound and balanced accounts of the contribution of ethnic groups to the vitality of America. The role of all ethnic groups is neglected but probably the most neglected is the Negro American. (Clark, foreword to Morris C. Goodman, *Junior History of the American Negro*, vol. 2: *The Civil War and the Civil Rights War* [New York: Fleet Press, 1970], 1.)

I welcome this opportunity to analyze the two major components of the proposed legislation—the funds requested for compensatory education and the moratorium on busing. . . . I am contending in the essence of my prepared statement that the whole discussion on busing moratorium is essentially a racist discussion. It is, in fact, an attempt to do by public passion and politics what the courts have refused to do; namely, to go back on or dilute or reverse *Brown*. There is no question that this is a passionate issue because race persists in being an American obsession. The President, whether he knows it or not, is using the emotional charge concerned with busing in the face of facts, in conflict with the facts as an aspect of exploiting for political purposes. I think this is a very dangerous thing for a public official to do. It is extremely dangerous for the President of the United States to do; namely, exploiting a dangerous racist reality in America for political purposes.

This is really playing with fire.

There is no evidence that transportation within reasonable time and distances has any unfavorable negative effect on the children transported. In fact, the children themselves talk about this in very positive terms. My own feeling is that transportation could be used even more effectively as part of the education process.

It disturbs me, therefore, that the President's proposal to prohibit the transportation of students for purposes of school desegregation is racially restrictive. A recent survey—Harris poll—reveals that the majority of black Americans do not support the President's anti-busing position in despite of the barrage of propaganda from white and black separatists. Some black separatist leaders make no pretense about this issue of segregation—they expect to inherit the educational budgets of black school districts for their own purposes. The division of America into two societies will be perpetuated as long as a dual school system prevails. (Clark, testimony before the House Committee on Education and Labor as a witness representing the American Civil Liberties Union, *Congressional Record*, April 13, 1972, 615–628.)

I believe that "open admissions" will contribute to an increase or deepening, and broadening, of standards, and that the open admissions policy can enrich and bring us closer to the real values of education. (Clark, "Open Admissions: The Pros and Cons" [address at a symposium sponsored by the Council for Basic Education, Washington, DC, October 29, 1971], 49.)

I will confess to you that in all the work I've been doing in calling attention to the need for raising standards and the quality of public education, I have been surprised by the number of people—including some of my colleagues on the [New York State] Board of Regents—who have told me to forget it: "Why," they ask, "are you always raising these issues?"

Let me tell [a story.] It concerns the *Washington Post*. The editorial-page people were fairly negative. Interestingly enough, reporters who covered this story over a period of time were positive in their reports. I went down and had lunch with a number of editorial board members, including Ben Bradlee, and they thought that the whole thing was idealistic, unreal. I was trying to reorganize the school system; it wouldn't work. I decided to call Kay Graham [the publisher]. I had served on the board of the University of Chicago with her; I thought I knew her. I said, "Kay, I'd like to talk with you about the negative editorials on the educational plan for Washington." She brushed me off, saying, "Kenneth, I do not like to interfere with the editorial department of the paper." I answered: "Look, you know there is such a gap between the editorial position and the news reporting—why?" Her response: "There's no point in our talking." (Clark, "Perspectives on Education," *Daedalus* [Fall 1984]: 229–235.)

At the turn of the century, the late W.E.B. Du Bois prophesized that the problem of race would be the dominant problem of the twentieth century. His prophecy is now seen to be alarmingly accurate. (Clark, "The Continuing Struggle to Desegregate U.S. Education," *Chronicle of Higher Education*, September 4, 1979, 64.)

The black power people have advanced to the point of caricature because they are attempting to deal with the reasons for the erosion of pride and confidence in the peripheral terms of African heritage. What they do not understand is that you cannot give pride to an adolescent who is four or five years retarded in reading and understanding and using English by trying to teach him the Swahili language or African tribal music. (Clark, quoted in "Ghetto Education," a special supplement of *Center Magazine* [November 1968]: 51.)

When he [my son, Hilton Clark][2] was about 14 years old I took him with me on a speaking engagement. I spoke before an assembly meeting of the Ethical Culture Society in Philadelphia on the psychological consequences of racial prejudice and discrimination. At the end of the meeting, we had a coffee hour and the audience was very gracious. Each person came up and told me how much he enjoyed my talk. I tried to smile, and I wondered how anyone could enjoy what I had said if he had listened.

But I decided to play the etiquette game of the invited speaker who speaks graciously to those who compliment him. After some minutes of this, I looked around for my son but could not find him. When I finally found him downstairs I suggested that we leave. He said that he had been ready for a long time.

When I asked him how he had enjoyed the talk, my 14-year-old son looked at me with a terrifying, unctuous smile. He came up, took my hand, and said, "Dr. Clark, I want to tell you how much I enjoyed your talk. I learned a very complex thing this morning. I learned that Negroes are human beings, too, and that if you are cruel to them they react the way other human beings react."

I was sick—sick at the penetrating, devastating truth my son had imposed upon me, and which has not left me since. Needless to say, he is having trouble. He is having trouble in this society because he would not accept my contention that if one is to survive one has to deal with the problems and frailties of human beings without the kind of crushing severity my son brought to the situation. (Clark, "The Negro in Turmoil," in Eli Ginzberg, ed., *The Negro Challenge to the Business Community* [New York: McGraw-Hill, 1964], 58.)

The pathos of black students in predominantly white colleges and universities who are demanding segregated social and academic facilities is matched only by the subtle guile and cynicism of white academic and administrative officials who grant these demands with a speed unprecedented in the tortuously slow and pedantic academic process. These segregated facilities in predominantly white colleges are, in fact, duplicating within campuses the process of institutionalized educational segregation. They are racist. They perpetuate the damage done to black youth. They make it difficult, if not impossible, for these young people to be competitive with others, academically and vocationally. They reduce the intellectual and psychological and human potential of even the brightest of these young people to an unacceptably inferior norm with the rationale of racial style, pride and "soul." In reinforcing this pattern of personal insecurity and frustration, and in exploiting the fears of black students, white college administrators and decision-makers are accessories to these illegal forms of segregation on their campuses and, intentionally or unintentionally, are agents of that dehumanization and intellectual inferiority being perpetrated on a whole generation of potential leaders of black people in the United States. (Clark, "Segregation—The Road to Desegregation?" *Crisis Magazine* [May 1974]: 159–160.)

It is a truism that the status of the Negro in America is the best single index of the vitality of the total American society. If Negro teachers can prepare Negro students for top level scholastic performance and for other creative use of their human potentials, they will give these students the only realistic basis for positive self-esteem. . . . The Negro teacher is pivotal in this inextricable relationship between sound education and desired social change. If he cannot assume this responsibility and these risks—without regard to the reasons he cannot—then he cannot contribute to the stability and survival of our society and he would not be worthy of respect. If he has the vision, clarity, integrity, and personal dignity and will which are necessary in order to make this contribution to a society desperately in need of stable moral guideposts and meaningful values and standards, then he would have earned the respect and gratitude of his fellow man. And this would reflect the ultimate paradox; that 300 years of oppression did not corrode the spirit of all of its victims but refined the inherent human dignity and strength of many. (Clark, "Negro Teachers in Contemporary America: A New and Challenging Role," excerpts from an unpublished paper, Clark Archives, Hastings-on-Hudson, NY, 1966, 15.)

I am not going to inflict upon you another version of education of the disadvantaged. I am now convinced that this is a phony issue; that the discussion itself perpetuates the phoniness; that in my continuing to deal with this issue as if it were absolutely real, I, Kenneth Clark, have been an accessory to the phoniness, the charade. I have continued and have been a part of setting up the smoke screen and obscuring what is the basic issue:

that we have a problem of education of the disadvantaged. We have a problem of education in the ghetto precisely because we insist upon having this problem, precisely because we insist on discussing it as if it were a problem and discussing seriously all of the alibis, the rationalizations, and the explanations offered for the default of the public education system, particularly in large urban centers, in fulfilling the one responsibility which schools have—namely, to teach children.

. . . I am really disturbed when I hear wonderful, warm, sensitive human beings tell me that minority group youngsters, low socio-economic status youngsters, should not be required to meet academic standards because it will frustrate them; it will disturb them and build up tensions and anxieties which are inimical to the kind of happiness which should be found in our schools. (Clark, "Education in the Ghetto: A Human Concern" [address, Urban Education Lecture Series, Teachers College, Columbia University, New York, January 13, 1970], 6–14.)

New York City, 20 years after the *Brown* decision, with official sanction and by virtue of a series of decisions made by the Board of Education and its paid professional staff, is operating a biracial public school system. No attempt has been made to implement even piecemeal plans. What the boards of education of New York City have done—there was a series of boards during the past 20 years—is for us to substitute for any serious attempt to obey the letter and the spirit of *Brown* [is to issue] a series of policy statements in favor of desegregation. The board's procedure is to accept reports and to file and forget reports. (Clark, "New York City Schools Segregated on Purpose 20 Years after Brown," testimony at public hearings of the New York City Commission on Human Rights, May 1974.)

While the argument about busing has been used as a reason for not bringing about desired changes in the racial composition of our schools, the mere fact is that there is more busing going on in public education in the United States to maintain racially isolated schools than there is to eliminate racially isolated schools. No one has raised the argument of busing as a horrible thing, when the function of that transportation was to maintain segregated schools. In many rural areas, the buses are as much a part of the educational process as are the schools themselves. The argument for the desegregation of our public schools must now be presented in terms of the damage which racially segregated schools inflict upon privileged white children for their rejection of authority; namely, their view of authority as morally hypocritical, insensitive, socially disturbing and unstablizing. One of the most disconcerting things for me is the extent to which these young privileged white people seek to escape the moral conflict and quandary which racial segregation practices impose upon them by not only rejecting authority and values, but at times even rejecting reason itself and the whole rational process. These, I suggest, are the defenses to escape the personal guilt. These are their attempts to avoid the sense of moral and ethical emptiness which a racist society imposes upon sensitive individuals. (Clark, testimony before Senator Walter F. Mondale's Select Committee on Equal Educational Opportunity, Washington, DC, December 1970, 4, 10.)

It is in fact ironic that in the last quarter of the twentieth century—a period in human history when man is capable of instantaneous communication throughout the world; has developed ultimate nuclear weapons; has constructed devices which have placed man on the moon and are capable of probing and exploring the planets within our solar system—there remains the anachronism of qualifying educational institutions and educational goals in terms of the stark, tribal superstitions of race. (Clark, "Obligations and Responsibility of Higher Education for Race Relations" [address, Leadership Conference, Jacksonville, FL, February 24, 1983].)

That black students taking the S.A.T.'s score, on the average, 100 points lower than the national norm should not be surprising. The disturbing fact of consistent academic retardation of black students has been the basis of debate for decades. The traditional "explanation" for blacks' consistently low academic achievement scores is that blacks are inherently inferior intellectually. This "explanation," in its subtle and gross forms, is a manifestation of the racism that lies at the core of, and perpetuates, this educational and social problem. (Clark, "Blacks' S.A.T. Scores" [opinion editorial], *New York Times*, October 21, 1982.)

One of the last, and probably most disturbing, comments made by Albert Einstein was, "The splitting of the atom has changed everything save our mode of thinking, and thus we drift toward unparalleled catastrophe." I am presumptuous enough to make a modification of Einstein's observation—a modification specific to the topic of our conference. We have not changed our approach to the goals and objectives of education. We have not changed our rationale for the construction and use of tests at all levels of our education process. And we have not changed our definition of the standards, quality, and goals of education. Our society as a whole, and specifically our educational institutions have not yet seen that the purpose of our various techniques for evaluating our fellow human beings is to help them and ourselves to develop and use our most positive human values and insights for the benefit of civilization. In the nuclear age, an amoral intelligence, the mere assimilation and regurgitation of facts, the boast and competition for military and scientific technological superiority, must now be seen as the major danger to human survival. Education can be the antidote to the extinction of human civilization only if it uses its instruments of evaluation to make disciplined intelligence a social trust. This is the quality of education and the purpose of examinations. (Clark, "Tests as Diagnostic and Not Rejective Instruments" [address to the Testing and Quality Assurance Conference, Miami–Dade Community College, February 12, 1986].)

The librarian is the guardian of the books which communicate our cultural heritage. The librarian is generally seen as the custodian of the chronicle of the human struggle for understanding—the joys, the tragedies, the poetry, the satire—which attempts to plumb the various levels of the human experience. As a child growing up in the center of Harlem, I had the good fortune of meeting Arthur Schomburg, the great collector of books and the founder of the Schomburg Collection located at 135th Street and Lenox Avenue. I met Schomburg when I was 12 years old, a crucial time of my life. Fortunately, my mother had taught me to read before I entered school. At that time teachers had not heard the complex theory of how frustrating and damaging it would be to hold underprivileged children from broken homes to the same high standards as privileged children. Since I could read, it was quite natural for me to gravitate toward the library. On one of my trips to the library, I decided that I was going to explore the third floor, that forbidden and mysterious area upstairs reserved for adults. I fully expected to be turned away unceremoniously. As I climbed the stairs, I felt the excitement of an interloper. I was prepared for the risk of rejection. When I entered the room, a large man, whom I later came to know as Arthur Schomburg, got up from his desk and came over to me and smiled. He didn't ask what I wanted. He merely put one arm around my shoulder and assumed that I was interested in books.

On that first day of meeting Arthur Schomburg, I knew I had met a friend. He did not ask me whether I had come from a broken home. He did not ask me whether my mother was poor. He never told me to improve myself. He merely looked and saw that I was a human being who was probably desperately hungry for the kind of nourishment to be found in books. He accepted me as a human being, and helped me by sharing with me his love and his excitement in the world of books.

Arthur Schomburg was one of my first heroes. I could identify with him because he identified with me. Arthur Schomburg was a rare person. He was not only wise and warm, but he was also incapable of condescension. He could not reject another human being for irrelevant reasons, nor was he self-righteous in his protestations of democratic behavior. In all the years that I knew him—from the time I was 12 years old until his death after I had finished college—I never heard him utter a bombastic or boastful or self-serving remark. Because of Arthur Schomburg, the Schomburg Collection of the New York Public Library at 135th Street became my haven. The library was my own, my haven and my place of peace.

It was there, through Arthur Schomburg, that I first learned about the excitement inherent in the struggle with words and ideas. This is an incalculable contribution to the life of another human being. Books became more important after I met him because anything that was important to anyone who was as wonderful as he had to be important to me. In the years later, when I was a student at Howard University and in charge of inviting a speaker for a conference on guidance for high school students, there was only one person I thought of asking. (Clark, "The Librarian: Role of the Emancipator" [address given at the New York Public Library Early Childhood Resource and Information Center, March 1, 1983].)

A truly educated person must have courage. He must have the courage necessary to dare to stand alone, to run the risk of alienation from a social system which seeks to distort him to fit its mold. He must dare the torture and anguish of moral commitment and certainly he must accept the risks inherent in testing his values through disciplined action. Only through the acceptance of these risks can intelligence and education become functional and socially meaningful. Social progress and decent human relations do not just happen. They are the products of individual human beings—acting as individuals or collectively—who maintain their adolescent idealism, enthusiasm, critical intelligence and courage. They come from the labors of individuals who are intellectually and passionately incapable of accepting injustice and cruelty as a way of life. They come from individuals who understand that wisdom and courage are inseparable, and that our society is desperately in need of both—now. If you can join this small group of pilgrims, you are, indeed, an educated person and worthy of the congratulations and gratitude of our country and mankind. (Clark, "On Being Educated in Today's World" [commencement address, Morgan State College, June 3, 1963].)

Under what circumstances is the Negro ever adjudged worthy or deserving of association with others, and how can he be expected to develop these traits of "worthiness" under conditions which tend to perpetuate characteristics of unworthiness as described by the proponents of this position themselves? In the belief, no doubt, that this was a statement of compassion, one white opponent of New York's school integration plan said: "If I were God, what would I do to improve the lot of the Negro? If I were God, I'd make everybody white." To sensitive Negroes, this betrays the ultimate condescension—the belief that to *be* Negro means irrevocable rejection. (Clark, quoted in Peter I. Rose, ed., *The Study of Society: An Integrated Anthology* [New York: Random House, 1967], 507.)

The educated woman should be so educated as to be able to articulate without apology the affirmative role of a new feminism—to assert those values, those positive feelings that are inherent to the woman as the most precious child-bearing being. . . . In the educated women, whether it be in all female colleges or coeducational colleges, the presence of the female should be a constant reminder of those values of love and kindness and tenderness which Nietzsche called the values of the weak and the feminine.

Somehow a way must be found to remove the pejorative implication of "feminine" as used in describing these values which are essential for man's acceptance of and respect for man. The unqualified concern with the value of life and love over all other considerations are not concerns which should ever be apologized for. A concern with beauty, a concern with justice, a concern with man's compassion and empathy must be affirmed as the core of the meaning of function of education.

In her role as wife, and mother, and teacher, and lover—in her role as artist, as writer, as dancer or worker or executive—in her overall role as the giver of that poetry which makes human life tolerable—women must insist upon unqualified and limitless love of man for man. She must communicate to her children, and all children, beginning with the fact that the symbol of the milk which flows from her breasts is the very essence of human survival. (Clark, "The Educated Woman in a Time of Crisis" [commencement address, Briarcliff College, May 31, 1970].)

One of the most devastating things a teacher can do to a lower-class child is to ask him: "What does your father do?" Such an inquiry, harmless enough in middle-class society, creates tremendous anxiety in the child. The child often responds with sheer fantasy, exaggerating his father's occupation, claiming that he is a policeman or a fireman or a clerk, or in another job that seems to the child to convey status. Almost never will he admit that his father is a porter or a dishwasher or an elevator operator. Rarely will he admit that his father does not live at home unless he disguises his absence by saying he is dead. (Clark, "Sex, Status, and Underemployment of the Negro Male," in Arthur M. Ross and Herbert Hill, eds., *Employment, Race, and Poverty: A Critical Study of the Disadvantaged Status of Negro Workers from 1865–1965* [New York: Harcourt, Brace & World, 1971], 138–147.)

I'm charging that all new members of the [New York State] Board of Regents were interviewed by the political leadership of the House and the Senate in the New York Legislature and among the ideas which were explored with them were their ideas concerning race, busing, quotas, et cetera. And I also charged that if it was fair to the leaders that new members or those who came up for re-election were fair on the desire to desegregate the schools by busing or any other rational means, the chances of their being selected were nil. I've said this over and over again in our debates in [Board of] Regents meetings.

It is absolute double talk. Because the fact is that the Board of Regents, on this issue, has become nothing more than a subcommittee of the Legislature reflecting what the political officials, the elected political officials, believe to be the desire of the majority of whites in New York State. And that is our role. We are now saying that the Board of Regents must be nothing more than a reflection of the existing prejudices and desires of the majority of whites in New York State. (Clark, statement at meeting of New York State Board of Regents, WNBC, Channel 4, January 26, 1970.)

Black children or any other group of children can't develop pride by just saying they have it, by singing a song about it, by saying I'm black and beautiful or I'm white and superior. (Clark, quoted in Christopher Lasch, *The Culture of Narcissism: American Life in an Age of Diminishing Expectations* [New York: W.W. Norton, 1978], 144.)

As one who was privileged to participate as a social psychologist in this historic litigation leading to the *Brown* decision, and as one who was identified by training and occupation as an educator and by birth as a black, I could not escape reflecting on the fact that these fundamental social, political, psychological, and educational insights into the broader aspects of the goals and the significance of education—the human and moral factors involved in racially segregated education—were being consistently expressed by lawyers and judges in our federal courts while educators collectively, and with a few notable exceptions, tended to remain silent. (Clark, "Obligations and Responsibility of Higher Education for Race Relations" [address before the Leadership Council, Jacksonville, FL, February 24, 1983].)

Just teach them to read. (Clark, "Kenneth Clark's Revolutionary Slogan," *New York Times*, March 17, 1983, 15.)

When I was teaching at City College, I had a class of graduate students taking a course in Social Psychology. Half of those students were policemen who were participating in a program of cooperation between the City College and the New York City Police Department. After the first week or so, when the ice was broken, those policemen began to participate quite freely in class discussions on social psychological problems in the New York City area. In a discussion on the possibility that policemen might be more prone to investigate alleged delinquency among minority youths than others, one policeman said, "It is just good police work if one sees a group of adolescents in a car to stop that car, particularly if the car is a late model driven by a minority group adolescent. The chances of this being a stolen car are great." Another one said, "Well, you know, actually policemen are part of the community, too. They tend to share the existing prejudices and stereotypes of the larger community." Some of the other members of the class pointed out that this type of activity might cause some hostility on the part of minority youngsters toward the police. They would believe they were being harassed. This in turn would cause some greater tendency toward anti-social behavior. It was pointed out that this factor might contribute to a cycle of hostility. (Clark, "The Study of Urban Violence: Some Reflections" [address given at the Center on Violence and Human Survival, John Jay College of Criminal Justice, October 2, 1989].)

The problem of educational illiteracy and its antidote have their roots in the preschool stages of development. Early childhood is probably the time when normal children are most sensitive and responsive to their environment. One need only observe that young children begin to understand and communicate in the language of their social environment, that this verbal facility increases within the support of the family and is reinforced by interaction in the first school experience, to see the importance of this early stage. . . .

The development of language usually occurs through auditory stimulation, and does not in itself require visual stimulation. The visual stimuli involved in learning to read need not be so difficult to learn. Yet, such a variety of theories exist on the matter, often generating self-fulfilling prophecies to explain the failure to accomplish the desired end, that one can only express surprise. If such controversies existed also with respect to verbal communication, there would be a need for a plethora of remedial oral language skills courses to supplement those that now exist for remedial reading. An embarrassingly simple approach to the remedy of illiteracy among children and adults would be to teach them to read with the natural ease and flair that is common when they learn to speak and communicate orally. (Clark, quoted in "Literacy in America," *Daedalus* 119.2 [Spring 1990]: 114.)

COMMENTARY

Gregory H. Williams

Kenneth Clark was a giant, in the academy and outside of it. As a scholar raised in a nation scarred by the divisive and disabling consequences of slavery and racism, he contributed immeasurably to America's understanding of itself. His scholarly research shed new light not only on "black" and "white" but on the human condition. That contribution secured his place in the history of knowledge and contributed inestimably to the long and arduous healing process.

I am pleased to claim both a professional and a personal connection to Dr. Clark. As the president of the City College of New York (CCNY), I can attest without reservation that Dr. Clark was among the brightest in the panoply of bright stars that have taught here at City. Much of his groundbreaking work was done during his thirty-three-year tenure at CCNY, the flagship college of the City University of New York. He was certainly one of the primary reasons that City's doctoral psychology program is ranked among the top ten in the nation. He was a force at the college and in the surrounding community of Harlem, where he touched the lives of countless students, faculty, and community members.

I also feel personally touched by Dr. Clark's seminal contribution to an understanding of the American psyche. His revolutionary research for the NAACP was the intellectual underpinning for *Brown v. Board of Education*. That decision came down in 1954—the same year that my African American father (who was "passing" in the vernacular of the time) and Caucasian mother split apart. That year, when I was ten years old, I learned that I was in fact "colored," and I went from a secure, middle-class "white" home in Virginia to live with my father's family in the black housing projects of Muncie, Indiana. My autobiography *Life on the Color Line: The True Story of a White Boy Who Discovered He Was Black* (1995) describes how my life was turned upside down and how everything that I had taken for granted was called into question.

I would not learn about Kenneth Clark's work until years later, when I was in college. But I recognized immediately, from personal experience as well as academic sources, that he was one of the towering figures of the twentieth century. Dr. Clark's dedication to civil and human rights, his willingness to fight for equality on all fronts, and his intellectual and moral courage changed America.

Johnnetta B. Cole

For over fifty years, Dr. Kenneth B. Clark has put his scholarship in the service of his people and in the interest of a more just and equitable world. He has helped us to better understand the damaging consequences of racism, especially on young children, and he has actively participated in efforts to attack that destructive system of inequality. Anyone who believes in freedom and equality for all peoples is in his debt.

NOTES

1. [*Editor's Note*: This letter was reported in a news story in the *New York Times*, May 23, 1969, under the headline: "Clark Scores Separatism at Antioch." The story began: "Dr. Kenneth B. Clark, whose studies helped convince the Su-

preme Court to ban racial segregation in public schools, has resigned as a trustee of Antioch College, decrying its 'racially organized and exclusionary' Afro-American Studies Institute."]

2. [*Editor's Note*: See Chapter 19, "Afterword," this volume.]

CHAPTER 7

The Role of the Courts

The Supreme Court decision—as important as it is—has not solved our problem of democracy. It has made it possible for us to begin to work on these problems in an atmosphere of hope and inspiration for our young people. (Clark, quoted on *NBC News* in the immediate aftermath of the *Brown* decision, May 28, 1954.)

The privileged delinquent does not come before the courts because his family generally can and does protect him from these forms of social discipline. It is difficult to obtain objective data on this form of delinquency because this form of pathology is so inextricably woven into the fabric of the valued and privileged aspect of our society. The behavior of the privileged delinquent may go unnoticed because it may be seen merely as a "normal and natural" pattern of a discriminative middle and upper class way of life.

Like the underprivileged delinquent, the privileged delinquent, too, is a victim of his society. His personality has been shackled to the competitive values of the quest for status and success. He has been disciplined and rewarded in terms of these goals from the competition for grades and approval in the elementary grades through the hectic anxiety in awaiting the competitive examination scores which will determine his admission to or rejection from a privileged college. Under these conditions others are likely to be seen as threats, competitors, or inferiors. (Clark, "Creative Discipline," in Eli Ginzberg, ed., *Values and Ideals of American Youth* [New York: Columbia University Press, 1961], 251.)

I think the crucial mistake that that Court made in its May 11, 1955, decision was the mistake of assuming that those in control of the political power of the states that maintained segregated education were in fact reasonable men. The "all deliberate speed" decree was interpreted by these men as an invitation to evasion, an indefinite postponement. It led some of them to state publicly that the Court could be ignored. It stimulated open defiance, massive resistance, and led to a Little Rock type of violence directed against even minimal and token desegregation. (Clark, "The Negro in Contemporary America" [address, Mills College, December 3, 1963].)

I recall that when I was writing a report for the Mid-Century White House Conference on Children and Youth in 1950, I tried to make the report very long, and very exhaustive and exhausting, on the assumption that none of the Advisory Committee would read it. One of the statements I made—and the Supreme Court cited the report in its 1954 decision but without including this statement, curiously enough—was that American racism was as profoundly American as the Declaration of Independence. I had just thought of this for the first time. A man by the name of Dr. [Benjamin] Spock and [Columbia University Professor] Otto Klineberg were members of that Advisory Committee. They were very disturbed about the statement, and they said, "Kenneth, do you really mean this?" I said, "I really haven't yet developed the habit of writing things I don't mean. I suppose with experience will come that habit." But [they asked] do you really believe that American racism is as profoundly and as dynamically significant, with the same dynamics as the Declaration of Independence and visa versa? And I said, "Yes, I do, because both are manifestations of the profound human dilemma of insecure beings, seeking desperately to find some basis for making their lives more tolerable, more acceptable. I didn't win the argument— they had me take out that sentence from the report on the grounds that Congress would not understand and I felt that it was above all important that Congress understood. (Clark, "The Dilemma of the Insecure" [address given as part of the 1969 Haynes Foundation Lecture Series, University of Southern California, April 7, 1969], 10.)

It may be of some value to point out that the earlier studies of the development of self identification and evaluation in children with Mamie Clark were not motivated by or conducted with any direct concern for their applied or policy implications and consequences. The fact that the United States Supreme Court in handing down the *Brown* decision in May 1954 cited these findings and other relevant research which I summarized in the document, *The Effects of Prejudice and Discrimination on Personality Development* [see Appendix 2, this volume], was a gratifying illustration of the possibility that even in the social and psychological sciences what is called "pure" research can sometimes have some direct social policy and applied social change effects. The *Dark Ghetto* research on the other hand, from its inception, was clearly motivated by the desire to influence social policy and influence the decisions of those with power to facilitate, block, or determine the rate of desired social change. The *Dark Ghetto* cannot be described with candor as an exercise in "pure" research.

. . . This study of the dynamics of a systematically dehumanizing community on the humanity and effectiveness of the personalities confined within it was not conducted without concern for the implications of these findings for social justice and social change. (Clark, "The Pathos of Power: A Psychological Perspective" [presidential address, American Psychological Association, Washington, DC, September 4, 1971].)

The insidious and persistent resistance of northern whites to the desegregation of the *de facto* segregated schools and the enforcement of this position by black separatists have now strengthened the resistance of southern segregationists to effective desegregation of American public schools. This new and unexpected alliance—this strange spectacle of interracial bedfellows—has confused, temporarily bewildered, or exploited the ambivalence of those southern and northern whites who assumed the risks necessary to obtain and attempt to implement effective school desegregation programs. A presently undetermined number of blacks—still a minority, no greater than 20 percent according to the latest surveys—seem bewildered and uncertain about whether the goals of desegregated schools are still worth pursuing. (Clark, "Public School Desegregation in the Seventies," *New South* 27.3 [Summer 1972]: 23.)

The demand for decentralization and community control of public schools interestingly enough came in the wake of the desegregation thrust of the '50s, which my own involvement in the NAACP following the public school desegregation, really forced me into an examination of the *de facto* public school desegregation in the public schools in the City of New York. In 1952, at a meeting, I literally was forced by lawyers for the State of Virginia into looking at the New York public schools, where I was blithely testifying about the *de jure*, effects of *de jure* segregation in South Carolina and in Virginia. I will never forget the lawyer's name, Justin Moore. He said, "Dr. Clark, how dare you come down and tell us in Virginia about the damaging effect of segregated schools in Virginia when you come from a city that has segregated schools?" And I was shocked. I came to know Justin Moore after that, but I never really told him what a jolt he gave me on the stand. When I came back to New York, Moore was right. And we precipitated a discussion and attempts to deal with the problem of the *de facto* segregation of schools in New York City and really got nowhere. (Clark, testimony before a meeting of the Temporary State Charter Revision Commission for the City of New York, typewritten minutes, November 22, 1972, 1350–1351.)

As one examines the various anti-busing legislation and constitutional amendments now being discussed in the United States Senate and in the White House, a common denominator for an inherent constitutional and moral crisis emerges. All of these proposals, including the Scott-Mansfield compromise, have as their central fact that for the first time since the Emancipation Proclamation, the legislative and executive branches of the federal government are seriously entertaining action to limit the rights of racial minorities to unqualified equality of opportunity—and are also attempting to limit the duty of the federal courts to assure and protect these rights. In past discussions concerning the similarities and differences between the American and South African forms of racial inhumanity, Americans—including this writer—could argue with some persuasive sincerity and legal logic that American racism was by no means as malignant because it was not reinforced by the legislative and official police power of the federal government. Indeed, up to the present it could be argued that American racism is contrary to the United States Constitution and is violative [*sic*] of federal and state civil rights laws.

. . . Neither political expediency, nor the often violated emotional slogans concerning the sanctity of the "neighborhood school" or the many forms of tribalism can be permitted to interfere with the rights of American children to that quality of education which would prepare them to live and contribute to a more humane world of the future. (Clark, quoted in "Fact Book on Pupil Transportation," a publication of the Metropolitan Applied Research Center, April 1972.)

The American people, unlike the Germans who said after the war that they did not know of the Jews' fate, cannot assert without subjecting themselves to tragic ridicule that they did not know that in consigning their children to the dung heap of segregated schools they were relentlessly destroying them. This stark problem involving the quality and character of the American people—the need to resolve this moral dilemma—is the inescapable reality of the twentieth anniversary of the *Brown* decisions. (Clark, "20 Years after *Brown*—The Unresolved Dilemma," *New York Times*, May 17, 1974, 38–39.)

Twenty years ago Chief Justice Earl Warren, writing for all of his colleagues on the United States Supreme Court, asked the following key question: Does segregation of children in public schools solely on the basis of race, even though the physical facilities and other "tangible" factors may be equal, deprive the children of the minority group of equal educational opportunities? In its answer to this question, the *Brown* decision established its claim to historic compassion and revealed a fundamental concern with the quality and requirements of humanity, not frequently found in legal discourses and decisions, by the simple, eloquent answer: To separate them from others of similar age and qualifications solely because of their race generates a feeling of inferiority as to their status in the community that may affect their hearts and minds in a way unlikely ever to be undone. Chief Justice Warren then quoted from the findings in the Kansas case: "Segregation of white and colored children in public schools has a detrimental effect upon the colored children . . . the policy of separating the races is usually interpreted as denoting the inferiority of the Negro group."[1] A sense of inferiority affects the motivation of a child to learn. The decision then concludes: Separate educational facilities are inherently unequal. These findings are as true today as they were in May of 1954. They will remain true as long as American children are required to attend racially segregated schools anywhere in this nation.[2]

This stark confrontation of the quality and character of the American people—this need to resolve this moral dilemma either positively or with the efficiency of their power—is the essential lesson of the twentieth anniversary of the *Brown* decisions. (Clark, "Some Reflections on the Twentieth Anniversary" [address, Manhattan County Day School, May 15, 1974].)

In 1950 I did the study, or the bringing together of the various studies, on the effects of segregation on personality development [see Appendix 3, this volume] for the Mid-Century White House Conference on Children. I was asked to do that by the committee that organized the conference and guess that's what I was doing. That was the basis of my first book, *Prejudice and Your Child*, which expanded my thoughts on the data that came from the doll tests with Mamie. So really the involvement in the relationship between social psychology, developmental psychology and social problems of race began to take form in the early 50s when I began the work for the Mid-Century White House Conference. Before that I was sort of an academic or pure psychologist, teaching and doing research with Mamie.

After that in 1950–51, I got involved with the lawyers of NAACP because of these data that I had done earlier for the Mid-Century White House Conference on Children. There was this convergence between my academic life and the social policy, social change life. You see this really was imposed by the demands of the Mid-Century White House Conference initially and then the lawyers of the NAACP. That's not wholly true, by the way, because in 1946 Mamie and I set up Northside Center.

My initial response was that of tremendous exhilaration. I just felt so enthusiastic. I felt proud to be an American. I was full of hope and optimism. I gave an interview to the school [City College], press and others saying that the decision should really eliminate all cynicism about whether the system works or not. If the Daughters of the American Revolution had asked me to give speeches, I would have gone around giving speeches for them. The Chamber of Commerce and other patriotic organizations could have had another recruit in me for nothing. I continued this kind of enthusiasm for quite awhile. In fact, I went around making speeches, and what's worse, writing articles to the effect that the racism system in America at least in terms of the institutionalization of racism would be turned around within five to 10 years. Obviously, it's not true. Looking back, I seriously underestimated the depth and venom of American racism.

I stated in "Desegregation: An Appraisal of the Evidence" [See Appendix 4, this volume] one of my major monographs that very few people know about but I consider one of the most important things I wrote—I state there that the social psychological theory that governed an understanding of the desegregation process was that it was not necessary to bring about attitudinal changes as an antecedent to behavioral changes but rather if one changed the institutional patterns this would in turn affect the attitudes. I still believe that theoretically but what's worrying me is what triggers genuine attempt to institutional change? And when I have to focus on that question, then I don't see any other than attitudinal change, as they are operative in the decision-makers. These people have been socialized in a racist society. They control the direction and the rate of institutional change so you are not going to get institutional change through generosity and clearly you don't get it by court decisions and I'm stuck. I am a much sadder, not wiser person in 1975 than I was in 1955. (Clark, transcript of an unpublished interview with Larry Nyman, City College of New York, June 19, 1975, 17–20, from the Clark Archives, Hastings-on-Hudson, NY.)

[*Editor's Note*: On the occasion of Dr. Clark's retirement from City College at age sixty-one in 1975, he was interviewed on "The *Brown* Decision," on radio station "Voice of America," June 10, 1975. Following are excerpts from that interview.]

Q: *What was your role in the* Brown *decision?*

A: I'm not modest about it, but I would like to point out that the *Brown* decision is a direct result of the tremendous work and planning of the lawyers, the legal defense fund of the NAACP. I am not modest, and I don't want to ever pretend any modesty, which I really don't feel. But reality has to be faced. The fact is that long before I was invited by those lawyers to provide a social science base for their legal arguments, they were planning these cases when I was an undergraduate at Howard University. The late Charles Houston was having seminars at the Howard University Law School on the matter of their eventual challenging of the system of segregation in the United States. I was surprised when in 1951 Thurgood Marshall and Robert Carter of the Legal Defense Fund of the NAACP [now a federal judge in New York] came to me and asked if there was anything that psychologists and other social scientists could offer by way of evidence as to the detrimental effect of racial segregation on human beings. They decided that the way in which they were going to overturn the *Plessy v. Ferguson* [1896] "separate but equal doctrine," which had maintained segregation in the institutions of the United States, was by trying to demonstrate that segregation was harmful. They couldn't approach it in terms of physical harm so it was their decision to see if it was possible to approach it in terms of psychological harm. It just so happened that when they came to me in, I think it was February of 1950, I had just completed, for the 1950 Mid-Century White House Conference on Children and Youth, a manuscript on the effects of segregation on personality development of American children.

When I was working on that document I didn't have the slightest notion that it would have any practical effect. I thought it was just going to be another academic treatise, written, discussed, filed and forgotten. When the lawyers came a few months later with their request and question, my answer was to give them the document that I had prepared for the Mid-Century White House Conference. And it was they who decided that this was what they wanted. Sheer coincidence, believe me. But from that point on, my life hasn't been the same because they got me involved almost as a professional expert witness and my wife and I had our personal lives practically dominated by those events.

Q: *Your life hasn't been the same. American education hasn't been the same.*

A: Well, when you listen to some of my critics, they say that with some bitterness. There is a new group of social scientists who look upon those of us who have been involved in providing evidence on the detrimental effect of segregated schools and other segregated institutions as the modern devils, disrupters of what was otherwise, from their point of view, placid, acceptable accommodation of racial discrimination in American society. To me this is the important new development in the last 10 or 15 years. A group of social scientists are now systematically seeking to undercut the work which the social scientists did in support of *Brown* by pointing out that our work was unscientific, that we disrupted otherwise acceptable education. What they are really saying is that the desegregation process is not unlike prohibition. In prohibition you had a situation in which the law was not enforceable and therefore had to be repealed. But implicitly what they're saying is that the masses of American whites are resisting desegregation of the schools, they're resisting "busing," which I have always felt was a spurious issue. Therefore, it won't work. Therefore, desegregation of the schools is wrong. As one of my colleagues, Professor Hylan Lewis, said when we were analyzing the recent position of [Secretary of Transportation William] Coleman in which he is saying publicly and with a report backing up his position, that busing is not only not leading to desegregation of the

schools but leading to intensification of segregation because whites are fleeing the cities. My colleague Professor Lewis said: "You know, what he is
saying is that democracy can't work. And when there is resistance, then
one should withdraw the democratic demands." I agree heartily and somewhat sadly with my colleague, Professor Lewis, because this, unfortunately,
is what too many contemporary social scientists are saying. And my personal feeling is that they are really responding to the neo-reactionary, the
period that has dominated American politics on the federal level in the last
10 years or so.

Q: *Surely, it doesn't stop and start with the question of black and white
children going to school together but the continuum that has brought black
people into the professional ranks in corporations, which are not involved
in it, and other positions of accomplishment.*

A: I don't think there's any question that there have been major positive
changes in race relations in America since the *Brown* decision that go beyond the school desegregation issue. By the way, I'm not one of those who
will ignore the fact that the significant changes have occurred in the southern states as far as segregated schools are concerned . . . [but] if you look
at what is happening in northern cities you could become rather pessimistic.
When you look beyond schools you do see that significant, positive changes
have occurred in race relations. There are an increasing percentage of
blacks in the middle class. There are jobs that are opening up and have
opened up to blacks in the private sector from which they were previously
excluded. Affirmative action is working, not as effectively as many of us
would want, but it's happening. Lyndon Johnson appointed a black, Thurgood Marshall, to the United States Supreme Court and he is there. There
was a black in the Cabinet, [Secretary of Housing and Urban Development]
Robert Weaver. And there is a black in Mr. [Gerald] Ford's Cabinet, Bill
Coleman [Secretary of Transportation]. (Clark, "The *Brown* Decision" interview, Voice of America, June 10, 1975, 5.)

May 17, 1954 was one of the happiest days of my life. About noon on
that day I received a telephone call from Thurgood Marshall[3] who had just
left the United States Supreme Court. Even before he told me the specifics
of the unanimous verdict I could tell by the joyous tone of his voice and
by the excitement which crackled over the telephone wires that America
had made a turning point in the struggle for justice and democracy. I listened to Thurgood but I do not remember his exact words. The aura of a
momentous victory dominated my senses, accelerated the beat of my heart
and took control of my body. Vaguely, I remember Thurgood saying that
we must celebrate and that we would all meet at a hotel in New York for
dinner and a not too sober assessment of the meaning of the decision.

(Clark, unpublished manuscript, Clark Archives, Hastings-on-Hudson, NY, 1976.)

Those of us who were privileged to participate in this historic case and in the preparation of this brief did so with enthusiasm, pride and a sense of personal involvement which we knew even at that time would be a monumental demonstration of the importance of the possible contribution of a value-oriented social science to social policy and the democratic process. We did so with a most positive sense that the discipline, research, methods and values of social science were in fact relevant instruments in man's ongoing struggle for truth, justice, equity and humanity. What is equally, if not more important is the statement [see Appendix 3, this volume] did not mislead the American people. The contribution of concerned social scientists could remain one of the blueprints and beacons in the continuing search for democracy and equality in our nation and in the world. (Clark, "25 Years after *Brown v. Board of Education*: Perspectives. The Preparation of the Social Scientists' Brief," symposium speech, Washington, DC, September 1, 1979.)

Twenty-five years after the *Brown* decision ruled that "separate educational facilities are inherently unequal," the majority of black students attending colleges in the southern states attend traditionally black colleges. In spite of the fact that the United States Supreme Court, in a series of decisions before and after, made it possible for an increasing number of black students to attend traditionally white state-supported colleges, universities, and professional schools, a dual and biracial system of publicly supported higher education is today the dominant and seemingly accepted educational reality in the south. The most visible and dramatic desegregation of traditionally white southern colleges are such varsity sports as basketball and football. (Clark, "Good Enough for Blacks," manuscript, Clark Archives, Hastings-on-Hudson, NY, 1979.)

[*Editor's Note*: The following is a transcript of an interview of Dr. Clark with Professor Richard L. Evans, Distinguished Professor of Social Psychology at the University of Houston and director of the Social Psychology Program and Social Psychology-Behavioral Medicine Research Group. It offers some unusual insight into the details of that Supreme Court decision as seen by Dr. Clark.]

Q: *Probably one of the most important decisions the Supreme Court has made during this century was the first time that social science data were seriously considered in the deliberations of the Supreme Court. Could you discuss the development of this study?*

A: The study originated with my wife, Mamie. It was her master's thesis subject at Howard University, She was interested in studying the development of self-awareness in human beings, and she had only black children available as subjects. This fact made her move toward looking at self-awareness as determined by race or color. Mamie's original methods were really a modification of the Horowitz and Horowitz Show-Me Test (1939). She finished her master's and came up to New York. (She later became the first black woman to earn her doctorate in psychology at Columbia.) I was so fascinated by this study that I said maybe we ought to continue. Then I developed an extension of the method, the Show-Me Method, and used the dolls and the color test. Our primary concern was trying to understand how human beings developed a sense of their own identity, and the racial color factor was a component.

Q: *Could we pause for a moment so that you might briefly describe the methodology and results of the study? As I recall the study, even black children showed a preference for white dolls, more often selecting them when asked which doll they would rather have to play with.*

A: At that time, there was no question about it. Two-thirds did. This was a disturbing study for both Mamie and me.

Q: *How old were the children?*

A: From three to seven years old.

Q: *So these were not infants. These were children who were already old enough to be significantly influenced by the culture.*

A: No question about it. We were measuring the effects of socialization when it is deleterious to self-esteem. I saw black children, in both the north and the south, being dominated by negative stereotypes about themselves. I then asked them the last question: "Now show me the doll which is like you." Some of these children would break down into tears. I remember one little girl who looked up at me as if to say, "How could you do this to another human being?" and broke down into tears and ran out of the room. In the south, that wasn't as frequent; they would laugh and say, "That's a Nigger; I'm a Nigger," or something of that sort. It was so disturbing to us personally that I found the report of the study difficult to write.

Q: *Now, let's move a little further. I mentioned at the beginning of this question the* Brown versus Board of Education *case. This was perhaps the first, and certainly an extremely important, instance of social science influencing a Supreme Court decision. How did that all come about?*

A: Well, it came about through the lawyers of the NAACP. They decided that they were going to challenge the constitutionality of segregation without regard to alleged equality of facilities. The only way they thought they could really repeal the separate but equal doctrine was by being able to demonstrate that there was damage inherent in segregation in spite of the equality of the facilities. Robert Carter, who was Thurgood Marshall's [attorney for the NAACP] assistant, spoke to me first. He said, "You know, it would be easy for us if we could demonstrate medical damage or broken bones or something that is concrete that everyone would agree on as damage, but the type of damage we're talking about is psychological damage, a much more subtle damage. And the only place for us to turn is to psychologists." First, they went to Otto Klineberg. Otto was a member of the Mid-Century White House Conference on Children and Youth (1950). This conference was concerned with the question of personality development. They asked me about two or three months before the conference to synthesize the literature on the effects of race, prejudice, discrimination, and segregation on personality development of American children, white and black. It didn't occur to me that this was going to have any practical significance. I gave Carter a copy of the monograph and said, "You read this, and if it is at all relevant to what you and Thurgood have in mind, then maybe I can help." He read it, and within a week he said to me, "Look, it's not only relevant, but it couldn't have been better if you had prepared it for us."

Q: *So one task covered the other.*

A: That's right. We started meeting and I advised him and the other lawyers of the group of social scientists whom we would need. I advised the lawyers as to those whom I thought would make good witnesses. Then later, after the trial, they said, "Look, we don't know whether the Supreme Court is going to accept this or not, but we want you to pull together in a social science brief the essential points of the testimony of the expert witness of the trial level." Well, I did.

Q: *You took the core statements of these testimonies and expert witnesses.*

A: That's right. And a summary of the White House Conference memorandum [Mid-Century White House Conference on Children and Youth (1950)]. It became the appendix to the legal brief that was the Social Science Brief [see Appendix 3, this volume] for the *Brown versus Board of Education* case of 1954.

Q: *That was to become a landmark involvement of the social sciences in law. Before this, the involvement of psychiatrists or clinical psychologists in sanity hearings was the typical contribution.*

A: And you know, there were times when one of the more puristic lawyers demanded what I could not give him: proof that segregated schools in themselves created the damage. To them, that was the legal point. And I said, "Look, I don't know of any social scientist who could give you that specific kind of information." We could say that segregated schools in the context of a segregated society are damaging, but not segregated schools in isolation, because, for one thing, segregated schools do not exist in isolation.

Q: *That's right.*

A: It is not an idyllic romance. I had to fight with the lawyers for the integrity of social science; not that they wanted me to pervert it, but some of them wanted me to make statements that I did not believe the evidence would support.

Q: *There is a fine distinction between internal and external validity of psychological data in the courtroom. Will the results of a single psychological investigation generalize to a broader societal situation? As you say, it is often impossible to demonstrate, and the scientist with integrity hesitates to make such generalizations.*

A: You're darn right. And I insisted upon pointing out to them that my value to them was directly related to the integrity and clarity of what I provided for them.

Q: *After the decision, there was a good deal of social legislation and social action, supplementing the decision to explore what could be done on a larger scale to remedy some of the things that your study suggested were being generated by our culture. At that time, having worked with President Kennedy's Committee on Delinquency and Youth Crime, I became acutely aware of the work that you were doing with your Harlem Youth Opportunities Unlimited, Inc. (HARYOU) in New York. The issue of delinquency and opportunity has been under some fire. The point of view of the Kennedy administration was that if you can change the environment and increase the opportunities for disadvantaged youth or children, you will increase the probability that they will become constructive members of society. How did you become involved in this issue and how did you perceive this idea? I can see that by then, of course, you could no longer be just a professor of social psychology at City University. You became intricately involved in the social problems.*

A: There is no question that by that time I was an involved social psychologist rather than an isolated ivory-tower academician. Around 1950 there was an excitement in being involved in real issues. But there was also conflict. As to my work at HARYOU, it stemmed directly from my work with the lawyers and my work with Mamie as a research director at a child guidance center in Harlem, the Northside Center for Child Development. In 1940, Mamie and I founded the Northside Center for one purpose: to provide underprivileged children in Harlem with the alleged benefits of psychiatric and psychological help in counseling. We knew that if we were going to save these children it was important to do something about the environment in which they were growing up. We also knew that you couldn't really do very much if you provided help under conditions that threatened their self-esteem, increased their sense of dependency, etc. Mamie contributed the notion and practice of building the sense of self as an integral part of our psychotherapy. (Clark, interview in Richard Evans, ed., *The Making of Social Psychology: Discussions with Creative Contributors* [New York: Gardner Press, 1980], 64–71.)

A summary analysis of the total pattern of responses of the blacks questioned in this survey [in *Ebony* magazine] revealed that whatever were the positive gains obtained by the civil rights movement of the 1950s and the 1960s these gains have not yet resulted in a consistently positive self-image for the majority of blacks. (Kenneth B. Clark and Mamie Phipps Clark, "What Do Blacks Think of Themselves?" *Ebony* [Special Issue] [November 1980]: 176.)

I continue to be an extremist. An extremist in persisting in believing that black kids can learn, and that segregation is one way in which they are prevented from learning. I remain an incorrigible integrationist. (Clark, quoted in Nat Hentoff, "The Integrationist," *The New Yorker*, August 23, 1982, 46.)

Our graduates must understand that as educated individuals they have the responsibility—the obligation—to communicate to their fellow human beings that in this nuclear age human survival will depend upon man's capacity to give and receive love, to be kind, to be empathetic, to be sensitive to the needs of their fellow human beings. These cannot be done by computers. As a matter of fact, they may be obscured—obfuscated—by computers. (Clark, "Thirty Years after the *Brown* Decision: Education in a Computer Age," paper, Clark Archives, Hastings-on-Hudson, NY, May 1984.)

The unanimous decision of the Supreme Court dealt with the problems of education, American racism, and human values as inextricable components of American democracy. Education and human values would be impaired by racism. The Court succinctly stated: "We conclude that in the field of public education the doctrine of 'separate but equal' has no place. Separate educational facilities are inherently unequal."[4]

This conclusion rejected the *Plessy v. Ferguson* doctrine which had sustained racial segregation in education and in all aspects of American life since 1896. This rejection extended the democratic protection of the Bill of Rights to black Americans. In its categorical rejection of the *Plessy* racist doctrine, the Court stated that the Negro plaintiffs are "by reason of the segregation complained of, deprived of the equal protection of the laws guaranteed by the Fourteenth Amendment."

In supporting this important Constitutional conclusion, the Court stated its view of the role of public education "in the light of its full development and its present place in American life throughout the nation."

In regard to the pivotal role of public education in maintaining the stability of American democracy, the words of the *Brown* decision are direct and explicit:

Today, education is perhaps the most important function of state and local governments. Compulsory school attendance laws and the great expenditure for education both demonstrate our recognition of the importance of education to our democratic society. . . . It is the very foundation of good citizenship. Today it is a principal instrument in awakening the child to cultural values, in preparing him for later professional training and in helping him adjust normally to his environment. In these days, it is doubtful that any child may reasonably be expected to succeed in life if he is denied the opportunity of an education. Such an opportunity, where the state has undertaken to provide it, is a right, which must be made available to all on equal terms.

In relating the purpose and function of education in our democratic society, the Court resorted to interrelated human concerns and values: "To separate them from others of similar age and qualifications solely because of their race generates a feeling of inferiority as to their status in the community that may affect their hearts and minds in a way unlikely ever to be undone."

In developing this human concern for the welfare and future of children, the Supreme Court quoted the specific educational finding of the Kansas federal court to the effect that:

A sense of inferiority affects the motivation of a child to learn. Segregation with the sanction of law, therefore, has a tendency to retard the educational and mental development of Negro children and to deprive them of some of the benefits they would receive in a racially integrated school system with the rights of minorities to participate actively in the political process.

The gains of blacks which emerged from the *Brown* decision helped to solidify the foundations of American democracy for the benefit and social education of all Americans. The positive results of the civil rights movement motivated and educated other groups of Americans. Legal purists and some social scientists have criticized the *Brown* decision for not relying solely on legal precedents, and for resorting to the "soft" findings of psychologists and social scientists. Implicit in some of their criticisms is the belief that the law and the constitutional decision would be contaminated by human values. Among the early critics was a serious student of jurisprudence, the late Professor Edmond Cahn, of New York University Law School.[5]

One of the first social scientists to publish a direct criticism of the role of social scientists in the *Brown* decision cases was Ernest van den Haag.

As early as 1957, he had written a critical rejection of the findings of the social scientists and expressed clearly his doubts about the wisdom of the *Brown* decision in general. He made clear his belief that racial segregation is not psychologically damaging. These criticisms highlighted the fact that the *Brown* decision was a momentous document which integrated education, racism, and human values. It was not an isolated legal document. It did not discuss education as if it were independent of its social and humane goals.

It is significant that the *Brown* decision, while specifically concerned with the problem of racial segregation in public schools, resulted in widespread social and racial changes in American life. Its broad social and human educational values soon became clear. Its assertion of fundamental social and psychological truths cleared the way for the removal of all state laws which required or permitted racial discrimination and segregation in public accommodations, public transportation, and publicly supported recreational facilities.

The pervasive human and social educational value of the *Brown* decision made it possible for the executive and legislative branches of the Federal Government to become active partners, without apology, in the ongoing struggle for social justice. Ten years after the *Brown* decision, the Congress of the United States passed the 1964 Civil Rights Act which sought to prohibit social discrimination in employment. A year later, in 1965, it passed the Voting Rights Act which sought to remove the traditional barriers and subterfuges which encouraged such groups as women, Hispanics, Native Americans, Asians, and gays, to seek unqualified justice and the removal of the remaining patterns of discrimination directed against them. It is ironic, however, that the problem presented to the United States Supreme Court concerned the specific education issue of the constitutionality of racially segregated public schools. Yet, observations of the results of the *Brown* decision during the past decades reveal that the beneficial consequences of that decision were more pronounced, pervasive, and observable in other aspects of the society than in the field of public education itself.

The pattern of resistance to any genuine compliance with the letter and the spirit of the *Brown* decision is pervasive and formidable. This is particularly true in those northern cities with a high percentage of ghettoized blacks. White middle-class parents have abandoned the public schools, enrolling their children in suburban schools or in private and parochial schools. To the extent that this pattern is followed by the more affluent black families, it causes the urban schools to become predominantly black, poor, and segregated.

In the light of the damage, which racially segregated schools inflict upon American children, this is particularly tragic. It restricts their ability to function constructively within the complexities of a demanding democratic society, in a diverse and interdependent world. There is no evidence that the damage is less in *de facto* segregated schools than it was when segregation was required by law. After the explicit educational and human assertions of the *Brown* decision, Americans who persist in the perpetuation of racially segregated schools, and who refuse to accept realistic remedies for the elimination of biracial educational systems, cannot now truthfully say that they are unaware of the fact that they are inflicting irreparable damage upon the "hearts and minds" of children who still are required to attend segregated schools.

It is disturbingly clear that educators as a whole, with a few notable exceptions, have defaulted in helping society to face, understand, and seek to resolve this critical educational and human problem.

If the fundamental objectives of the *Brown* decision are ever to be obtained, educators must explain that the goals of education go beyond the teaching of cognitive skills. These skills, important as they are, must be integrated into the total pattern of understanding, which includes the acceptance of human values. The critical purpose of education in this broad and total sense is to free the human mind of ignorance, superstition, irrational fears and hatred, tribalisms, parochialisms, and hostilities that interfere with the ability of human beings to interact constructively with their fellow human beings.

The *Brown* decision was most explicit in stating the damage inflicted upon minority children. It was unfortunate, however, that the Court omitted from its most eloquent and humane statement the section concerning the equally dehumanizing educational and human damage inflicted upon white children.

In the *Appendix to Appellant's Briefs* [see Appendix 3, this volume], prepared by the social scientists and submitted to the Supreme Court by the NAACP lawyers for the plaintiffs, it was stated, "that segregation, prejudices and discrimination, and their social concomitants potentially damage the personality of all children—the children of the majority group in a somewhat different way than the more obvious damaged children of the minority group."

The social, psychological, and human value damage inflicted upon white children was clearly summarized in the Social Science Brief as follows:

Those children who learn the prejudices of our society are also being taught to gain personal status in an unrealistic and non-adaptive way. When comparing themselves to members of the minority group, they are not required to evaluate themselves in terms of the more basic standards of actual personal ability and achievement. The culture permits and, at times, encourages them to direct their feelings of hostility and aggression against whole groups of people the members of which are perceived as weaker than themselves. They often develop patterns of guilt feelings, rationalizations and other mechanisms, which they must use in an attempt to protect themselves from recognizing the essential injustice of their unrealistic fears and hatreds of minority groups.[6]

The report indicates further that confusion, conflict, moral cynicism, and disrespect for authority may arise in majority group children as a consequence of being taught the moral, religious and democratic principles of the brotherhood of man and the importance of justice and fair play by the same persons and institutions who, in their support of racial segregation and related practices, seem to be acting in a prejudiced and discriminatory manner. Some individuals may attempt to resolve this conflict by intensifying their hostility toward the minority group. Still others react by developing an unwholesome, rigid, and uncritical idealization of all authority figures—their parents, strong political and economic leaders. As described in *The Authoritarian Personality*, they despise the weak, while they obsequiously and unquestioningly conform to the demands of the strong whom they also, paradoxically, subconsciously hate. (Clark, "The Brown Decision: Racism, Education, and Human Values" [paper presented at the annual Charles H. Thompson Lecture-Colloquium, School of Education, Howard University, November 4, 1987], 126–128.)

I was full of optimism at the time of the *Brown* decision.[7] Thurgood Marshall and the other lawyers, and my social science colleagues, whom I involved in working with me, thought this was going to be a turning point. How naive I was! (Clark, quoted in Studs Terkel, *RACE: How Blacks & Whites Think & Feel about the American Obsession* [New York: The New Press, 1992], 334.)

The Supreme Court's 1954 decision in *Brown v. Board of Education* spawned a collective hope and dream for an end to racial segregation in American public schools. I joined in the optimism. I spoke and wrote buoyantly, confident in our future. At the time, I believed there would be positive changes within a decade or more. I thought that I, and the small group of like-minded persons with whom I worked, successfully would raise these issues, combat all signs of segregation, and remain persistent in opposing racism in our local schools.

Although I knew of the *de facto* pattern of segregation that existed at that time in the New York City public school system, I thought the problem of segregation essentially was a southern problem. I now confess this was naive. I recall being oblivious of the extent to which the board of education and school officials, including the commissioner of education, had developed curious subtle and covert social maneuvers for maintaining segregated schools in New York City. As a social psychologist, I can say now that wishful thinking colored my ideas and beliefs. I did not realize how deeply endemic racism was in the American culture.

At that time, the North rationalized its racism by contending that racially segregated schools were a manifestation of a larger pattern of our racial culture. Segregation in housing patterns and racially segregated communities created segregated schools. I thought that taking important steps in modifying the racial housing pattern would address the segregated housing problem. This, in turn, would resolve the reorganization of our public school system seriously and successfully. I did not understand, however, that the maintenance of segregated housing not only excused persistent patterns of school segregation, but that segregated housing itself represented a form of deeply embedded racism that resisted all attempts at desegregation—ironically, particularly in the North, I was perplexed. Thus, while in writings and speeches I highlighted the gains in our society, such as the civil rights gains, affirmative action, and the increasing numbers of elected black political officials—very important developments, but I underestimated the significance of racism's staunch hold on the American people.

Recent developments have made me reflect on the early stages following the Court's *Brown* decision. I now see more clearly the curious way that our early optimism prevented us from anticipating how racial progress would result in a form of backlash. The current resistance to affirmative action, for example, reflects the depth of American racism. We now are confronted with various manifestations of the belief that affirmative action essentially represents a rejection of or penalty against white males. This argument, however, conceals the fact that affirmative action was designed to remedy the past rejection, prejudice, and exclusion of minorities, particularly blacks. It is disheartening to see that these attempts to remedy social injustices now are being used to maintain those prior injustices.

As another example, segregated schools and segregated housing still pervade the American landscape, but they are not being discussed as manifestations of racism. Similarly, desegregation and integration are not being discussed as attempts to resolve former and persistent forms of injustice. Instead, these issues are discussed as issues of poverty and choice rather than as lasting symbols of our history of racism. Significantly, many liberals and many Supreme Court decisions now follow this pattern of racial exclusion. In fact, institutions of higher learning explain racial isolation in terms of beneficial conditions for blacks in general, despite the earlier beliefs that segregation not only damaged black children, but also interfered with the human growth and development of white children. I am particularly fascinated by the fact that some blacks approve of segregated living quarters and segregated communities. The rise of the black separatist movement in the 1960s manifested blacks' identification with the reasoning of their oppressor. Black separatists internalized the reasoning of the proponents of racial separation.

It is clear to me, however, that the failure to desegregate our schools at all levels—at the elementary, high school, and college levels, despite our awareness of the harm that segregation inflicted on all of our children, has demoralized our society. It has weakened our social fabric. Yet we are being told that segregated schools and segregated housing in ghettos are not only desirable, but that blacks should feel grateful.

I often wonder how Thurgood Marshall and Robert Carter would present their case today before the present Supreme Court. How would they cope with the present pattern of resegregation that so pervades our society? As one of the social scientists who worked with Marshall and Carter during the *Brown* cases, I would argue that segregation, not only in Clarendon County, South Carolina, but also in New York City, in the Twin Cities, and in America at large, is as damaging now as it was then. The dream so long deferred should be re-examined, but not because the premise of the *Brown* decision has changed. The Supreme Court in *Brown* said: "We conclude that in the field of public education the doctrine of 'separate but equal' has no place. Separate educational facilities are inherently unequal." Earlier, the Court noted: "To separate [black students] from others of similar age and qualifications solely because of their race generates a feeling of inferiority as to their status in the community that may affect their hearts and minds in a way unlikely ever to be undone." Those words still ring true today.

In the 40 years since those statements, we have seen copious examples of the harm inflicted upon our society by the racism onto which we have held. It is time that educators, who have been dormant for so long, assume their role as leaders in this campaign for justice. Educators can become crucial participants in helping society protect our children and protect itself from the persistent damage of racism and segregation. Our schools, our neighborhoods, and, in fact, our society as a whole must be mobilized. We cannot apologize about freeing ourselves from the damage that is being done to our children and to the very fabric of our society. Our society desperately needs rejuvenation and a renaissance of positive and constructive policies by which we can all become constructive partners. (Clark, "In Pursuit of a Dream Deferred: Linking Housing and Education, Beyond *Brown v. Board of Education*, Housing and Education in the Year 2000." *Minnesota Law Review* 80.4 [April 1996]: 745–748.)

"Kenneth Clark, when asked in 1995, 'What is the best thing for blacks to call themselves?' He answered, 'White.' " (Clark, quoted by Sam Roberts, *New York Times*, sec. 4, May 7, 1995, 7.)

[*Editor's Note*: Kenneth Clark was one of many participants in the civil rights struggle who, in time, became pessimistic when looking back at *Brown*. In 1993, he wrote:]

I am forced to face the likely possibility that the United States will never rid itself of racism and reach true integration. I look back and shudder at how naïve we all were in our belief in the steady progress racial minorities would make through programs of litigation and education. (Clark, quoted in James T. Patterson, *Brown v. Board of Education, a Civil Rights Milestone and Its Troubled Legacy* [New York: Oxford University Press, 2001], xxviii.)

COMMENTARY

Nicholas deB. Katzenbach

In the early 1950s Dr. Kenneth Clark was a young psychologist in New York—one of a handful of black Ph.D.s with serious academic credentials. It was to him that Thurgood Marshall and the Legal Defense Fund turned for help in the battle to overturn the Supreme Court's holding in *Plessy v. Ferguson* that the Constitution was satisfied if the white majority provided blacks with "separate but equal" facilities. Young Dr. Clark became a frequent expert witness in the effort to desegregate public schools around the country, opining that segregation in education gave black children feelings of inferiority and lack of self-confidence and recounting among other things his own novel experiments with black and white dolls in the hands of very young black children.

That testimony was seized upon by a unanimous Supreme Court as an important basis for its opinion in *Brown v. Board of Education* and declared segregated public education unconstitutional. Dr. Clark believes that the *Brown* decision ranks with the Declaration of Independence and Lincoln's Emancipation Proclamation as one of the great affirmations of American democracy. Given his important role in persuading the *Brown* Court, it would be understandable if pride led Dr. Clark to exaggerate its importance. But, with the advantage of almost a half century of experience, I am inclined to think it is, if anything, an understatement of *Brown*'s importance.

While Dr. Clark, educator that he is, tends to emphasize the importance of equal education for all in desegregated schools, *Brown* stands for even more—essentially a desegregated society as a whole. We have not yet in fact desegregated all our schools in our still de facto segregated society. But *Brown* was instrumental in breaking down formal segregation in the South and became the intellectual foundation for the Civil Rights Acts of the 1960s and this nation's commitment to an integrated society.

In *Brown* the Court invited the country to see a different vision of democracy, and the Congress and most of the country responded.

Burke Marshall

I got to know Kenneth Clark and advise him and his work during the middle of the 1960s. He was a fine, intelligent, articulate, determined, pervasive, and effective leader and organizer. I was for a while on the board of his Metropolitan Research Center, and I always marveled at his ability to get the most out of his board members.[8]

Robert L. Carter

I turned to Kenneth Clark for help because we needed to show that segregation had an adverse effect on the educational development of black children. We had no precedents to rely on and, unlike higher education, no alumni or public opinion evidencing the inferiority of the black schools. We needed social scientists to testify that segregated education marked the black child as inferior. Kenneth testified to that effect in the South Carolina and Virginia cases and helped us secure the services of psychiatrists who testified to similar effect in the Topeka and Delaware cases. He also secured the support of the social science community for our basic and critical contention that the racial segregation of black children denied them their constitutional right to equal educational opportunity. To that end, a social science brief was filed and signed by the leading social scientists in the nation, which asserted that racial segregation had a deleterious impact on the development of black children based on social science data and findings derived from studies, tests, and experience in the field. The Supreme Court explicitly relied on the views of these social scientists in its ruling. Kenneth Clark's help was thus critical to our success. Monday morning quarterbacks, who afforded no advice as we sought to frame a winning approach to the High Court, were prone to assert that we could have won without Kenneth Clark's help and without the use of social science data. I conceptualized our argument in *Brown*, and I have never wavered in the belief that social science data supplied the essential ingredient needed for success in *Brown*. Without Kenneth's help that ingredient would never have been presented to the Supreme Court.

NOTES

1. [*Editor's Note*: Kenneth B. Clark, "The Effects of Prejudice and Discrimination on Personality Development," Fact-Finding Report, Mid-Century White House Conference on Children and Youth, 1950, mimeographed. See Appendix 2, this volume.]

2. [*Editor's Note*: The following is excerpted from J. Harvie Wilkinson III, *From Brown to Bakke: The Supreme Court and School Integration, 1954–1978* (New York: Oxford University Press, 1979), 32.

Applying social science to active controversies is also playing with fire. Most justices lack strong backgrounds in economics, psychology, or sociology; they are not familiar with the current state of the art; they can but poorly distinguish what is reputable methodology from what is sham. For every study that appears to support a justice's conclusions, another might be found to contradict or seriously qualify them. The force of the Court's views may be blunted, as in *Brown*, by a collateral debate on the veracity of its sources. And the social sciences lend to constitutional law a mushy bottom; if the cited authorities are later discredited, should not the opinion that cited them be also? All this is not to say that social sciences have no place in constitutional law—they do—but that for the untutored, caution is advisable. *Brown*, however, cast caution aside. It appeared to lean on social science for its central thesis—otherwise unexplained—that segregation damaged the personal and mental development of Negro school children. The first studies cited in footnote eleven for this proposition dealt with dolls. Professor Kenneth Clark had shown drawings of otherwise identical black and white dolls to segregated Negro school children between the ages of six and nine. When asked to select the "nice" doll, more children than not chose the white doll, supposedly evidence that school segregation implanted in blacks a negative image of their own race at a tender age. Almost immediately, questions emerged about Clark's study, even from friendly critics.

See Appendixes 7 and 8, this volume.]

3. [*Editor's Note*: At the time, Mr. Justice Marshall was chief counsel of the NAACP, representing the complainant.]

4. [*Editor's Note*: *Brown v. Board of Education*, 347 U.S. 483 (1954). "Text of the Supreme Court Opinions, May 17, 1954." See Appendix 5, this volume.]

5. [*Editor's Note*: Edmond Cahn, "Jurisprudence," *New York University Law Review* 30 (1955): 150–159.]

6. K.B. Clark, "Appendix to Appelant's Briefs—The Effects of Segregation and the Consequences of Desegregation: A Social Science Statement," September 22, 1952.

7. [*Editor's Note*: The following is from Ben Keppel, *The Work of Democracy: Ralph Bunche, Kenneth B. Clark, Lorraine Hansberry, and the Cultural Politics of Race* (Cambridge, MA: Harvard University Press, 1995).]

Clark trained in the 1930s at two centers of politically activist social science: Howard University; and Columbia University, where Clark worked under Otto Klineberg. In the three years prior to *Brown v. Board of Education*, Dr. Clark took a leading role in recruiting social scientists as expert witnesses in the appellate courts to buttress the National Association for Colored People's case against segregation. He was responsible for summarizing the relevant psychological research for presentation to the Supreme Court. One of his papers, the "Effects of Prejudice on Personality Development," was the first source cited by Warren in footnote 11 of his decision; the last in the footnote was Gunnar Myrdal's *An American Dilemma*. Myrdal was another of Dr. Clark's friends and mentors. Clark's involvement with *Brown* grew directly from his years at Howard University and Columbia University. The words that Warren paraphrased in the most quoted section of *Brown* had been written by Clark four years earlier . . . for presentation to the Mid-Century White House Conference on Children and Youth. One year later, Klineberg, Clark's chair [of the Psychology Department] at Columbia, told Robert Carter of the Legal Defense and Education Fund about Clark's work on the psychological effects of prejudice upon African-American children. From this contact Clark became the principal advisor on social science to the Legal Defense and Education Fund; as a member of the NAACP's legal defense team, Clark brought the concept of the inferiority complex into the litigation.

8. [*Editor's Note*: letter to the editor, October 6, 2002.]

CHAPTER 8

Race, Politics, and the Democratic Process

This, the middle of the twentieth century, the beginning of the Atomic Age, may well become known as the period of paradox. This is a period in which man may achieve either peace or the ultimate social psychosis of mass suicide. This is a period in which the fruits of human intelligence will either provide the leisure, comforts, and challenge for creative living or will increase intolerably the tensions, fears, and conflicts of life. In this period of world history the promises of the democratic ideal will be fulfilled for all men everywhere—in Mississippi, New York, South Carolina, or South Africa—or human beings everywhere will be doomed to an Orwellian existence of social and spiritual stagnation. (Clark, "The Crisis of American Democracy and the Negro" [address at the annual luncheon of the National Committee for Rural Schools, New York, November 19, 1955], 7.)

Democracy is a peculiar form of social and political organization which cannot be obtained and sustained by default. Apparently democracy is the most challenging form of governmental organization because it requires apparently constant concern and constant vigilance, and it maybe is a type of society that requires that people continuously sacrifice for it. And apparently only those who understand the delicacy of the equilibrium that is democratic society are able to mobilize the strength to fight for it.

I think, however, that it is the most challenging and maybe in the long run the most effective system of government or social system that man has devised. The paradox of it is, though, that in its pure and effective form, democracy and human decency must be color-blind. It has to be blind to arbitrary differences and distinctions among men. Part of the delicacy, the irony and the paradox, is that democracy is a system which must either benefit all of the individuals who are part of it, or it cannot benefit anyone, and it must be maintained by all of the groups or individuals who are part of that system or it cannot be maintained at all. The Negro-American has no choice except to continue to try to save American democracy, because if he doesn't do his stint to save this democracy, he is lost. (Clark, "The Role of Whites in the Civil Rights Struggle" [address presented at the World Affairs Conference, Mills College, December 4, 1963].)

Harlem Youth Opportunities, Inc. (HARYOU) is a creature of controversy. It was conceived in the general conflict, the normative turmoil, the persistent tensions, which comprise the Harlem ghetto. It was made inevitable by increasing evidence that the pathological forces within the ghetto were influencing and determining the patterns of adjustment of a rising and intolerably large number of young people of the community. . . . Public officials periodically announced bold new programs, which somehow never managed to have any perceptible effects. . . . Out of this cacophony of conflict and misunderstanding, where the one constant was increasing evidence of the deterioration of Harlem youth, the HARYOU program emerged. The inviolable, undebatable theme of HARYOU is that the youth of Harlem are not expendable. (Clark, *Youth in the Ghetto: A Study of the Consequences of Powerlessness and a Blueprint for Change* [New York: Harlem Youth Opportunities Unlimited, Inc., 1964], 21–41.)

As was stated in the HARYOU document, *Youth in the Ghetto*—a prototype for the national [federal] anti-poverty program—effective programs for the poor must be geared to developing in the victims of the ghetto the ability and the power to bring about desired social change through intelligent systematic and responsible social action. (Clark, "Community Power Structure and the War on Poverty" [address, Gertrude Folks Zimond Memorial Lecture, Vassar College, October 10, 1967].)

It must be demonstrated that a nation which presents itself to the world as the guardian of democracy and the protector of human values throughout the world cannot itself make a mockery of significant ethical principles by dooming one-tenth of its own population to a lifetime of inhumane futility because of remediable educational deficiencies in its public schools. (Clark, "Monopoly and Inefficient Public Schools" [address, Stanford University, July 13, 1967], 5.)

The predicament of the Negro in America and the destiny of our nation are much too critical in these times for the Negro public official to confuse histrionics with the hard thinking and work necessary for effectiveness. If the Negro in America is to survive—and if he does not survive America cannot survive—then the cold calculating realism of the Negro elected public official must be combined with the values and concern for humanity necessary to make survival possible. (Clark, "The Negro Elected Public Official in the Changing American Scene" [address given at the National Conference of Negro Elected Officials at the Center for Continuing Education, University of Chicago, September 30, 1967].)

A serious war against poverty, like any other war, eventually has to be judged in terms of its results. It is the ultimate victory that counts. By this standard, the war on poverty must now be seen as approaching defeat. (Clark, "Elimination of Poverty in the Decent Society," White Paper, Clark Archives, Hastings-on-Hudson, NY, 1968.)

In general terms, law and order used today, and particularly by political officials, generally means containing the disruptions of the ghetto. Or protecting privileged people from the irrational outbursts of underprivileged people. (Clark, guest on *What's Happening to America?* hosted by Edwin Newman, NBC Television, July 12, 1968.)

One of our best hopes is something that has caused our conflicts. Jeffersonian democracy is the "monkey on our back." This nation has been caught by the idealistic words of its founding fathers and we'll never be free of them. Jeffersonian democracy was a major development, a major experiment in government. As a political system with an essentially moral, ethical basis, one that stated that the rights of human beings were its concern. Unfortunately, that policy was being contradicted even as it was being articulated. Even a sophisticated civilized man like Jefferson was caught up in the American web of moral schizophrenia. Slavery was clearly a violation of all the wonderful words in the Declaration of Independence and the first 10 amendments of the Constitution. But those words did exist, they were written. And they did exist. And they form the basis for the torture of America. (Clark, in Mary Harrington, "A Conversation with Kenneth B. Clark," *Psychology Today* 2.1 [June 1968]: 21–22.)

The fact that America was the first nation which dared to develop a political system on a moral, philosophical creed was one part of its dilemma. But the other part was the fact that at the same time that America verbalized its morality, the rhetoric for a democratic political system in its Constitution and its Declaration of Independence, it was confronted with the reality of slavery. African slaves in America were not considered persons, human beings who had the right and the privileges eloquently stated in the Founding Fathers' rationale. (Clark, "The Dilemma of the Insecure" [address, 1969 Haynes Foundation Lecture Series, University of Southern California, April 7, 1969], 2–4.)

Negro elected officials have, in a significant sense, become the new leaders of the civil rights movement in America. . . . as the number and power of Negro elected and appointed governmental officials increase, their problems and challenges will increase. As the proportion of Negroes in the large industrial cities increases, the number of Negroes in political decision-making positions on the local, state, and national level will increase. These officials must find ways of retaining and increasing a critical percentage of white support since the future of the Negro in politics cannot be restricted to the racially segregated ghettos. The Negro political official must be pre-pared for the realities and the problems of a politics of integration. Within this inescapable context of biracialism, the Negro must compete on single standards to gain and retain political power as the most potent instrument whereby the promises of racial justice can be made real. Intelligent and responsible use of political power is the basis of meaningful economic power. "Black capitalism" and "black economic development" will remain merely titillating words if they are not a part of the total pattern of solid political activity among Negroes.

At this demanding, put-up-or-shut-up stage of the civil rights struggle the Negro political official will be required to prepare himself to bear the ad-ditional burdens of helping America to save itself from its past racial and urban mistakes and helping to develop new and higher standards of polit-ical morality and performance. This challenge may be difficult, but it is unavoidable for the leaders of an oppressed minority. If he is to be relevant and effective, in the continuing and intensified struggle for racial justice in America, the Negro elected official cannot be just another politician. While he must be realistic, he cannot be expedient. His realism must be the realism of unswerving and uncompromising concern with the problems of social and racial justice in America; the Negro elected official cannot be just an-other politician. (Kenneth B. Clark, Julian Bond, and Richard G. Hatcher, "The Black Man in American Politics, Three Views," a publication of MARC, Inc., December 1969, 10–18.)

Boiled down to a few sentences, it [my testimony] was presented in the beginning and the end of the written Kerner Commission [1968] report—namely, my feeling that inquiries, conferences, investigations were endless in dealing with serious social problems and, particularly, racial problems. Our society has devised the technique of investigations, inquiries, and re-ports. Social scientists have become more affluent, if not more powerful, as a result of being hired to make these studies. But these studies have tended to repeat themselves. I was assured by the prestigious gentlemen there that it would be different from the Kerner Commission. The Kerner Commission did do a much better job in publicizing the report than the previous ones, but its effect so far has not been any different. It has been read, discussed, and forgotten, in terms of action. (Clark, "Education in the Ghetto: A Human Concern" [address, Urban Education Lecture Series, Teachers College, Columbia University, NY, January 13, 1970].)

I have had some contact with the Nixon administration. Last fall, I was involved in a black elected officials conference which was held in Washington—totally bipartisan. I was sort of a technician and helper, and my Metropolitan Applied Research Center was the vehicle through which the black elected officials moved to bring themselves together in a conference. The Republican and Democratic officials who met there were greeted by the President in the White House, in the Rose Garden. The President and his official family were quite gracious in meeting the group for about an hour. A number of Cabinet members actually attended the session. But at the end of the conference, we were never really able to get back to the White House to provide the President a summary of our concerns. My feeling was that those [elected black] officials were really seriously interested in trying to communicate to the President their feelings about dangers in administration policy and strategy, which if the White House had accepted or considered seriously at that time might have helped in preventing some of the widening alienation and negative reactions of not only blacks but students. I think maybe people around the President tried to protect him from inconvenience, and people who were bringing uncomfortable and difficult problems to his attention. We had hoped that would have been followed by a small group getting back to the White House and viewing problems of segregation in the schools, the new federalism or new approach to the states, and the implication of this for blacks in southern states. But we were never able to get back. (Clark, guest on *Speaking Freely*, hosted by Edwin Newman, NBC-TV, transcript, May 31, 1970.)

I welcome this opportunity to analyze the two major components of the proposed legislation—the funds requested for compensatory education and the moratorium on busing. My considered conclusion is that both guarantee *unequal* education for minority children. It is clear that the President's proposals to prohibit the transportation of students for purposes of school desegregation are racially restrictive. In seeking to turn back the clock of racial progress in America, this Administration must be aware of the fact that [this bill] threatens the Constitutional protections of all Americans. The President [Richard M. Nixon] is attempting to substitute a government in which the tyranny of whim and passion replaces government under law. . . . To protect all of our children, I call upon you to defeat this bill. (Clark, testimony before the House Education and Labor Committee, April 12, 1972.)

Social scientists are indistinguishable from politicians. And certainly they then tend to become dependent upon the politicians for small consultant favors or public exposure, and seemingly for political influence. Under these conditions social scientists, in spite of their scientific pretensions, are no more dependable in the quest for social justice than are other citizens. (Clark, "Social Policy, Power, and Social Science Research," *Harvard Educational Review* 43.1 [February 1973]: 120.)

Watergate highlights the complexity of the American illness in that these crimes were planned and committed by successful—not overtly disadvantaged—Americans. These crimes were committed by men who daily preached about the importance of preserving the American democratic way of life. They preached about "law and order" even as they pandered to the prejudices and exploited the ignorance of the majority of the American electorate for political process. These were pragmatic men who themselves were symbols of the success of the upward mobility promises of America. These were men who boasted about their own virtue and sneered at the frailties of less successful human beings as they flaunted their friendships with such affluent and successful religious leaders as Billy Graham and Norman Vincent Peale. These were men who were dominated by an insatiable hunger for power and domination, as values which must take precedence over elementary decency, justice, humanity, love and truth. These men demonstrated by their acts the depth of their frustrations, the pathetic emptiness within them, the futility of seeking affirmation of the value and quality of the self through material acquisitions and the endless pursuit of power. These men are Americans. These men are very sick. (Clark, "How Sick Is America?" [address, Bayerischer Rundfunk, Munich, Germany, July 11, 1973].)

It is a testament to the American democratic system, that once the federal courts made it clear that the promise of democracy could not be qualified by arbitrary and irrelevant grounds of race or color, the legislative and executive branches followed suit. The Congress of the United States passed important civil rights legislation in the latter part of the 1950s and the 1960s. In spite of his personal opinions, President Dwight D. Eisenhower ordered federal troops to enforce the desegregation decision in Little Rock, Arkansas. President John F. Kennedy, in later years of his aborted administration, provided an atmosphere of positive movement toward strengthening civil rights and civil liberties as desirable and long-delayed goals in the fulfillment of American democracy. And were it not for his entanglement in the tragic ambiguities of the purposeless Vietnam War, it would even now be clear that President Lyndon B. Johnson contributed more to racial progress in America than any other President in the 200 years of American history. (Clark, "How Sick Is America?" [address, Bayerischer Rundfunk, Munich, Germany, July 11, 1973].)

When a reporter for *The New York Times* asked me to comment on the fact that America had landed the first human beings on the moon I was forced to reply that, unlike so many others who saw this as a major triumph and demonstration of American status and achievement, I was sad. I was sad not because of this successful adventure but I was sad because the filth, the decay of American slums remained ignored as we congratulated ourselves on this triumph in space. The problem which continues to face concerned human beings is not the conquest of outer space, but the conquest of inner space wherein resides human conscience, sensitivity, and concern for the welfare of our fellow human beings. If America found the way to make this difficult political commitment it will be a most fitting celebration for the Bicentennial of the American. (Clark, "Toward a Slum Free America: Contemporary Forms of the Politics of Utopia" [address, Temple University Department of Political Science Lecture Series, Philadelphia, PA, May 15, 1975].)

It should be possible to help the American people to understand and act upon the understanding that, to borrow from [Alexis] de Tocqueville, "It depends upon themselves whether the principle of equality [democracy] is to lead them to servitude or freedom, to knowledge or barbarism, to prosperity or to wretchedness." (Clark, "Democratic Politics and Popular Education" [address, Bicentennial of the United States of America, The Little Red Schoolhouse, St. Charles, MN, April 24, 1976].)

In terms of raising the consciousness of the people to the need to include more blacks, both John Kennedy and Lyndon Johnson were in a category by themselves. Kennedy because he seized the opportunity to lead the movement early by announcing the Plans for Progress program in 1962. Johnson because he was thrust into a position of leadership and made a major contribution to race relations as a reflection of a national conscience. During these two Administrations, the Federal Government undertook serious affirmative action programs The process may well have started, I think, with an unpublicized meeting on May 15, 1963, in New York, with the then Attorney General, Robert F. Kennedy. So were James Baldwin, Harry Belafonte, Lena Horne, Lorraine Hansberry, and about a dozen other black people from various fields.

"What do you people want?" Robert Kennedy asked us directly.

"Jobs, and to be fully included in the American economic system," somebody replied.

"That's what the Negro wants."

Bob Kennedy told us it was "politically unrealistic" for the president to take a public position on this issue. The meeting ran on more than five hours. Kennedy did not give us much encouragement that time. But he listened.

Fifteen days later, however, L.B.J.—as vice president—gave a speech on civil rights. It included, word for word, some of the things we said to Bob Kennedy. I was convinced then, and I am still, that Johnson had been asked to test the political winds. The response was good. Soon after, Jack Kennedy helped spark the movement. These two men, perhaps more than any others in power in America, helped open up the economic mainstream to blacks. (Clark, "Long Time Coming," IBM's *Think* magazine, July 1976, 68.)

The Kennedy-Johnson period in American history was a period of hope, of promises, of concern with making the American democratic system more effective, more real. It was a period when one sought to extend the benefits of democracy to groups of human beings who previously had been either excluded or involved only to a minimal degree. It is appropriate that the Kennedy-Johnson period of 1961 through 1968 was designated as the period of "The New Frontier" and "The Great Society." Summing up the positives and the negatives of the Kennedy-Johnson social programs, one can objectively conclude that their overall effect remains positive. The problems that arose demonstrate that social progress and the struggle for social equality do not proceed on a straight, upward line. Social progress must be charted with ups and downs, but with the general trend toward up. Future historians will interpret these governmentally supported social programs as a reflection of two Presidents who were, in fact, deeply concerned with raising the status and the quality of life of their fellow human beings. (Clark, address, "Community Action and the Social Programs of the 1960s," in David C. Warner, ed., *Toward New Human Rights: The Social Policies of the Kennedy and Johnson Administrations* [Austin, TX: Lyndon B. Johnson School of Public Affairs, 1977], 95, 107.)

These [Little Rock, Arkansas] students have reacted extraordinarily well to the tensions, threats and anxiety surrounding their attendance at Central High School. They are aware of the problems and dangers. Many of them have borne directly the brunt of organized harassment and hostility perpetuated by a hard core of about 50 white students in Central High School. In general, they react to the jostling, name calling, taunts, and threats with disciplined restraint . . . all of the students, with possibly one exception, seem to be reacting most positively to being thrown into the public spotlight. There seems to be no evidence of any severe distortion in their perspective of themselves. In short, they do not seem to be suffering from a celebrity psychosis. Their relations with their former classmates and the community in general also seem to be quite good.

In general, these nine students are quite aware of the importance of their pioneer role. They have been made so keenly aware of this that they are willing to accept the personal discomforts and abuse so that other Negro students will have an easier time. (Clark, "Present Complexities in American Race Relations: Symptoms of Conflict and the Sickness-Success Syndrome" [address, The Merimon Lecture, No. 20, School of Medicine of the University of North Carolina at Chapel Hill, November 20, 1980], 1–12.)[1]

Race relations has been a critical and unavoidable index of the stability and health of American democracy. It has been a central fact of its history. (Clark, "Present Complexities in American Race Relations: Symptoms of Conflict and the Sickness-Success Syndrome" [address, The Merimon Lecture, No. 20, School of Medicine of the University of North Carolina at Chapel Hill, November 20, 1980], 2.)

It is a clear fact that the Reagan Administration has sought to reverse the positive goals and procedures for remedying past racial discrimination in employment. While the executive branch of the federal government, including the Civil Rights Division of the Department of Justice and the U.S. Civil Rights Commission, consistently seeks to dilute the positives of affirmative action, it is significant that—so far—the United States Supreme Court and the Federal courts have not followed this trend. (Clark, "Affirmative Action at the Crossroads: A Manifest for Change" [address at a meeting sponsored by the Board of Governors, California Community Colleges, San Jose City College, September 26, 1986].)

COMMENTARY

Charles B. Rangel

Dr. Kenneth Clark's *Youth in the Ghetto* blueprint for saving young people in Harlem was a carefully conceived document that should be preserved as part of history. It became the model for the entire nation. It enabled young people to leave the ghetto; it gave them a chance in life.

NOTE

1. [*Editor's Note*: Based on Kenneth B. Clark, "Some General Observations in the Negro Community of Little Rock, Arkansas," White Paper, after Dr. Clark visited there in 1958. From the Clark Archives, Hastings-on-Hudson, NY, February 6, 1958.]

CHAPTER 9

Breaking the Barriers Through Legislation

Obviously, laws and courts cannot handle this [racism] problem totally, but they are very important. The Supreme Court of the United States has been the most significant factor in precipitating the present confrontation between whites and Negroes on the moral and constitutional issues of race in America. But the Supreme Court cannot enforce, itself. It is up to the executive and legislative branches of our Government to see that the laws are, in fact, implemented. And, of course, in this case, there is also the Negro. The Negro is now taking into his own hands the responsibility for seeing that his rights are not ignored. (Clark, quoted in "Racism and the Courts," *U.S. News & World Report*, June 10, 1963, 39.)

Attitudes are complex and often irrational things. It is precisely because of the difficulty in controlling man's attitudes toward his fellow man that we have created laws and established police powers which seek to control man's behavior. Racial prejudice is not only non-rational, but it also seeks to defend itself by menacing virtues out of distortion, unreality and primitive emotions under the guise of protecting superiority and civilization. (Clark, quoted in *New York Times Magazine*, August 28, 1963, 57.)

The passage of a meaningful civil rights bill by the United States Senate is mandatory. The symbolic significance over and above the practical and realistic imperatives for the passage of this bill without emasculating amendments is indicated by the catastrophic despair and frustrations which will erupt in the Negro people if this bill can get killed by a small cynical group of senators. (Clark, "One Hundred Years after Emancipation: A

Time for Hope or Despair?" [address given at the seventh annual National Workshop for Religious Liberals, Washington, DC, July 1964].)

Certainly the President's declaration of the war against poverty was a clear statement of purpose, and the Congress passed the legislation . . . but I think we must be clear that we are not now fulfilling these promises. Any misunderstandings about the present limitations of the program could do great harm, and I think the chief harm that we must address ourselves to here would be that these programs raised hopes. They have been well publicized, the poor and others have been told that there is something positive that the Government is doing for them, and I think we will be providing a real powder keg, and intensifying the danger of that powder keg by raising these hopes and then not fulfilling them. (Clark, excerpt from testimony examining War on Poverty, *Hearings before the Subcommittee on Employment, Manpower, and Poverty of the Committee on Labor and Public Welfare*, U.S. Senate, 90th Cong., March 13, 1967.)[1]

The nature of the civil rights reality since the summer of 1963 has been confusing, contradictory, obscure, and at times seemingly chaotic. The dignity of the non-violent sit-in movement from 1955 aroused the conscience of white Americans and resulted in the passage of the strong civil rights and voting rights legislation by Congress in 1964 and 1965. But these were the years in which the center of gravity of the civil rights movement shifted from the southern to northern cities. The television portrayal of the stark brutalities of "Bull" Connor in Birmingham, the barbarities of Jim Clark in Selma, and white southern policemen using dogs and cattle prods against Negroes who now refused to cooperate with racial segregation gave way, after 1964, to the standard summer TV fare of scenes of major ghetto riots in New York, Buffalo, Rochester, Watts, Philadelphia, Newark, Plainfield, Cambridge, and Detroit, and minor eruptions elsewhere.

These riots revealed, among other things, that the "victories" won by the dignified non-violent protests of the southern Negro and civil rights legislation were not relevant to the predicament of the northern Negro, and did not remedy the pervasive forms of racism which afflicted him in his northern city ghettos. Most Negroes now live in the north where they have the right to vote and where there are laws which ostensibly protect their rights to fair employment, to purchase any house which they can afford, and to assure their children equal and non-segregated educational opportunities. (Clark, "Where It's At: Civil Rights," *Vogue*, April 1, 1968, 178.)

Despite the high hopes of the youthful Kennedy Administration, and its holdovers under Johnson, the campaign for massive feasible participation by the poor in the anti-poverty program must now be seen as a charade, an exhilarating intellectual game whose players never understood the nature of power and the reluctance of those who have it to share it. It seems apparent that canny political leadership—national and city—never intended fundamental social reorganization. The political participation of the poor in their own affairs was not to be a serious sharing of power after all.

Congressional reaction against the challenge of community action programs, the Johnson Administration's executive pre-occupation with Vietnam and its loss of interest in the War on Poverty, its refusal to acknowledge the imperatives of the Kerner Commission Report, the inadequacy of that Administration's reaction to the series of northern urban riots, and the more recent growing resistance of Congress to foundation involvement in voter education and registration—all are indicative of the superficiality of the official engagement with the poor. (Clark, with Jeanette Hopkins, *A Relevant War Against Poverty: A Study of Community Action Programs and Observable Social Change* [New York: Harper & Row, 1969], v.)

Anti-discrimination and equal opportunities legislation have not alleviated the [jobs] condition. Where legislation is in effect, job discrimination persists, only in a more subtle form. One must assume, therefore, that the manner in which covert discrimination operates makes it relatively immune to the laws that have abolished its cruder manifestations. In addition to rigorous enforcement of legislation, techniques must be used that are as subtle and as pervasive as the social evil they seek to overcome. (Clark, "Sex, Status, and Underemployment of the Negro Male," in Arthur M. Ross and Herbert Hill, eds., *Employment, Race, and Poverty: A Critical Study of the Disadvantaged Negro Workers from 1865–1965* [New York: Harcourt, Brace & World, 1971], 14.)

If it is true that affirmative action is now judged as imposing discrimination upon those who benefited from such discrimination in the past, then one has no remedy. One has to accept the fact that the consequences of past discrimination will have to continue into the present and into the future. . . . Quotas [are] another example of what I call the "semantic diversion." Traditionally, quotas had a meaning as exclusion. Government-enforced affirmative action programs should continue until they are no longer necessary. They are means toward an end. (Clark, "The Costs of Discrimination," *Challenge* [May–June 1977]: 33, 35.)

In spite of this critical error in planning and perspective, the [federal] antipoverty movement did leave a positive residue of, admittedly imperfect, community control, concerns, rhetoric, and organizations among the poor. Groups of individuals in economically depressed areas did become more concerned with what was happening to their children in their neighborhood public schools. It would not seem to be an exaggeration to say that the movement toward the decentralization and community control of the public schools in New York City is a direct spillover from the community action component of the anti-poverty programs. Unfortunately, the evidence today reveals that this decentralization and community control has not yet resulted in any observable increase in the academic achievement of poor children in these public schools. While one cannot with absolute confidence conclude on the basis of available evidence that the rise of systematic political activity among minorities is a direct consequence of the anti-poverty programs of the Sixties, the passage of the Voting Rights Act of 1965 caused a marked increase in the number of black elected officials throughout the United States. (Clark, address, "Community Action and the Social Programs of the 1960s," in David C. Warner, ed., *Toward New Human Rights: The Social Policies of the Kennedy and Johnson Administrations* [Austin, TX: Lyndon B. Johnson School of Public Affairs, 1977], 105.)

There is little question that the most complex problems related to enforcement of the affirmative action and equal opportunities laws are those which reflect the present manifestations of flagrant and subtle racist backlash. The resistance to equal employment opportunity and affirmative action should be expected, given the fact that the laws were required. Obviously, if equal opportunities were practiced, there would be no need for corrective legislation. While it is true that the more flagrant forms of white backlash rarely expressed themselves in terms of racial epithets and overt racial stereotyping, it is also true that in reacting against effective enforcement of these rules and regulations, thinly disguised and more subtle forms of racism were resorted to. For example, it has been stated that effective compliance with affirmative action would result in the reduction of standards and efficiency, and would interfere with the primary priorities and objectives of the corporation and institution. In the attempt to remedy the effects of past racism in the area of employment, a new semantics of racism has developed. It has become fashionable to state that increasing the number and percentage of minorities and females in positions from which they had been previously excluded was a form of "reverse discrimination" and "preferential treatment." The common denominator of these code terms was that all effective attempts at remedying past discrimination are inherently racist and violative of anti-discrimination laws. (Clark, unpublished paper presented to the U.S. Commission on Civil Rights, March 10, 1981.)[2]

COMMENTARY

Bill Bradley

Dr. Kenneth Clark has written and spoken about race in America for over fifty years. His body of work shows the insight of a psychologist and educator and the commitment of a civil rights warrior. With candor he confronted America with its continuing racism while at the same time taking black political leaders to task for being unable to increase "humanity and justice" for those left behind in America's inner cities. Above all, he maintained the hope of a patriot who knows that the promise of America includes everyone and that our ideals will be fully realized only when all Americans share the realization of that promise.

NOTES

1. [*Editor's Note*: The statement is a summary of a study that Dr. Clark conducted of twelve community action programs around the nation during the 1964–1966 period.]

2. [*Editor's Note*: Dr. Clark was speaking as president, Clark, Phipps, Clark & Harris, Inc., an equal employment/affirmative action consulting firm based in New York.]

CHAPTER 10

The Civil Rights Movement

An investigation of intergroup attitudes in one of the larger, more isolated communities that make up metropolitan New York found that nearly 60 percent of the Jews held some unfavorable stereotyped reaction toward Negroes and 70 percent of Negroes had some unfavorable stereotyped reaction towards Jews. Those Jews who looked unfavorably upon Negroes found that they "have no ambition—they are lazy—they drink a lot—they have low intelligence—they are low class, rowdy, dirty, and noisy." Negroes antagonistic toward Jews tended to feel that, "Jews own everything—they are more aggressive—they engage in sharp business practices." (Clark, "Candor about Negro-Jewish Relations," *Commentary* 8 [February 1945]: 13–14.)

The assimilation process is made possible and facilitated by the basic American assumption and the reality of social and economic upward mobility. It should be pointed out that the reality of upward mobility characteristic of the American scene seemed dependent upon the fact that the American culture until relatively recently was a growing, expanding and essentially a frontier culture. This new culture not only offered opportunities to new migrants to better themselves, but welcomed them as new partners in the challenging effort of building a new nation which was destined to become great through the success of their efforts. . . . As the culture continued to develop and opportunities decreased, this competition for status seemed generally to increase. Each new wave of white European immigrants found itself initially at the bottom of the American status hierarchy—with only the Negro as a caste-like rejected group which it could look down on.

(Clark, "Racial Prejudice among American Minorities," *International Social Science Bulletin* 2 [Winter 1950]: 4–5.)

It is a distinct privilege and honor for me to have the opportunity to introduce to you this afternoon the Rev. Dr. Martin Luther King Jr. He is a young man. . . . I believe that he has within him the potential for truly great leadership. Not just leadership of the American Negro. He has the potential for leadership of the spiritual, ethical and moral sort that all the American people sorely need. (Clark, introducing Dr. Martin Luther King, Jr., to the National Committee for the Rural Schools in New York, Clark Archives, Hastings-on-Hudson, NY, December 21, 1956.)

He [Dr. King] is . . . articulate, intelligent . . . with an inherent dignity and calm. He discusses the issues of the boycott and the general problems of race relations in Alabama and the south, not only without venom, but without apparent emotion. He recognizes the relationship between the success or failure of the Montgomery Negroes . . . the total problem of racial justice in America and the more complex problems of international relations. . . . He is profoundly concerned with the fundamental issues of the nature of justice and democracy. He is neither cynical nor sentimental; he does not expect miracles nor does he accept the clichés of gradualism or, "We are not ready." He contends that human beings are always ready for justice. (Clark, report to the Unitarian Service Committee, Inc. Community Service—USA, Boston, MA, issued on May 15, 1956.)

It [the *Brown* decision] provided the full and sustained motivation for the nonviolent civil-disobedience movement coordinated with brilliance and imagination by the Rev. Martin Luther King Jr. Within the decade immediately following the *Brown* decision, American civil rights leadership sustained the momentum in behalf of racial justice and obtained objectives unmatched in American history.

During that period, James Farmer, A. Philip Randolph, Dorothy I. Height, Dr. King, John Lewis, Whitney M. Young Jr., Roy Wilkins, Malcolm X and other black and white civil rights activists demonstrated that, in spite of some differences, it was possible to combine all resources, approaches and styles and to forge a leadership cadre. Civil rights victories, including the 1964 Civil Rights Act and the 1965 Voting Rights Act, were the result. (Clark, "The Role of Race," *New York Times Magazine*, October 5, 1960, 26.)

Probably the most dramatic example of effective personal leadership among Negroes in recent years is the emergence of the Rev. Martin Luther King Jr., a symbol of the Negro's resistance to the stigma and humiliation of racial segregation. Rev. King's role in organizing, directing, and controlling the Montgomery bus boycott outlawing segregation in intrastate transportation catapulted him into national and international prominence. He captured the imagination of liberals and opponents of injustice throughout the world and justifiably won the loyalties and affection of American Negroes. (Clark, "The Negro in the North," in Mathew A. Ahmann, ed., *The New Negro* [Notre Dame, IN: Fides Publishers, 1961], 35–36.)

How do I—a Negro in America who throughout his undergraduate years and the early part of his professional life identified himself with liberalism—how do I now see American liberalism? I must confess bluntly that I now see white American liberalism primarily in terms of the adjective, "white." And I think one of the important things Negro Americans will have to do is learn how they can deal with a curious and insidious adversary—much more insidious than the out-and-out bigot. The public schools in New York City are not headed by bigots, they're not headed by people who say outwardly, "I believe that Negroes are inferior, that they can't learn." They're headed by liberals. Most principals in the New York City public schools and most of the principals in Harlem schools say, "I am a liberal, I vote the Democratic ticket." Some of them might even say, "I'm a little socialist inclined." But the fact is that these schools are woefully inferior. They are not getting better; the evidence is that they are getting worse and worse. And the people who are directly responsible for this are self-identified liberals. (Clark, "Liberalism and the Negro," *Commentary* [March 1961]: 39.)

This observer has no doubts that Martin Luther King's philosophy of love for the oppressor is a genuine aspect of his being. He personally does not differentiate between the philosophy and the effectiveness of the nonviolent direct-action approach to the attainment of racial justice, which he personifies and leads. For him, the philosophy is not just a strategy; it's a truth, it is his assertion of the philosophical position that one cannot differentiate means from ends. The quiet, contemplative, at times exasperatingly academic style is truly Dr. King. He is a paradox of the scholar and the effective man of social action. (Clark, *The Negro Protest* [Boston: Beacon Press, 1963], 35.)

Malcolm X is a very careful man. He seems to speak spontaneously but I think Malcolm X chooses his words very carefully. His attitude toward Martin Luther King certainly would seem to reflect that the Muslims do not respect non-violence. They believe that non-violence is another sign of the stereotyped meek Negro. To be perfectly accurate, though, I think we would have to say that there is no evidence that the Muslims preach violence in the sense of organizing Negroes for violent revolt. (Clark, "The

Negro in Contemporary America" [address delivered at Mills College, December 3, 1963].)

James Baldwin is someone whom I admire not only as a writer but as a person. I'm sometimes quite fearful that he will destroy himself by giving too much of himself, working too hard. . . . Baldwin has become a major irritant because his truth cannot be ignored. His words have clarity, a grace, a style and a penetration which make it impossible for our religious leaders to continue their pattern of perfunctory verbalization against racial sin, while they actually accept [it]. . . . I believe that Baldwin remains a towering and major figure in the present racial confrontation. As a writer he has mobilized the powerful weapon of words and the systematic presentation of ideas, as another weapon in the Negro's struggle for justice. (Clark, "The Negro in Contemporary America" [address delivered at Mills College, December 3, 1963].)

This present crisis or confrontation or revolution [in the 1960s], if you will, is unique in that it is being fought not with military weapons but with the more powerful weapons of the democratic ideology. (Clark, "The Negro in Contemporary America" [address delivered at Mills College, December 3, 1963].)

Before World War II, there was another big [civil rights] spurt with A. Philip Randolph—president of the Brotherhood of Sleeping Car Porters Union—[and leader of] the March-on-Washington movement that brought out of President Roosevelt the first executive order for a Fair Employment Practices Committee. Randolph at that period was the most militant Negro leader, and he was really anticipating the direct action approach which is now being used so effectively. (Clark, quoted in *Pageant* magazine, October 1963, 34.)

One hundred years after the Emancipation Proclamation, Negroes in the United States are at least being taken seriously. (Clark, "A Relevant Celebration of the Emancipation Centennial," *Ebony*, September 19, 1963, 23.)

The poetic irony of American race relations is that the rejected Negro must somehow also find the strength to free the privileged white. (Clark, "Black and White: The Ghetto Inside," *Boston Magazine*, October 1965, 35.)

The great tragedy—but possibly the great salvation, too—of the Negro and white in America is that neither one can be free of the other. The Negro is a little bit white and every white is a little bit Negro, in the sense that neither is totally alien from the other. Both are caught in a common human predicament. Each needs the other, the white to be free of his guilt, the

Negro to be free of fear. . . . The Negro alone cannot win this fight that transcends the "civil rights struggle." (Clark, *Dark Ghetto: Dilemmas of Social Power* [New York: Harper & Row, 1965], 223, 240.)

[Congressman] Adam Clayton Powell's effectiveness in the ghetto is a consequence, in part, of his suave charm. Here is a man who is always in complete control of his gesture and posture, as sensitive to his role as an actor on a stage. He is narcissistic, but even his narcissism is under control. He holds sway over his predominately female congregation at the Abyssinian Baptist Church by dramatizing himself as the prototype of the desirable male aware of his power. He uses his appeal without apology. But Powell must be understood also in terms of this massive pathology of the ghetto, where a powerless people seek a concrete hero who will fight the battles they cannot fight for themselves. All the better if the hero defies and taunts the white enemy. Here is the gratifying joy of vicarious revenge without the attendant penalties of a real encounter.

In his flamboyant personal behavior, Powell has been to the Negroes a symbol of all that life has denied them. The Negro can in fantasy journey with Adam to the Riviera, enjoy a home in Puerto Rico, have beautiful girls at his beck and call, change wives "like rich white folks." Powell plays the role the Hollywood star may for whites but even more powerfully, for added to the magic and glamour of personal fame is the excitement and virtues of defiant racial protest.

The Negro masses do not see Powell as amoral but as defiantly honest in his protest against the myths and hypocrisies of racism. What whites regard as Powell's violation of elemental ethics, Negroes view as effective and amusing defiance. Whatever is the personal ethical moral standard of the individual Negro, it tends to be suspended in judgment of Powell. He is important precisely because his *is* a caricature, a burlesque, of the personal exploitation of power. His behavior merely focuses on the fact that certain respectable white congressmen, too, may use public funds for personal junkets or put their wives on the public payroll. The white power structure never successfully calls him to account and the Negro sees this and applauds.

In the genuine thrust of the civil rights movement, Powell is a has-been, still seeking to give the impression of leadership. The fascinating thing is that this façade becomes something more because whites in positions of power still respond to Powell as though he were able to deliver or withhold Negro votes. When U.S. Attorney General Robert Kennedy was faced with the possibility that Powell might attempt to exploit the HARYOU program in development of Harlem for personal political gain, Kennedy was quoted in the daily press as saying, "I have no fault to find with Adam Clayton Powell." (Clark, *Dark Ghetto: Dilemmas of Social Power* [New York: Harper & Row, 1965], 163, 165–166.)

What surprises me is that there have not been more Adam Clayton Powells. ... We cannot be as pure as Caesar's wife. We are human, too. (Clark, quoted in Neil Hickey and Ed Edwin, *Adam Clayton Powell and the Politics of Race* [New York: Fleet Publishing Corporation, 1965], 293.)

As Senator [Robert F.] Kennedy warned: "All these places—Harlem, Watts, South Side—are riots waiting to happen. (Clark, "The Wonder Is There Have Been So Few Riots," *New York Times Magazine*, September 5, 1956, 187.)

I am now sharing with you some of the thoughts that went through my mind as I watched enviously the time being given to an analysis of the meaning of "Black Power." I think it is an ambiguous concept. As I think about power, the one characteristic it does not have is color. This term is not definable except in terms of its opposite. "Black Power" cannot be defined with precision because it has no objective reference point other than the common predicament of Negro Americans who share only their lack of power and their resentment and anger at being denied equality and justice in the American democratic system. The inherent contradiction of this slogan is that it had to be defined realistically in terms of the lack of power. Were this not true the slogan would not have been needed. I thought also that it was a slogan that was more effective as an emotional stimulus for mass consumption than as a basis for hard, tough, substantive and pragmatic approaches which I believe to be necessary to move the civil rights movement out of its present explosive doldrums. (Clark, "Social Power and Social Change in Contemporary America" [address given as a consultant to the Foreign Affairs Scholars Program, Department of State, Agency for International Development, and the United States Information Agency, Washington, DC, July 18, 1966].)

[Black Power:] "It is the civil rights version of Watusi." (Clark, quoted in William Brink and Louis Harris, *Black and White: A Study of U.S. Racial Attitudes Today* [New York: Simon & Schuster, 1966], 66.)

In the area of consumer merchant relationships, [anti-Semitism] is a fact documented by many studies of the past, and more recent studies that Negroes in the ghettos are economically victimized in being required to pay higher prices for shoddy products and are also victimized by usurious interest rates in installment buying. Rightly or wrongly, it has become part of the mores of the folk Negro to associate this form of economic exploitation with the small merchant whom he invariably perceived as Jewish. A similar perception which becomes a part of the folk vocabulary and reality applies in the area of slum housing. It may not be an exaggeration to say that this has become so much a psychological reality that even a Negro slumlord may be perceived and described as "a Jewish landlord." (Clark, address before the American Jewish Congress National Governing Council, New York, December 3, 1967.)

America is moving closer each day to separate societies, one rich, self-indulgent, smug, cruel, callous, inhuman; the other poor, frustrated, bitter, angry, dehumanized. (Clark, "Elimination of Poverty in the Decent Society," manuscript, Clark Archives, Hastings-on-Hudson, NY, September 1968.)

Martin Luther King was the closest to a genuine saint that I have ever known. I used to get almost angry with him, because he made me feel so inadequate by really believing all the things he said about human beings and white Americans. His public position was identical to his private position. In the last year or so of his life, in private conversations with friends, he began to express his concern about America, his concern for her strength. But I never heard him make a nasty, disparaging or mean remark about any individual. Even when he was angry at the thoughtless or cruel things people said or did, he never expressed his anger by rejecting the person. If the civil rights movement in America does nothing but produce Martin Luther King, it has justified itself. Great human beings are rare. I think he is among the greatest spirits civilization has produced. (Clark, in Mary Harrington Hall, "A Conversation with Kenneth B. Clark," *Psychology Today* 2.1 [June 1968]: 23.)

The recent series of ghetto eruptions, which started in Harlem in 1964, and continued through Watts, Newark, Detroit, Chicago, Cleveland, including in its prairie-like wake, almost all major, and some not so major, northern American cities, is the most dramatic manifestation that the battle for racial justice is now being fought out in northern cities. It is no longer a purely southern anomaly. Many northern whites who previously considered themselves allies of the Negroes, as they fought the more flagrant and remote battles of race in the South, tended to retreat behind their suburban barricades and their rationalizations of white backlash. (Clark, "The Dilemma of the Negro" [address given as part of the 1969 Haynes Foundation Lecture Series, University of Southern California, April 10, 1969].)

The Negro intellectual must clearly differentiate his role from the equally important roles of others. He cannot confuse his role with that of the politician or the mass leader. He cannot hope to be successful by imitating or adopting their techniques or their slogans. He certainly cannot appeal to the man in the street through the uncritical use of slogans, emotional phrases, and other devices which have been found effective in arousing the emotions and allegiances of the crowd. On the contrary he is obligated to scrutinize the ideology, the motivation, and the methods of the popular leaders. He must interpret them and repudiate or accept them when the evidence so demands. The Negro intellectual would reduce his effectiveness if he sought to compete with others more competent and more suited in temperament and background for the status of popular leader. His role is to interpret, supplement, and give substance to the work of these leaders. He must content himself with the limited role of speaking to a minority at any given point in history. This, however, does not mean that the Negro intellectual can use this required division of labor as an excuse for withdrawal from social action. The dangers and imperatives of our times require that thought and responsible action merge into a single pattern of commitment. It is the fate of the Negro intellectual that he has no choice but to accept the challenge of trying to help America survive. (Clark, "The Duty of the Intellectual," in *Pathos of Power* [New York: Harper & Row, 1974], 23–29.)

A few months after *Brown*, I was in the office with Thurgood [Marshall] and he was very, very sad. I said, "What's the matter?" He said, "Well, we had the decision, but now our problem is how do we get it implemented? The law and the court decisions can't, in themselves, change patterns of behavior. The fight has just begun." So I said, "Yeah." At the time, of course, I was pretty optimistic that if we change the institutional patterns, it'll bring about changes in attitudes. And that was a theoretical position which I took as a psychologist and published. But Thurgood was really down. Three or four years before, we were going through the trial level of the cases, and he maintained an impression of light-heartedness, matter-of-factness, joking. Those of us who knew him knew that was just a facade—his jokes, and his casualness . . . he was a very serious human being. So I said, "All right, Thurgood, I want you to know that I've been taking notes on this process all along, and taking notes on you . . . and one of these days I'm going to write about you." And then he looked me right in the eye and said, "All right, Kenneth, I want you to know that truth is no defense against libel." (Clark, notes preparing for CBS program script on the Bicentennial, Clark Archives, Hastings-on-Hudson, NY, September 3, 1975.)

[Ralph Bunche] forcefully articulated that racism was to be understood not in terms of the black man's deficiencies but in terms of the white man's. (Clark, quoted in Richard Kluger, *Simple Justice: The History of* Brown v. Board of Education, *and Black America's Struggle for Equality* [New York: Alfred A. Knopf, 1976], 130.)

[In preparing for the *Brown* case] Thurgood [Marshall] kept his options open. He played the role of conductor beautifully. It was clear that Bob Carter was the most persistent, consistent advocate of the involvement of the social scientists at the trial level. Bob was way out on the limb, pretty much by himself. Most of the other lawyers felt this approach was, at best, a luxury and irrelevant. Thurgood didn't tip his hand, except that he did let Bob and me go ahead with the dolls. By the time we actually went to Charleston, the battle had been basically won.

[*Editor's Note*: The trip to Charleston took place on May 23, 1951—Marshall, Carter, and Clark traveling by train together. Following, Dr. Clark's recollections of that train ride:]

Thurgood had this unique capacity to deal with profoundly serious matters and then alleviate the mood with a remark that cut to the human predicament at the core of the problem. . . . I saw the battle fatigue. I had known him on and off for 10 years, and 'till then I had always thought he was inexhaustible and that he would just naturally keep on fighting. But he said to me then, "You know, Kenneth, sometimes I get awfully tired of trying to save the white man's soul." I said something innocuous back, like, "You have no choice." And he said, "I'm not so sure." He was resolved, of course, to see the segregation case through—"and then I've got to rest," he said. I sensed the complexity of the man for the first time then. (Clark, quoted in Richard Kluger, *Simple Justice: The History of* Brown v. Board of Education *and Black America's Struggle for Equality* [New York: Alfred A. Knopf, 1976], 321–324.)

In February, 1951 Robert L. Carter, the senior assistant to Thurgood Marshall, the then Director of the Legal Defense and Education Fund of the NAACP, visited me in my office at Northside Center for Child Development to discuss a matter which literally changed the course of my life. He stated that the Legal Defense Fund had decided to challenge before the Federal courts the constitutionality of segregated public schools. He said that these important cases would seek to repeal the "separate but equal" doctrine. The specific purpose of Carter's visit with me was related to the problem of the NAACP lawyer's need to demonstrate that segregated public schools damaged the human beings who were being segregated. He stated that only if it were possible to present evidence concerning damage to the plaintiffs would it be possible for the courts to rule that even if the separate facilities were equal the very fact of separation and segregation was unconstitutional. Within two weeks after this meeting Robert Carter called me and said, most enthusiastically, "Kenneth, that report could not have been more relevant for us if we had commissioned you to prepare it for us. Thurgood wants to see you. Can you come down to our office right away?" Within a matter of an hour or two I was talking with Robert Carter and Thurgood Marshall in the offices of the NAACP Legal Defense Fund. (Clark, Symposium: 25 Years After *Brown v. Board of Education*: Perspectives, "The Preparation of the Social Scientists' Brief," address to the 87th Annual Convention of Social Scientists, New York, September 1, 1979.)

The overall question "What do blacks now think of themselves?" can be answered by the evidence that, at best, blacks in general are still ambivalent in evaluating themselves and other blacks. Like all other human beings, blacks want to see and accept themselves in positive terms but they have deep and persistent conflicts. (Kenneth B. Clark and Mamie Phipps Clark, "What Do Blacks Think of Themselves?" *Ebony* [Special Issue] [November 1980]: 177.)

For the past 60 years American democracy has been reinforced by the existence of the American Civil Liberties Union. The ACLU has persisted in meeting the most difficult tests of being the moral conscience of our nation. It has protected the fundamental political and human rights of all Americans—indeed of all human beings within our jurisdiction. Its operational ideology has been and continues to be that all ideologies and all beliefs must have equal freedom of expression; no human being or group of human beings can be permitted to restrict or suppress the rights of other human beings. As expected, the ACLU has been criticized, threatened and ridiculed. But the power of its moral strength is demonstrated by the fact that the greater the risks and threats, the greater its clarity, its courage and its persistence. In fulfilling this difficult role, the ACLU will continue to give substance to American democracy and will help us to distinguish between social barbarism and civilization. (Clark, "The Moral Conscience of Our Nation," *Civil Liberties* [September 1980]: 14.)

As I was driving down to Rutgers, I thought about one of the outstanding— great intellect, great artist, great athlete, a great person concerned with dignity and with justice for human beings—one of the outstanding alumni of Rutgers. Every time I think of Rutgers, I think of Paul Robeson. Maybe one of these days Rutgers will be sufficiently mature and courageous to state publicly and proudly that Paul Robeson was an outstanding alumnus. (Clark, "Civil Rights in the 80s" [address, 100 Black Men of Rutgers, Rutgers University, April 20, 1981].)

During the past two decades, and particularly in the eight years of the Reagan administration, civil rights progress has become stagnant, if not regressed. The Reagan administration used the Civil Rights Commission, the Justice Department, and hard-won civil rights laws to reverse racial justice. We were confronted with the fact that again the power of the executive branch of government was being used to continue the inferior status of blacks. White backlash became a dominant political reality. As Rosalynn

Carter stated, the Reagan administration succeeded in making racial intolerance again acceptable. This combination of governmental white backlash and overly publicized black separatism now provide the halt and retreat of the progress of the civil rights movement. (Clark, "Civil Rights: The Past, the Present, and the Future" [address before the Community Relations Commission, Baltimore, MD, May 10, 1989].)

James Farmer, executive director of the Congress of Racial Equality (CORE), was formerly a Methodist minister. He combines the appearance of personal calm and tolerant objectivity with a surprising forthrightness and fervent commitment. He makes no diplomatic accommodation to power figures, but demands uncompromising equality. In CORE's loose confederation of militant and seemingly undisciplined local chapters under a permissive national board, Farmer is a stabilizing influence, a convergence point; he holds power by virtue of his personal example of commitment. (Clark, "Introduction: The Civil Rights Movement: Momentum and Organizations," in Talcott Parsons and Kenneth B. Clark, eds., *The Negro American* [Boston: Beacon Press, 1965], 609.)

Malcolm X is a punctual man. He arrived at the television studio with two of his closest advisors, at the precise time of our appointment. He and his friends were immaculately dressed, with no outward sign of their belonging to a separate sect or ministry. Minister Malcolm (and he insists upon being called "Minister Malcolm") is a tall, handsome man in his late thirties. He is clearly a dominant personality whose disciplined power seems all the more evident in contrast to the studied deference paid by his associates. He is conscious of the impression of power which he seeks to convey, and one suspects that he does not permit himself to become too casual in his relations with others. (Clark, *The Negro Protest* [Boston: Beacon Press, 1963], 17.)

It took me two whole years to force the [New York] State Education Department to release the Pupil Evaluation Program scores, and when they did I found out why they had been so reluctant to do it. In the ghetto areas of New York City, from 80 to 85 percent of the children were not only below the norm but *significantly* below. I asked that those scores be made available to the legislators. At the time, Charles Rangel, now a congressman, was the assemblyman from a Harlem district. When he looked at the scores in the Harlem schools, he shouted: "My God! My district is an educational disaster area." (Clark, quoted in *The New Yorker Magazine* as a member of the New York State Board of Regents, August 23, 1982, 37.)

In seeking to understand the contributions of Martin Luther King Jr., we must go beyond the popular perspective of Martin as civil rights leader. He made nonviolence a prevailing term, even if not a fact in the daily lives of the masses of human beings. For his personal commitment, Martin Luther King received the Nobel Peace Prize at a time when conflicts were dominating Europe, Asia, and Africa. Yet, respect for one's fellow human beings has not noticeably increased. As a matter of fact, the evidence is disturbingly clear that the fundamental logic of Martin's concerns with the ability of groups of human beings—races, clans, nationality groups—to work together and to interact even among themselves with subtle and overt nonviolence has not been embraced. The philosophy, the principles, the humanity, the basic sensitivity of Martin Luther King have been ignored. More practical men in politics, diplomacy, and education continue to dominate the functioning realities. (Clark, "Martin Luther King, Jr.: The Humanist" [address before the Coordinating Council for Minority Issues, University of Chicago, January 18, 1993].)

Martin Luther King, with associates, including Andrew Young, would discuss with us problems he had to deal with in his increasing role as a leader in the struggle for racial justice. One of the most important of these discussions occurred in 1968 when Martin expressed to a number of us, including Whitney Young and Roy Wilkins, his desire to take a public position against the Vietnam War. Wilkins and, to a lesser degree, Young believed that this would be a mistake. They felt it would confuse the issue of civil rights with a nonrelevant international and military dispute. They felt that Martin and other civil rights leaders should concentrate on the specific problems of seeking racial justice in the United States. A number of us agreed with Martin. We believed that the issue of racial justice in the United States could not be isolated from the issue of the role the United States played in Asia and Africa. We also believed that there was a fundamental moral issue in America's military aggression in Vietnam that was not unlike the basic moral problem of America's racism. It was clear that Martin had already made his own decision to state publicly, in a speech at Riverside Church, his anti–Vietnam war position.

The private conflict between Martin and Roy Wilkins persisted and was quietly festering. At one point, a number of us felt that it was necessary to bring them together with other civil rights leaders. The first of these discussions took place at my home, in 1968, with Martin, Roy Wilkins, Whitney Young, Hylan Lewis, Floyd McKissick (then head of CORE), and myself. It was the only time I saw Martin get quite emotional, as he accused Roy of publicly misrepresenting and distorting his views. The candor of these talks was clearly therapeutic. Roy stated and restated his position that Martin's anti–Vietnam war position was confusing the civil rights issues while alienating influential governmental supporters in the Johnson administration. Whitney Young assumed a conciliatory role. His training as a social worker helped him defuse, as much as possible, the emotional conflict between Roy and Martin. Both Roy and Martin agreed that the opportunity to share points of view with each other was of value. At the end of these discussions, there seemed to be a clearer understanding, even if no agreement, among these leaders. (Clark, *King, Malcolm, Baldwin: Three Interviews* [Middletown, CT: Wesleyan University Press, 1985], 8–10.)

Probably the most remarkable aspect of my relationship with Jim Baldwin was a meeting we had with Robert Kennedy. Jim invited me to be part of a group he had organized to meet with President Kennedy's Attorney General. This meeting [in New York City] on May 24, 1963, was by all odds the most dramatic meeting I have ever attended. Jim Baldwin began by stating that President Kennedy and Robert Kennedy had asked him to bring together a group of Negroes who would explain the desires of blacks. Robert Kennedy stated that he and his brother, the President, were sympathetic to the aspirations of blacks and that blacks, in turn, should understand this and be more responsive. This opened up the discussion.

Robert Kennedy and Burke Marshall were stunned. . . . The impasse was, unfortunately, made all the more difficult when Kennedy pointed out that other Americans also had to endure periods of oppression. In support of this fact he noted that his grandfather was an Irish immigrant. Jim Baldwin responded with the most scornful, candid comments: "You do not understand at all. Your grandfather came as an immigrant from Ireland and your brother is President of the United States. Generations before your family came as immigrants, my ancestors came to this country in chains, as slaves. We are still required to supplicate and beg you for justice and decency."

At Baldwin's outburst, Robert Kennedy's face turned purple but he remained silent. The meeting could not be put back on the track of amicable discourse. Jim Baldwin and his associates insisted repeatedly that what was required was for the President of the United States and the United States government, as a whole, to use their full power and force to obtain unqualified justice for Negro citizens. Specifically, they suggested that President Kennedy walk arm in arm with some black children to take them to newly integrated schools. Robert Kennedy concluded that this was unrealistic and transparent game playing. After more than three hours, the meeting ended. It had achieved some cathartic emotionality, but seemingly little understanding. (Clark, *King, Malcolm, Baldwin: Three Interviews* [Middletown, CT: Wesleyan University Press, 1985], 13–15.)[1]

Whitney M. Young, Jr., who had been dean of the Atlanta School of Social Work, before his appointment as executive director of the national Urban League, has been recognized by Negroes and whites as one of the most thoughtful, balanced, and forthright of Negro leaders. Under his leadership, the Urban League has learned to talk without equivocation with the princes of economic power in the white society." (Clark, *King, Malcolm, Baldwin: Three Interviews* [Middletown, CT: Wesleyan University Press, 1985], 167.)

One of the most devastating blows to the civil rights movement was, of course, the loss of its key leaders during the late 1960s and later. Malcolm X was assassinated in 1965 and Martin Luther King in 1968. Whitney Young died in 1971 and Roy Wilkins died in 1981. During this period the nation also lost the potential Democratic leadership of John and Robert Kennedy—theirs were voices of dynamic, even though differential, optimism. Martin Luther King's persistent assertion of eventual moral victory and Malcolm X's—to use [James] Baldwin's words—"more sinister" and "much more effective" militant demands were silenced by their assassination. Baldwin—the only survivor of the three—retreated to Europe and took with him his outraged anguish and the call for a moral rebirth in white America. (Clark, *King, Malcolm, Baldwin: Three Interviews* [Middletown, CT: Wesleyan University Press, 1985], 3–6.)

I first met Martin Luther King Jr. in early 1956, when my wife and I were traveling by train from Atlanta, Georgia, to Birmingham, Alabama. A Pullman-car porter told us that the Reverend King was on the same train. It was at the beginning of King's leadership in the Montgomery bus boycott. We asked the porter to bring him to our compartment, and he introduced us. Martin was most gracious and charming. He said he had heard of our role as expert witnesses in the *Brown* decision cases. This first meeting was characterized by warmth and friendliness, as if we had known each other before. He shared with us the challenges and the risks involved in the Montgomery bus boycott. He invited us to come to his home on our way back. I accepted the invitation, and met his wife [Coretta Scott King] and their infant, and also some of his associates, including Mr. Nixon, the train porter who had, in fact, initiated the boycott and had urged Martin to assume leadership of this protest. As I visited with Martin and his wife, I became aware of the excessive demands this new responsibility was imposing on both of them. What kind of help would they need, I asked. They replied that they would appreciate help with the housework. (In large social movements, the need for such practical help is generally overlooked.) I told them of a group in New York, the National Committee for Rural Schools, to which I belonged, which had a flexible program for providing help for children and for individuals in the rural South. I said that when I returned to New York, I would suggest to the advisory board and, in particular, to Ray Brandstein, the executive director, and Benjamin McLaurin, an associate of A. Philip Randolph's and chairman of the board of the National

Committee for Rural Schools, that the group finance the salary of a house-keeper/mother's helper. . . . This suggestion was unanimously accepted later by the advisory board. I believe that this may have been the first outside financial help provided to Martin Luther King Jr. and his family in support of his leadership in the Montgomery bus boycott.

My relationship with Martin continued for a number of years. When he was invited to be a keynote speaker at the December 1956 annual luncheon of the National Committee for Rural Schools, I had the privilege of introducing him. It was his first public appearance in New York City. Our relationship became friendlier and warmer as the years went by. He and his wife visited my family in our home in Hastings. We spent an enjoyable few days together in Montego Bay, Jamaica, in June 1965. He had a delightful sense of humor, which permeated even our most serious discussions of the problems and challenges in the ongoing struggle for racial justice. When I was director of the Metropolitan Applied Research Center (MARC), Martin was a nonresident Fellow of the organization. While my relationship with Martin was at all times friendly, and while I agreed from the beginning with his position on Vietnam, our views did not always coincide. For example, I frequently discussed with him the question of the extent to which he could expect blacks in America, who were oppressed, to be able to muster the ability "to love their oppressors." I would argue that this placed an additional burden on the masses of Negroes. It required a level of maturity and sophistication that I, as a psychologist, did not believe most human beings had. Martin would respond to these concerns by explaining the philosophical meaning of his concept of love. Essentially, he felt, love meant not being dehumanized by oppression, but, rather, seeking to tap the humanity and the conscience of the oppressor. I always felt as though Martin were a member of my family. I admired and respected him, and knew that his public positions were completely compatible with his private personality. He was a genuine human being, who, against the advice of some of us, was able to go to J. Edgar Hoover in December 1964 and offer him an olive branch of peace and understanding, in spite of the obscenities Hoover directed toward Martin. For these and many other reasons, I personally felt inadequate in Martin's presence. (Clark, *King, Malcolm, Baldwin: Three Interviews* [Middletown, CT: Wesleyan University Press, 1985], 7–10.)

There is no question that Arthur Schomburg played a profound role and had great impact upon my intellectual, cultural and personal growth . . . probably without knowing to what extent because he was so easy, so matter-of-fact, so soft-spoken . . . [so] low-keyed.[2] (Clark, quoted in Elinor Des Verney Sinnette, *Arthur Alfonso Schomburg: Black Bibliophile & Collector, a biography* [New York and Detroit, MI: New York Public Library and Wayne State University, 1989], 36.)

Adam [Powell] was very realistic. He did not believe, and I guess he was right, that I, as a leader of HARYOU could overcome any objections or attacks which he would have. He was right, I guess. As things turned out, he was absolutely right in terms of his relationship with Bobby Kennedy. I was in Adam's office one day when the telephone rang, and Adam's secretary said, "It's Kennedy calling." Adam, who was fascinating, said, "All right. Put him on; put the open part of the phone on." The secretary did, and Adam said, "How are you, Mr. Kennedy?" Bobby and Dave Hackett [a Kennedy aide] said, "Look, we have decided to go along with you, and we can arrange it so that your operation will be dominant in Harlem." They made it clear—I don't remember exactly what the words were, that Adam didn't have to worry about me. Of course, he didn't. I was shocked. "See. I told you where the political power was, and the lack of power for you," Adam said. And I had to accept this because I heard it. I mean, he didn't tell me secondarily. I heard it over the phone. I realized then that HARYOU was going to be subordinated to Adam's Associated Community Teams (ACT), that HARYOU would not have any power unless it was subordinated to ACT. By the way, I accepted that realism, and I resigned. . . . I was naïve in the area of political conspiracy and realism. (Clark, interview with Noel A. Cazenava in *The Oral History* [Columbia University], January 7, 1992.)

Reluctantly, I am forced to face the likely possibility that the United States will never rid itself of racism and reach true integration. (Clark, "Racial Progress and Retreat: A Personal Memoir," in Herbert Hill and James E. Jones, Jr., eds., *Race in America: The Struggle for Equality* [Madison: University of Wisconsin Press, 1993], 3–18.)

COMMENTARY

John Lewis

I met Kenneth Clark many years ago, and I have spent time in his home. I know his son, Hilton, and his daughter, Kate, and his son-in-law, Don Harris, is one of my closest and dearest friends. I think Dr. Clark was right in describing Martin Luther King, Jr., as a "paradox of the scholar and the effective man of social action." Martin Luther King, Jr., had the capacity, had the ability, to use his intellect and to mix it with passion and emotion, to get people to buy into a vision that he had for Americans. He spoke at the March on Washington in 1963; he said, "I have a dream. It is a dream deeply rooted in the American dream." That was a statement of his vision, but he was able to say it in a way to get others, the masses, to share this vision and to participate in this effort to move toward the realization of integration. On the one hand, Martin Luther King, Jr., was at home at the highest levels of academia and the highest levels of government, and at the same time, he was at home with nonviolent direct action in the streets of Birmingham or on the highway between Selma and Montgomery.

I agree with Dr. Clark when he calls the 1960s "unique." The 1960s represent an extraordinary, unbelievable, and amazing period in the history of our country in the long struggle for equality. It must be looked upon as the decade of civil rights, the decade of human rights, the decade of taking that great leap forward; it was a decade of fulfillment and optimism. During the past forty years, we have come a distance. We have made a tremendous amount of progress toward understanding the dilemma of race in building what I like to call "the beloved community," the truly interracial democracy and open society. Forty years ago all across the South, there was so much fear, so much overt discrimination and hate, that today we live in a better place. The signs that I saw forty years ago that said "white waiting" and "colored waiting" or "white man" and "colored man" or "white woman" and "colored woman"—those signs are gone and that fear is gone. I hear young people, young children, and some not so young, especially in the African American community, who say nothing has changed. And sometimes I feel like saying to these young people, "Come and walk in my shoes, and I will show you we live in a different place in a different world." I think that what Dr. Clark had to say years ago was important, and it's too bad that more people don't know of his writings because this man, in a sense, was ahead of his time, and I know that Thurgood Marshall and others used some of his ideas and suggestions in *Brown v. Board of Education*. Whether it is his book *Dark Ghetto* or a speech made, a letter he wrote, or some other text, he was on the point.

Hugh Price

Dr. Kenneth Clark was a giant among scholars. His research and writings deeply influenced generations of protégés in academia. More important, his work helped provide the intellectual arguments and evidentiary basis for outlawing segregation once and for all. Precious few scholars ever reach that pinnacle of societal impact.

Kweisi Mfume

Among his many achievements and highly justified accolades, in 1961 Dr. Kenneth B. Clark was the recipient of the NAACP's Spingarn Medal, our nation's most prestigious civil rights award. This book will help those unfamiliar with his great body of work understand precisely why.

Roy Innis

Dr. Kenneth Clark will hold a well-deserved place in American history as an eloquent and dedicated spokesman for the desegregation of America through integration.

A. Philip Randolph

The Negro, though in the fires of racial hate, must never say die and must never strike to kill even a hating and hateful foe. Stress by Dr. Clark upon this Gandhian principle gives this statement the force of prophecy.

Nadine Strossen

Dr. Kenneth Clark, longtime chair of the American Civil Liberties Union's National Advisory Council, has been a lifelong champion of the ACLU's signature mission: to protect all fundamental freedoms for all people. Although he is best known for his historic role in the fight against African-American apartheid, his work reflects his passionate commitment to liberty and equality for everyone. His prolific writings powerfully convey his dedication to the neutral defense of rights even—indeed, especially—when they are most embattled. His words are particularly inspiring now, given the enormous threats to civil rights and liberties in the "war on terrorism."

NOTES

1. [*Editor's Note*: The meeting in Robert F. Kennedy's apartment on Central Park South in New York, on May 24, 1963, was attended by Burke Marshall, Kennedy's assistant attorney general for civil rights, Dr. Clark, James Baldwin, Lorraine Hansberry, Lena Horne, and Harry Belafonte, among others. At the time, Dr. Clark commented: "The fact that Bobby Kennedy sat through such an ordeal for three hours proves he is among the best the white power structure has to offer. There were no villains in that room—only the past of our society." From Anthony Lewis and *New York Times, Portrait of a Decade: The Second American Revolution* (New York: Random House, 1953), 252.]

2. [*Editor's Note*: The Schomburg Center for Research in Black Culture, located at 135th Street and Lenox Avenue in Harlem, part of the New York Public Library system, is named after Alfonso Schomburg (1874–1938), black bibliophile, curator, and self-taught historian.]

CHAPTER 11

Civil Rights and the Church

There is a need to examine the degree to which the often repeated verbal position of the Church on this issue of race relations has been translated into social action and has in fact influenced the patterns of race relations in the larger society and within the structure of the Church itself. During the course of this [Advisory] Committee's activity, it discovered a number of significant racial problems and practices within the Protestant Episcopal Church which seemed relevant to many resolutions adopted by the Church.

Using the method of discussion and interviews with significant members of the staff of the National Council, it was able to explore and pinpoint some of these problems in depth. Among the many serious and still unresolved problems are the following: (1) A substantial number of social welfare agencies, hospitals, schools, and other social institutions, publicly identified with or incorporating into their name or designation, the name of the Protestant Episcopal Church, do, in fact, practice various forms of racial segregation, discrimination, or exclusions. (2) The Protestant Episcopal Church continues to support four Negro colleges under the auspices of the Church Institute for Negroes. By any reasonable educational standard, these colleges provide inadequate, if not inferior, collegiate education for Negro students. It would not be overly severe to state that schools with these inadequate standards and facilities would not be supported by the Protestant Episcopal Church if they were schools for white students.

During the recent period of major racial turbulence in the south following the *Brown* decision of the United States Supreme Court, some individual members of the Protestant Episcopal clergy have dared to take a forthright stand in support of the Supreme Court's decision as being consistent with the witness and the theology of the Church. Some of these individuals were required to pay the price of this moral and spiritual courage by the loss of their parishes.

About a year ago, the Presiding Bishop of the Protestant Church made a forthright statement on the role of the Church in demanding that no church-related school be used to evade demands for desegregation of the public schools in any given community. During the past year, at a time when many individuals were being imprisoned in Mississippi and other southern states for asserting their right to non-segregation in places of public accommodation, certain members of this committee attempted to prevail upon the Presiding Bishop to make some forthright public statement in support of the goals of the Freedom Riders and the "sit-in" movement. It was felt that the weight and spiritual prestige of his office could be used effectively in a visit with the President of the United States and the Attorney General. At such a visit, he could express publicly the concern of the Church over the fact that human beings were being jailed in America merely because they were asking for equality and justice. The Presiding Bishop did not consider it wise to express his personal feelings on this matter, or to restate the witness of the Church to the political leaders of our land.

The most recent and stark evidence of the discrepancy between the Church's verbalization on matters of race and its willingness to act decisively in this area is to be found in the correspondence between members of this committee and the Presiding Bishop when the committee sought some way of communicating its sense of urgency on matters of race relations to the House of Bishops. The significance of the correspondence can most effectively be seen by the actual letters themselves. The Presiding Bishop wrote on October 4, 1961, "I am afraid this will take up all our available time besides that which is needed for the transaction of business. I am very sorry about this, but these are directives from the Bishops."

Conclusions: A careful examination of the role of the Protestant Episcopal Church in America in the area of racial problems and justice reveals the Church's role as being restricted to the area of verbal resolutions. Effective action toward the goal of implementing the general principles asserted in these resolutions has been minimal. The lack of systematic action toward racial justice within the Church, or the lack of any effective role of the Church toward the resolution of these problems in the larger society, seems to reflect the conflicting forces which operate within the Church itself. So far, the powerful forces which interfere with a positive and assertive role on the part of the Church have not been identified. Together with the lack of commitment and intensity of concern about this problem and on the part of the identified decision-makers, these forces have been successful in keeping the Church impotent in the area of race. Decision-makers within the Church may be reacting to the possible loss of financial support, or anxiety concerning the risk involved in eliciting controversy and conflict within the Church, or may be reflecting their own ambivalence on the issue. Whatever the causes, the fact remains that the Protestant Episcopal Church in America continues to give lip service to the serious problem of racial justice, but so far has not demonstrated the courage, integrity, or creativity required to develop a strong and systematic program in support of its own resolutions.

These racial problems are real, persistent, and will not disappear short of complete justice and equality. The Church as an integral part of our society cannot continue to ignore them. The choice between being involved in attempts at positive resolution of these problems and the preservation of the power and the apparent efficiency of the Church as an organization is not a real choice. The oneness of the spiritual power and survival of the Church and the goals of racial justice in America makes the present posture of inactivity and timidity of the Protestant Episcopal Church a self-defeating mockery. The problem which remains is how this fact can be meaningfully communicated to those who are in the decision-making positions of the Church. The preservation of the Church as a social institution at the price of moral and spiritual emptiness confuses means with ends. A significant role of the Church on matters of unqualified racial justice in America is consistent with the Christian witness for which the Church ostensibly stands. Weakness, vacillation, passivity, and equivocation on the part of those in authority weaken and threaten to destroy the real power and significance of the Church—without regard to the maintenance of the facade or order, efficiency, and morally empty peace. This is practical impotence and mockery of the spirit of Christ. (Clark, "Policy and Implementation—Problems of Race Relations in the Protestant Episcopal Church," Report of the Advisory Committee on Intergroup Relations, Department of Christian Social Relations, The National Council, October 9, 1962.)[1]

Religious groups have become more seriously involved in action geared toward elimination of racism in our society. The activities of the National Council of Churches of Christ in America, and the intensified activities of the Catholic Church, together with the clear commitment of the organized Jewish groups have contributed significantly to the awakening of the dormant conscience of the American people. (Clark, "100 Years after Emancipation: A Time for Hope or Despair?" [address given at the Seventh Annual Workshop for Religious Liberals, Washington, DC, March 21, 1964].)

The value of the church in providing personal affirmation and self-esteem for Negroes is great enough to permit them to tolerate almost any degree of personal, theological, or educational inadequacy upon the part of their minister, so long as he holds the church together as a successful social and financial institution. Many Negro ministers have managed to mobilize the positive power potential of their churches and have harnessed it to the democratic and idealistic ideologies of religion for effective racial protest and action. It was inevitable that, in addition to their escape function, Negro churches would have a direct protest role.

Such Negro ministers as Adam Clayton Powell, Martin Luther King Jr., Ralph Abernathy, and Fred Shuttlesworth in the Negro protest movement reflect the historical and unavoidable relationship between Negro religion and Negro protest. The role of the Negro church in the early stages of the Negro movement may have owed its strength to the fact that the Negro church was the only institution in which the Negro was allowed that degree of autonomy and freedom from white domination which permitted even a minimal degree of organization for a sustained protest movement.

For the Negro, his church is his instrument of escape, his weapon of protest, his protective fortress behind which he seeks to withstand the assaults of a hostile world and within which he plans his strategies of defiance, harassment, and, at times, his frontal attacks against racial barriers. The ministers and laymen of the white Christian churches are responsible for making the Negro churches effective as vehicles of racial protest by their historic unwillingness to incorporate Negroes into their houses of Christ and by their inability to share with the Negro his passion and action for justice and equality. (Clark, *Dark Ghetto: Dilemmas of Social Power* [New York: Harper & Row, 1965], 174–176.)

A segregated church must be seen as an integral part of the total pattern of residential, educational and other forms of segregation which dominate our society. I submit that it is the ultimate in sentimental unrealism to believe that it will be possible to desegregate the churches or I would even contend it may not even be desirable to desegregate the churches in American society, without at the same time, addressing ourselves to the total system.

American whites are uncomfortable when confronted with the Negro whom he cannot escape. The Negro is a horrible reminder of problems which we would just as soon not be reminded of. Every Negro in an integrated church disturbs the equanimity of the church—whether he be obsequious in his pathetic wish to be accepted by you or whether he be bumptiously militant in his insistence that you recognize some special privileges and claim which he has upon your affection. (Clark, "De Facto Segregation and Parish Education" [address to the Board of Christian Education United Presbyterian Church, New York, April 1965], 12.)

One of the earliest civil rights controversies, dating back to the beginning of human slavery in the New World, was the argument whether the African slaves should be taught to read and converted to Christianity. A paradox of Protestantism, the dominant religion of the early North American colonists, was the need to reconcile the practical fact of human slavery with the ideals of Christian brotherhood. The advantages of slavery demanded that the religious and moral conflicts of the early American Christians be handled by the comparatively simple device of denying to the African slave the status of a fully developed human being. The contemporary Negro churches, whether in an all-Negro denomination or as part of a white denomination, are concrete symbols and citadels of this exclusion and rejection. (Clark, *Dark Ghetto: Dilemmas of Social Power* [New York: Harper & Row, 1965], 176.)

Certainly the church has not found the formula for developing or instituting any effective program even to contain the pathology of the ghetto, much less reverse it. We have to content ourselves with church resolutions—verbal pieties which do not really affect the day-to-day lives of the prisoners of the ghettoes or those who contain prisoners within their ghetto prisons. (Clark, "The Social Challenge to Big Business" [address given at the General Electric Public Affairs Conference, New York, May 3, 1968].)

Traditionally, the realm of social morality was left to religion and the churches as guardians or custodians. But their failure to fulfill this responsibility and their yielding to the seductive lures of the men of wealth and pomp and power are documented by the history of the last two thousand years and have now resulted in the irrelevant "God Is Dead" theological rhetoric. (Clark, quoted in John D. Margolis, *The Campus in the Modern World* [New York: Macmillan, 1969], 26–27.)

The stark fact is that less than one-half of one percent of Negro Protestant Christians in the United States worship regularly in non-segregated churches. The bulk of white and Negro children therefore may well view their churches as cloistered islands of racial exclusion. These children inevitably observe that their churches not only reflect, but appear to intensify, the pattern of racial segregation that exists in the larger community. Under these circumstances the church focuses for the child the moral dilemma inherent in preaching the ideals of brotherhood while practicing racial segregation. This discrepancy between ideals and practice is all the more conspicuous in churches and religious institutions, since their reason for existence is their moral and ethical role. . . .

Probably American churches, like American schools and colleges, have generally failed to offer moral guidance in terms of concrete action programs for the improvement of race relations because the church, like secular institutions, feels compelled to conform to the existing patterns of social attitudes, values, and norms found in the larger society. If the church permits itself to become a captive of the more practical and materialistic pressures of the larger society, then it will be unable to provide for our children the example of positive race relations which they need. (Clark, *Prejudice and Your Child* [Boston: Beacon Press, 1955], 105, 108.)

COMMENTARY

Calvin O. Butts III

Kenneth Clark was a hands-on intellectual whose power had a profound impact on the progress of people of African descent. He helped all Americans come to grips with the issues of race and poverty. He recognized the important role the church plays. Thank God for the work that he did.[2]

NOTES

1. [*Editor's Note*: A member of the Episcopal Church himself, Dr. Clark was an original member of the Advisory Committee of the National Council when the Committee was formed in 1960.]

2. [*Editor's Note*: Interview with the author, July 9, 2002.]

CHAPTER 12

The Role of Social Scientists

The hope for a dynamically stable, progressive, and constructive society lies in the ability of the social scientist to attack [social] problems with a vigor, a tough-mindedness, and a scrupulous regard for scientific integrity and freedom compatible with the immediate urgency of our contemporary social crisis. (Clark, "Social Science and Social Tensions" [address given at the 38th Annual Meeting of the National Committee for Mental Hygiene, New York, November 13, 1947].)

The social scientist who participates in civil rights or civil liberties litigation as an expert witness must exercise the maximum degree of care and objectivity in the collection and interpretation of the relevant data. Further, he must be clear and courageous in his social values and he must be willing to assume social responsibilities even under conditions that would place him in a position contrary to the social beliefs which are popular at a particular time and place.

As the collaboration between social science and the legal profession increases, it will be necessary for the professional societies among the social and psychological sciences to develop safeguards against possible ethical abuses; e.g., flagrant manifestations of prejudice, distortion of data and deliberately misleading interpretations. It would be impossible to prevent honest disagreement among social scientists reflecting differences in interpretations and emphasis. It is nonetheless important to minimize the possibility of the presentation of conflicting testimony by equally competent scientists concerning the available facts. (Clark, "The Social Scientist as an Expert Witness in Civil Rights Litigation," *Social Problems* 1.1 [1953]: 9.)

One of the most consistent of the legal critics is the distinguished professor of jurisprudence, Edmond Cahn, of New York University Law School. . . . Whatever might be one's degree of agreement or disagreement with Professor Cahn's estimate of the worth of the social scientists' testimony in these cases or the degree of the Court's regard for the social scientists' material presented in the brief or in the trial records, one must take seriously his arguments that the constitutional rights of Negroes or other Americans should not rest on social scientists' testimony alone. If he had concentrated and elaborated on this issue on a high level of academic discourse, he might have made an important contribution to thought in the field in which he is competent. When he leaves the area of law, constitutional rights, and matters of jurisprudence and invades the area of social sciences, making broad and general comments about the validity of social science methods, premises, approaches, findings and conclusions, and when he explicitly or implicitly attacks or suggests that the social scientists who participated in these cases as witnesses and consultants did not do so with the utmost personal and scientific integrity, he gratuitously leaves his field of competence and communicates his personal opinions, biases and misconceptions as if they were facts. His prestige is in a field in which he has been trained, thereby disguising his ignorance in a field in which he has no training.

Professor Cahn implies that the primary motive of the social psychologists who participated in these cases was not "strictly fidelity to objective truth." This is a serious, grave, and shocking charge. Professor Cahn did not present evidence to support his implication that the social scientists who participated in these cases, and particularly this writer, betrayed their trusts as scientists. (Clark, "The Desegregation Cases: Criticism of the Social Scientist's Role," *Villanova Law Review* 5 [Winter 1959–1960]: 226–228.)

It is almost 10 years to the day since the United States Supreme Court handed down one of its historic decisions, a decision which has had a great impact and probably will have an even greater impact upon American society than the Civil War itself. In these 10 years, many things have happened. The reactions to decisions have been varied; at least insofar as race is concerned the actual changes in the organization of schools have probably not been too great, but the great change brought about by the *Brown* decision has been in the morale of the Negro in the United States and that change is reflected in what has been called the Negro Revolution. . . .

We did have in our [*Brown* case] brief a whole area ignored by the Court in the *Brown* decision—ignored in the sense of not specifically being alluded to and that was the area in which we attempted to summarize the effects of segregation and discrimination on personality patterns of whites. It might have been too much to have expected even the Warren Supreme

Court to face the more painful aspects of our evidence—namely that a racist society corrodes the alleged beneficiaries. (Clark, address presented at the Symposium on School Integration, Michigan State University, May 8, 1964.)[1]

Rational planning is not to be confused with mechanistic control of man and society. The use of the approach and methods of a truly relevant social science for the development of a democratic social technology can increase human effectiveness, and is probably essential to social survival; and it can be consistent with human dignity. . . . The ultimate question, asked by Plato centuries ago, is, can the rational and intellectual powers of man provide the power to control the irrational primitive and destructive forces? Upon the answer to this question rests the destiny of human civilization. (Clark, "Problems of Power and Social Change: Toward a Relevant Social Psychology" [address given as the recipient of the Kurt Lewin Memorial Award from The Society for the Psychological Study of Social Issues, July 1965].)[2]

My work has enabled me to make a small contribution to human knowledge. In my mind, there is nothing more important than the acquisition and transmission of human knowledge, for out of knowledge comes power and wisdom. Knowledge is the base of the pyramid that is society, the structure on which stands all else that is important in life. To me, the chief enemy of life and social stability is ignorance. It is . . . an enemy that is always standing in the wings ready to pounce and tear down the structure of civilization that for thousands of years society has worked to build. We must fight ignorance to maintain the stability of life. This is the function of higher learning. And the agents of that function are the college professors, the teachers, as well as the press, the communications media and artists.

In my own field, psychology, I have found a special satisfaction. Here, too, you can deal not only in ideas, but in the active kind of scholarship that can be a power for good, for social justice. My emphasis in research is social action. I deal with people and movements, race and conflict, and ideas about social movements and social conflicts. And because my research interest is in the problems involved in these areas, I have moved into social action. . . . Your subject must burn inside you. It must be flaming so brightly that, like art, it becomes more important than everything else. (Clark, "Education: My Way of Life," *Boys' Life* [November 1965]: 12.)

How did I become interested in the problem of social power? I suppose because for a long time I have been interested in trying to understand the dynamics of the American civil rights movement and trying to analyze and speculate about the chances of meaningful and significant changes in the status of the Negro in American life. And for some peculiar reason—probably related to the "scrambled" or "inspired" egghead—not finding myself satisfied with attempting to understand the American civil rights movement, or its future, primarily in terms of its more dramatic form of protest; or for that matter, primarily in terms stated by Gunnar Myrdal in the 1940s in *The American Dilemma* [*sic*], considered at that time and still considered by many the classic work on the American race problem. The theme of *The American Dilemma* was that the American creed, the American ideals, would make the difference in terms of a positive resolution of the American race problem. I had the privilege of working with Myrdal and his staff in gathering the data, which led to the classic, *The American Dilemma*. (Clark, "Social Power and Social Change in Contemporary America" [address before an audience of summer interns working in the Department of State, the Agency for International Development, and the United States Information Agency, Washington, DC, July 18, 1966].)

The role of social science in the *Brown* decision was crucial, in the Court's opinion, in supplying persuasive evidence that segregation itself means inequality. . . . The United States Supreme Court, however, having once accepted social science data, not only opened the door to further use of such data but placed a heavy burden of responsibility upon individual social scientists and their professional associations. (Clark, introduction to Louis Friedman, ed., *The History-Making Decision That Sparked the Civil Rights Revolution in the United States. Argument: The Complete Oral Argument before the Supreme Court in Brown v. Board of Education of Topeka, 1952–1955* [New York: Chelsea House Publishers, 1969], xxxvi–xxxvii.)

Major things have happened between 1940 and 1970, to the point where it is my considered judgment that all the social sciences, including education, must now accept—because they can no longer avoid—the responsibility of providing for this society moral guidelines that emerge out of the methods of science, the approaches of science, the respect of science for logical, rational, and systematic thought. This is an obligation we cannot avoid. We can no longer say that religion must do it, because certainly religion has not and cannot do it. We can no longer say that philosophers must do it, because philosophy merely defines the problem. In the latter part of the twentieth century, if social scientists do not directly address themselves to the problems of social justice and social responsibility and if they do not assume all of the risks involved in so doing, this will not be a passive act. Such failure will be an active act to being accessory to our society being defeated by irrationality, to our society being a victim of uncontrolled passions and prejudices and cruelties. We have no other choice except to find the formula whereby science becomes an instrument for social change in the direction of social justice. (Clark, address given on the occasion of Dr. Clark accepting the Award for Creative Leadership presented by the Alumni Association of New York City College School of Education, October 15, 1970.)

My first serious scientific involvement in the larger theoretical concerns with the nature of man and society emerged as a result of the need to interpret the findings of the early research on the nature and development of the self and the problems of ego and racial identification. In these studies I was a collaborator with my wife, Dr. Mamie Clark. This fascinating and somewhat illusive "pure" research problem was initially my wife's Master's thesis problem. As she saw the larger implications of the first stages of this work, she was kind enough to invite me to join her in a more probing empirical and theoretical exploration of the nature and determinants of the self-image.

The present generation of human beings is required to develop psychological and social sciences with that degree of precision, predictability and moral control essential to the survival of man. The awesome advances in the physical and biological sciences have made psychotechnology imperative. Man can no longer afford the luxuries of a leisurely, trial-and-error, trivia-dominated approach to the behavioral sciences. The behavioral sciences are now the critical sciences; they will determine the answer to the ultimate moral question of human survival. (Clark, "The Pathos of Power: A Psychological Perspective" [presidential address before the American Psychological Association, Washington, DC, September 4, 1971].)

After the [*Brown*] case we would meet with the lawyers and evaluate the testimony. It was a period of optimism and belief. I don't think there was a single one of us—lawyer or social scientist—who in the cases that led to the *Brown* decision didn't believe we would win by preparing the briefs on the human aspects of a legal problem. This was a period of joy and hope. I remember on May 18, 1954, when the campus reporter at City College interviewed me, I said, "I'm certainly proud to be an American. We used the American democratic machine to make a major breakthrough on an institutionalized form of rejection. This," I said, "is a beginning of a new era, a new period when the promises of American democracy—that have been so long withheld from blacks now, through the power of the judicial branch, will be extended to the blacks." I was euphoric. This is an example of the manner and style of the lawyers—Bob Carter, Thurgood Marshall, Bill Coleman, Jack Winestein—as well as of the social scientists. (Clark, "School Desegregation in the North: The Current Battlefront," Metropolitian Applied Research Center, New York, NY, October 24, 1973.)

In August 1945, military personnel of the United States dropped an atomic bomb on the civilian population of Hiroshima. My immediate reaction was complicated bewilderment. I was starkly aware that hundreds of thousands of human beings had been destroyed by this single volitional act of warfare; my awareness was compounded and confused by a sense that this mass destruction of human beings was qualitatively different from all earlier forms of military destruction. In my turbulent attempts to understand what the United States had inflicted upon the Japanese people and the rest of humanity there remained a permeating sense of personal and collective guilt. But the justification for this personal guilt was defiantly illusive. I was tempted, almost successfully, to accept the common rationalizations against collective guilt—"this saved American lives," "this shortened the War," "this is no different from other forms of bombing of civilian populations in World War I and World War II."

These rationalizations would not work for me. The moral and ethical questions became more intense and more clear. They became for me the fundamental reality of the atomic and nuclear age. The dark yet blinding mushroom cloud of atomic destruction at Hiroshima and Nagasaki is a symbol of the new capacity of man to unleash total destruction upon his fellow human beings. This visible emblem demands re-examination of all past ideological, moral, and ethical premises. Its mocking reality requires a redefinition of the "realistic," the "practical," even the "imperative" in human affairs.

In one of his most beautiful essays, Bertrand Russell said that if he were to be asked what he considered to be the most important single answer to the solution of human problems—personal, social, and international—he would be embarrassed to give the answer because it is so simple. It is kindness. Kindness is not a lazy tolerance. Kindness requires courage; the courage to express and accept love; the courage to resist the blandness, passivity, or condescensions which betray a basic indifference to the positive capacity of others; and kindness demands the courage to believe in and accept the totality of another and to help a human being dare to be that which is good within him. This is the kindness that I believe could save the world from mindless, tragic nothingness. (Clark, *Pathos of Power* [New York: Harper & Row, 1974], ix–xiii.)

It required years of labor and billions of dollars to gain the secret of the atom. It will take a still greater investment to gain the secrets of man's irrational nature. (Clark, quoted in Gordon W. Allport, *The Nature of Prejudice* [Boston: Perseus Publishing, 1979], ix–xi.)

One of the things that fascinates me about discussions on the role of the social sciences is the fact that all such discussions seem to start on the uncritically accepted assumption that the connection between the social sciences and the law started with *Brown*. While the Supreme Court was never as explicit indicating the relationship of the social sciences approach to its findings, one finds, looking back to the history of the Law and Supreme Court decisions, that the social sciences did play a role before *Brown*. The fascinating thing, however, is that the role that social scientists played in the pre-*Brown* influence on social issues was subtle. It is a role not explicitly stated as a social science contribution, but, nevertheless, a very effective role. In such decisions as *Dred Scott*, or for that matter, *Plessy v. Ferguson*, what the Courts were saying was what social scientists of that time were saying, namely, that minorities, particularly blacks, were inferior. A host of social science theories and conclusions were essential in *Dred Scott*.

I had completed that study for the Mid-Century White House Conference and had written it up in the form of a monograph. When the lawyers told Otto [Klineberg] what they intended to do, Otto told them that a former student of his had just completed a monograph which might be of interest to him. He suggested that they talk to me to see if the monograph was relevant to their objectives and goals. The counsel for the NAACP's Legal Defense Fund was Thurgood Marshall. His chief assistant, Robert Carter, came to visit me and told me what Otto had said. His specific question was whether social scientists and psychologists could help them demonstrate before the courts that segregation damaged children.

I had not had very much contact with lawyers at that time, so I was very careful with my answer. My answer was a very simple one. I said, "I don't know. I don't know whether we can help you or not."

Keep in mind that this report and the studies which I had summarized, and from which I developed conclusions, had not been conducted for litigation purposes. There were a number of studies that were part of the report. One of them, "The Doll Study," I had conducted with my wife, Dr. Mamie Phipps Clark.

About two weeks after that first interview, Bob Carter came back. He said the monograph I had prepared for the White House Conference could not have been more relevant for their purposes if it had been written for them. He asked me to work with them and to help them gather my colleagues in the social sciences to work with the NAACP Legal Defense Fund as expert witnesses on the trial level of the cases they were developing in South Carolina, Delaware, Virginia and Kansas.

I said, "OK." And that changed my life. What I did was to contact some of the outstanding social scientists of the period on this matter and told them what the NAACP planned to do. I asked them if they would assume the role of expert witnesses on the effects of prejudice, discrimination, and segregation on personality development. I asked them if they would feel comfortable in extracting from their research the notion that racial rejection and segregation damaged human personality.

It is interesting, looking back on that period, that not a single one of the individuals I approached rejected the request. The closest to a rejection came from Gordon Allport, a distinguished professor at Harvard. He had written *The Nature of Prejudice*. Gordon responded that there was no question that he accepted the conclusions of my monograph and report, but he felt he didn't have the personality to be an effective witness in Court. As much as I respected him, knowing Gordon, I knew that was true. He just didn't feel he could battle with lawyers.

A number of social scientists who did get up on the stand for the *Brown* cases withstood the pressure of direct examination and the greater pressure of cross-examination. In two of the *Brown* decision cases, the one in Delaware and the one in Kansas, which was the *Brown* v. *Board of Education of Topeka, Kansas* case, the lower courts accepted uncritically the testimony of the social scientists. This is generally not known. In fact, the Delaware case was the only one in which the decision at the trial level was in favor of the plaintiffs . . . the Supreme Court took all four of the trial cases together and came up with the *Brown* decision.

I thought that the demands that Thurgood Marshall and Bob Carter placed upon me for bringing together the expert witnesses for the trial level of these cases were over once we were finished with that process.

I thought that from that point on, the lawyers would take over. As illiterate as I was about the law, I, at least, knew that they didn't need witnesses before the Supreme Court. So, when we finished with the trial level, I thought all I had to do was sit in and listen to the lawyers argue among themselves about how they are going to present the case to the Supreme Court. By the way, that was fun. I found there was no homogeneity among the lawyers. They spent most of the time arguing about what I considered rather simple phrases. I soon learned that what they wanted after the trial cases was for us to write a social science brief which would be a summary of what had been presented to the trial level. I had never before heard of a social science brief. They kept talking about "the Brandeis brief." I listened. I found that what they wanted of us was something beyond a Brandeis-type brief. In *Mueller v. Oregon*, Brandeis integrated the social science evidence in his legal brief. That was much simpler than what they were asking us to do. They were asking us not to contaminate their legal brief. If you read the briefs that were presented to the Supreme Court in *Brown*, you will see that they separated us. They had a respectable legal brief, and they also presented the highlight of what the social scientists had said at the trial level. By this time, I really was taking orders.

So I agreed that if two or three of my associates could go along with me, we would write the first draft of a legal brief, which was in effect a summary of our testimony. Stewart Cook, who was then chairman of the Department of Psychology of New York University, and Isadore Chein, who was a colleague of mine at City College, and I prepared the social science brief which we submitted to the NAACP lawyers under the title, "The Effects of Segregation and the Consequences of Desegregation: A Social

Science Statement." This was an Appendix to the Appellant's Brief submitted to the Supreme Court. [See Appendix 3, this volume.]

There is another thing I would like to tell you about. It is the fascinating relationship between the social scientists and the lawyers. It should be clear that the social scientists were at the bidding of the lawyers, but we were not asked to defend our position, except once. Some of the lawyers who were part of a group that had been working with the NAACP for quite a while asserted that the social science position and the social science brief could not be of *any* value if we did not clearly indicate that segregated schools in themselves produced this type of damage in the plaintiffs. One attorney, who was particularly adamant in this regard, had the status of having been the first and only black law clerk to a Supreme Court Justice. We all had to listen to him. He said that [Justice Felix] Frankfurter would not pay any attention to generalities about social effects as damaging unless we could demonstrate to him that the specific problem that is before the Court, namely, segregated schools, caused the damage. That was the biggest and longest argument I had with the lawyers. The social scientists finally prevailed in our argument that we could not distill a specific aspect of the total pattern of racism and segregation and say that this particular form of racism results in this form of damage.

We also did not know whether the Court was going to accept the social science appendix. The lawyers were quite clear in saying to us that it was a risk; the Court might say that it was irrelevant and would not consider it. Much to our surprise, they did accept it. Thurgood Marshall made it quite clear that the fact that they accepted the appendix didn't mean anything either. They could have accepted it, filed it in the round file, and addressed themselves only to the law. They not only accepted it, but, as you can see in Footnote 11, the Court took it seriously as well.

Needless to say, we were all very happy. After a few months, I began to hear from lawyers. A couple who were associated with the Rutgers Law School raised questions about whether the Court should have paid any attention to a social science argument. What I was reading from the lawyers who were raising these questions was that the social scientists were contaminating the purity of the law, that the law should never be diluted. One of the most serious objections which I paid a great deal of attention to, and had to write a response to, came from the distinguished professor of jurisprudence at the New York University [NYU] Law School, Edmond Cahn. Some of my former students who went from my class at City College to NYU Law School were apparently sentimentally loyal for they were disturbed at the things that this professor was saying about [me] hoodwinking and contaminating the law with my report. One student insisted that I have lunch with Professor Cahn and show him that I was a human being.

At our luncheon, Professor Cahn assured me that he was in favor of the decision, but he thought it would have been a much stronger decision without Footnote 11. He felt that constitutional rights should not be based on the flimsy findings of the social scientists. At that luncheon, we were genuinely friendly. I said, "I presume you believe that the constitutional rights of American citizens should be based on the solidity and absolute truth that is not debatable and questionable, a truth that is found in the Law." He smiled and I smiled. I asked him, "How would you deal with *Dred Scott*? How would you deal with *Plessy*? What is so absolute about the Law that it took us this long to reverse *Plessy*?"

I still think that Professor Cahn's statement, and the social science backlash that followed, deserves very serious study. On what can one base "Constitutional rights?" I suppose one thing that we can base it on is what we have been basing it on all along: It is whatever the Supreme Court says, and whatever the Supreme Court uses as its basis for saying what it says.

Perhaps you lawyers will have to think through very carefully how one prevents this not so subtle erosion of the law as stated by the Supreme Court. Perhaps by the time you do that, the Supreme Court will have came out honestly by preventing the legislative and executive branches from eroding *Brown*. Or the Court itself might say, "Look, we have the power to erode *Brown* ourselves." Then all three branches of government will have more quickly repealed *Brown* than repealed *Plessy*. This is the prediction of a social scientist with a very foggy crystal ball. (Clark, "Equal Protection Law from *Brown* to *Bakke*" [address, Rutgers Law School Seminar, Rutgers State University, New Brunswick, NJ, April 8, 1986].)

From the very beginning I saw social science, and particularly social psychology, as being quite relevant and quite important to problems of social justice and equality. My wife and I never lost that interest and that focus—seeing our work, our research, as not being abstract or detached, but very much a part of concerns with justice. (Clark, interview with Noel A. Cazenava, *Oral History* [Columbia University], January 7, 1992.)

COMMENTARY

Henry Louis Gates, Jr.

Kenneth Bancroft Clark is one of the great social scientists of our time. Unlike most academics, however, the work of Kenneth Clark transcended the laboratory and the classroom decisively to influence vital social issues of the day. How many psychologists are cited in the footnotes of a U.S. Supreme Court decision? How many scholars can be said to be the intellectual force behind such a momentous social change as the racial desegregation of an American public institution? Kenneth Clark is a giant, and it behooves us to know the life of his mind.

NOTES

1. [*Editor's Note*: See Thurgood Marshall, "An Evaluation of Recent Efforts to Achieve Racial Integration in Education through Resort to the Court," *Journal of Negro Education* (Summer 1952): 315–325).]

2. [*Editor's Note*: Kurt Lewin, a noted psychologist during World War II, helped to clarify the social psychological implications of autocracy and democracy, worked toward the reduction of anti-Semitism, and promoted the development and integration of psychological research and social action.]

CHAPTER 13

Civil Rights and the Military

Negro life in America in 1943 is fraught with the same racial tensions as were found in 1917. Institutionalized patterns of segregation and Jim Crow have not appreciably lessened. Segregation and discrimination are still the basic racial policy of the United States Army, Navy, Marine and Air Corps.

The morale of the Negro in World War II is not good fundamental morale. It does, however, contain the characteristics of primarily synthetic morale which were apparent in the expressed morale of Negroes in World War I. Morale today is more reality bound—tends to express directly the objective realities of the Negro's status in American life. Since this status is low the morale is also low. Negro morale in 1917 had less reality determinants and higher components of fantasy and wishful thinking.

The factor of positive hope played a large role in determining the pattern of the morale in the last war probably because this was a manifestation of the wishes of the group. In this war positive hope is complicated by negative hope but neither appears to play a dominant role in the morale pattern. The Negro today is more cynical, he tends to question more the meanings and realities of the slogans, appeals and symbols to which he is subjected. His past disappointments and racial experiences have made him less susceptible to a positive reaction to them.

There is less eagerness and ability of Negroes to identify themselves with the common cause (the goals and aspirations of the nation). This is so, not because he does not desire to do so, but because he is prevented from doing so. The barriers of segregation and the wounds of racial discrimination and humiliation have made him more militant. He has also restricted his attitudes, motivations and reactions more to these realities of his situation rather than to his wishes. There is evidence that this inability to identify with the common cause also involves an increase in the amount of racial ethnocentricism, which may probably be interpreted as a form of group withdrawal in the face of general and specific social frustration.

In the light of these considerations, therefore, it becomes necessary for the government to face squarely its responsibilities for maintaining a wholesome attitude in its people—not only Negroes but also whites. The present realities of the Negro's morale is an indictment of the principles of democracy as a desirable basis, upon which human beings may interact efficiently.

The problem of building an adequate, high morale in Negroes is not the same today as it was in 1917. Techniques compatible with the nature of the morale at that time could be used with success then. It would be a blundering mistake, however, to attempt to use those methods now and expect positive results. Morale based on, and reflecting fundamental realities, cannot be significantly influenced by synthetic and externalized appeal. In speaking of his responsibilities for promoting the morale of the Negro, [white officers] were delegated to visit camps where colored soldiers were ... first, for the purpose of learning as to the conditions existing likely to affect their patriotism, and, second, for the purpose of *delivering addresses such as would be calculated to promote the continued loyalty and a healthy morale among the members of this racial group* [italics Clark].

It is necessary to emphasize that attempts to raise the morale of Negroes, during the present war, through speeches calculated to promote [their] continued loyalty and patriotism, as if these were entities which could be subjectively divorced from their conditions of life, would be dismal failures regardless of the success of this procedure in 1917.

The Office of War Information has recently issued a pamphlet, which was probably calculated to raise the morale of Negroes. The reaction of Lester Granger, Executive Secretary of the National Urban League, to this effect is illuminating:

The recent O.W.I. publication called *The Negro and the War* is a monumental mistake and a disservice to the government and the Negro. I say this ... because it is like kicking a man who is down, and congratulating him because he is not yet dead.

This reaction (the degree to which it is typical is not known) can best be interpreted as indicating that the pamphlet was basically stimuli for synthetic morale and could not essentially fulfill, or substitute for, the conditions of fundamental morale. (Clark, "Morale of the Negro on the Home Front: World Wars I and II," *Journal of Negro Education* 12.3 [1943]: 424–428.)

There is no doubt that a new image of the Negro has emerged in the years following World War II. ... Among the factors are ... the participation of

Negroes in two major World Wars for democracy within this generation and their unwillingness to give their lives for democracy elsewhere while they are denied the benefits of democracy in their own land. (Clark, "The Negro in the North," in Mathew A. Ahmann, ed., *The New Negro* [Notre Dame, IN: Fides Publishers, 1961], 27.)[1]

You can't take human beings—and in the lifetime of many Negroes they saw these two wars and they heard the arguments—you can't do that, on the one hand, and then say, "Well, look, be content with the lack of democracy for yourself in your own homeland." And if nothing else happened to the Negro, he grew up in the sense that he said, "Well, all right, if they want me to give my life for democracy for others, I am prepared to give my life for my own equality and democracy." And he found he wasn't afraid.

If you were to ask me for the most significant difference between the Negro today and the Negro at the turn of the century or around World War I, to me it's that the Negro today is not afraid. And he cannot be intimidated by grown people running around in nightshirts. He has seen enough of death, he has heard enough about how people do not gain democracy to know that this applies to him, too. (Clark, quoted in *Pageant* magazine [October 1963]: 148.)

The historical and contemporary predicament of the Negro in America provides no basis for systematic military revolution. But beyond that lies the fact that violence, as a means of changing or maintaining status, is no longer acceptable in the latter part of the twentieth century. (Clark, "Introduction: The Civil Rights Movement: Momentum and Organizations," in Talcott Parsons and Kenneth B. Clark, eds., *The Negro American* [Boston: Beacon Press, 1965], xvi.)

A man gets tired of seeing no results. Way back in World War II, I was writing documents on Negro morale for the Office of War Information. Nothing happened. (Clark, in Mary Harrington Hall, "A Conversation with Kenneth B. Clark," *Psychology Today* 2.1 [1968]: 25.)

COMMENTARY

Clifford L. Alexander, Jr.

Kenneth Clark's comments about blacks in the military are accurate. It's a continuous complaint. Ironically, American black soldiers were treated with hostility at home during World War II—they were segregated on trains when they were moved in the United States, while German prisoners traveled with American white officers. It's been an uneven history. During the Civil War, blacks and whites fought alongside each other in the North and the South. It was not until Harry Truman's desegregation order in 1952 that the Armed services were officially integrated.

NOTE

1. [*Editor's Note*: In the aftermath of the war, President Harry S Truman issued an Executive Order on July 26, 1948, stating: "It is hereby declared to be the policy of the President that there shall be equality of treatment and opportunity for all persons in the armed services without regard to race, color, religion or national origin." Kenneth B. Clark, "The New Negro in the North," in Mathew A. Ahmann, ed., *The New Negro* (Notre Dame, IN: Fides Publishers, 1961), 27.]

CHAPTER 14

The Challenge to Business and Labor

In corporate America . . . many of these new black managers and executives are assigned to such race-related jobs. It "created" such areas as "community affairs" and "special markets." They are rarely found in line positions concerned with developing or controlling production, supervising the work of large numbers of whites or competing with their white "peers" for significant promotions.

These black employees jeopardize what little power they have if they seek to exercise it too aggressively in behalf of other blacks. It is generally understood by blacks in these positions, and by their white "benefactors," that the cause of personal racial justice can best be served if blacks can demonstrate that they are "objective," "balanced," "moderate" and not too pushy on racial issues. As a consultant to private corporations on affirmative action, I have often observed that, with some noticeable exceptions, black affirmative action officers of corporate and educational institutions are more likely to be cautious in the performance of their roles than many whites in similar positions. (Clark, "The Role of Race," *New York Times*, October 5, 1960, 30.)

The job discrimination against Negroes [in business] has been so widespread and has continued for so long that you may have to engage in some kind of compensatory positive discrimination to overcome the effects of this long-standing injustice. I think that employers will have to go out and actively recruit Negroes as Negroes.

During this transition period from injustice to justice, it is my personal opinion that we cannot pretend that there are no consequences of past injustices. We've got to face those consequences and do whatever is necessary to rectify them. Even if it means becoming color conscious. Absolutely, because the problems are problems that resulted from color consciousness. (Clark, "The Negro Is Tired of Waiting," *U.S. News & World Report*, June 10, 1963, 40.)

The city has failed its Negro youth. There are evidences of it all around us. They've failed in the apprenticeship program and most of all the city has consistently failed to stimulate the kids to help themselves. But the city has its back against the wall now. It can't turn away. It's got to act—and act soon. The city doesn't have any choices left. (Clark, quoted in Barry Gottehrer and the Staff of the *New York Herald-Tribune*, *New York City in Crisis* [New York: WCC Books/Pocket Books, Inc., and David McKay and Company, 1965], 29.)

Racism has been one of the persistently debilitating facts in the American labor movement. After Eugene Debs, the American labor movement was never really a solid force, a movement in which the total rights and concerns of all workingmen were protected. The American Federation of Labor's (AFL) position was one of no direct involvement in politics and one of apology when it did hesitatingly enter the political arena. It refused to become a significant part or core of any labor party. The Congress of Industrial Organizations (CIO) was more politically active but also uninterested in a labor party. After the initial stages the labor movement organized itself in terms of respectable nonproletarian models. . . . The American labor movement is basically a vehicle by which the workingman seeks to realize his aspirations to be a boss. It is a ringing refutation of the Marxian premise of categorical cleavages between economic classes. It is inextricably bound up in the American dream of success, of upward mobility. Unions are seen as escalators to management, not just as the protector of the working class. The presence of Negroes on the American scene has given some objective support to this belief, for whites have moved up—in large measure—by excluding Negroes from the competition, from the unions, and hence from the better-paying jobs.

Negroes have been effectively segregated in American labor, much as in American churches, with their "own" unions, such as the railroad Brotherhood of Sleeping Car Porters, for workers in jobs almost exclusively reserved for Negroes. Where Negroes are singled out as labor representatives, they hold these posts at the pleasure of white leadership. Even in unions where most workers are Negro or Puerto Rican, the actual top leadership is predominantly white and often seems responsive more to the wishes of management than to the people they allegedly serve.

A significant example of the powerlessness of the Negro worker in a major trade union with a "liberal" reputation is found in the status of Negroes in the International Ladies' Garment Workers Union in New York

City. The ILGWU is unique in many respects. The ILGWU is probably the most decisive force in the ladies' garment industry in New York City because it has rationalized and stabilized industry practices and established union control over a scattered multiplicity of small, highly competitive shops. Both employers and the workers regard the union as the major power in the industry. (Clark, "White Unions, Black Proletariat," in *Dark Ghetto: Dilemmas of Social Power* [New York: Harper & Row, 1965], 42–43.)

[Editor's Note: The following is excerpted from *Nation's Business*.]

Q: *Dr. Clark, what role can businesses play in finding answers to rioting?*

A: Business and industry are our last hope. They are the most realistic elements of our society. Other areas in our society—government, education, churches, labor—have defaulted in dealing with Negro problems. It is now up to business. . . . Business is the least segregated, least discriminatory, most fair, of the areas of our society—better than education, religion, unions or government. Business has had to [act] because of the need for resources and consumption. Consider the possibilities of economic growth of all companies in the light of increasing economic levels of the Negro population. Prospects are terrific. Business and industry, on the other hand, have tolerated the exclusion of Negroes from certain unions. Business did not argue or shout loud enough about this.

Q: *What blame, if any, do you assign business for the rioting?*

A: The main blame I would assign to business is that of insensitivity, apathy, indifference, and a Pilate type of washing one's hands, the unwillingness to become involved.

Q: *What are some of the immediate things business can do to stave off future rioting?*

A: Simply cleaning up the ghettos so that the areas where Negroes live are not as dehumanizingly dirty and drab and then putting something into the area which is more aesthetic.

Q: *Over the long pull what can business and industry do?*

A: Business and industry act out of enlightened self-interest and there is nothing wrong with that. The best interest of business calls for racial peace and one very important way of helping bring this about is to help find a formula of translating civil rights legislation into what happens to human beings. My own hunch is that this is what the riots are all about. (Clark, quoted in *Nation's Business* [Washington, DC] [October 1967]: 67–69.)

When you get right down to the blood and guts of the American economic and political system, there is only so much foolishness that business will tolerate when it affects the general stability of the total society. I believe business is our last hope because it deals with basics, the realities of social stability, and stability is the only basis upon which business can function effectively. With this as our perspective, we are no longer talking about being nice to Negroes; we're no longer talking about the differences be-tween the number of Negro children who die in infancy and the number of white children who die in infancy; we're no longer talking about the number of Negro adolescents who are seduced into narcotic addiction in order to make the drug dealer a profitable one.

Instead, we are beginning to see in rather cold, hard, pragmatic terms that the privileged cannot permit an intolerable discrepancy to exist be-tween them and the underprivileged because this jeopardizes their privi-leged status. When I say this to some of my liberal intellectual friends, they say that this sounds tough, hard, bitter and non-idealistic. I look them square in the eye and I say, "You're right; that's precisely what it is." (Clark, "Business—the Last Hope" [address given at an AT&T meeting, New York, 1968].)

Our economy is held back, retarded by segregation. White suburbs cannot exist without impact on other parts of the economy—without detrimental impact. For example, you can't understand the exclusive New York City suburbs like Scarsdale or Bronxville except in terms of the deterioration of the inner city. It's a damnable shortsighted perspective on the part of whites to believe that they can have white sanctuaries without paying an exces-sively high price—the suburbanite's taxes are not really just restricted to the beautiful lawns of Scarsdale. He's paying taxes here also. He's paying taxes in a monetary sense, and he's paying taxes in what he is storing up in social problems later on. I will confess that this kind of argument is hard to communicate. Because most people tend to see all the issues in the sim-plest possible way. For example, the man who lives in Scarsdale. To him, the problem of a Negro moving next door to him is seen only in terms of what he can sell his house for the next month after the Negro moves in.

When a man thinks like that, how can you show him what's happening to the world, what's happening even to the metropolitan region. The Ford Foundation gave a lot of money to the Fund for the Republic, which in turn gave a lot of money to some scholars to do a study on race and housing. After a great deal of money was spent and after a great deal of activity, they came up with a conclusion, mainly this: that property values don't fall when Negroes move in a community. (Clark, "Criteria for a Serious Program for Business and Industrial Recruitment and Training of the Ghetto Youth" [address to the New York State Psychological Associ-ation, New York, May 2, 1968].)

Since business can do almost anything it really wants to do, here is a chal-lenge in good faith—the long-range goal of seeking to eliminate slums and ghettos from American life. Any nation that can work the variety of economic and industrial and technological miracles which this nation has worked within the last three or four decades can certainly be equal to Sweden in creating a slum-free and a ghetto-free society. (Clark, quoted in Eli Ginzberg, ed., *Business Leadership and the Negro Crisis* [New York: McGraw–Hill, 1968], 31.)

Not long ago, I discussed the relationship of business and industry to social change with the president of Western Electric. I said, "Please don't tell me that you are interested in civil rights because of your ideals, please tell me that you are interested in these problems because you see that it is necessary on the basis of hard, tough efficiency." He looked at me and replied, "Dr. Clark, I want you to know that we are not just cold businessmen, we have ideals, and our movement into the civil rights area is based upon ideals." He did not understand why I responded as I did. I said, "Oh, my God!" I wanted to add that ideals clearly are shaky. They do not work in institutions as he expected them to work. (Clark, "Minority Motivation, Jobs and Technology" [address given at the International Conference on Technological Change and Human Development, New York, April 15, 1969].)

Unions, organized to help the powerless win justice, succeeded in their goal for white urban workers, but they are not yet willing to complete their social revolution by including groups which have not benefited, by insisting that the same rights be made available to the Negro. At present, the trade union movement is more retarded in terms of racial justice than a number of other areas of society, as for example, organized sports and higher education. Unions, labor and industry must take the initiative in challenging the low quality of education now provided for minority group children in ghetto public schools. It is in the self-interest of labor and management to insist that workers be able to compete effectively without the need for permanent programs of costly intensive re-education and re-training programs that attempt to compensate for the inadequacy of public education. (Clark, "Changing Spheres of Minority Influence" [address to the Collective Bargaining Forum, New York, May 12, 1969].)

For several years, I have argued that American business is the last hope for any serious, realistic, hard-nosed attempt to change the predicament of life in American slums. I do not come to this conclusion in the conviction that the business community is more empathetic to the day-to-day problems of the slum, nor because I believe businessmen are more idealistic or morally or ethically sensitive to this than others. I took this position rather because businessmen are clear about their goals. They are not bemused with moral self-righteousness. They are usually unsentimental about their concern for profits and productivity. Even racial discrimination may fall victim to their single-minded search for efficiency and economic viability. (Clark, quoted in "Job Training: A Time for Seriousness," *Wall Street Journal*, September 25, 1969.)

The traditional status of the Negro in American life is determined by the work he has been permitted to perform. For the American Negro, occupational status and human status have been one from the time of slavery up to the most recent civil rights protest. The slogan of the March on Washington in August 1963, "Jobs and Freedom Now," was not only a demand for equal employment opportunities but an assertion of the Negro's desire for acceptance as a total human being. In demanding that the opportunities for mobility and free competition in the economic and job market be opened to him, the Negro is also demanding to be included in the American Protestant ethic that constructive work is the basis of human dignity and provides the basis for one's manhood. He is in fact demanding that that myth be discarded which was essential for the support of human slavery and its successor, racial discrimination—the myth that the Negro was less than human and that his sub-humanity had to be dealt with by a caste-like restriction to certain occupations. (Clark, quoted in Arthur M. Ross and Herbert Hill, eds., *Employment, Race, and Poverty: A Critical Study of the Disadvantaged Status of Negro Workers from 1865 to 1965* [New York: Harcourt, Brace & World, 1971], 138.)

I am a cynical optimist. I believe that my optimism is based on the assumption that sooner or later self-interest will be put into our calculators and computers and on the basis of the right information we'll come out with answers which will show that the most practical, self-interested, if you will, materialistic thing for our society to do now is to fulfill the promises of democracy for all of its people. If the society doesn't do that, I believe that it's in a Hell of a fix, if not a terminal illness. (Clark, "Social Responsibility in the Corporate World" [interview with Tony Farina and Ross Williams in *Industrial Resources Counselors*, November 15, 1975], 14.)

[*Editor's Note*: The following appeared in *Challenge* magazine.]

Q: *How pervasive and effective do you think affirmative action programs now are in business and industry?*

A: The picture is spotty. The sheer weight of complaints before the Equal Employment Opportunity Commission (EEOC) leads one to believe that it's impossible for their job to be other than spotty. . . . I do not believe that you have compliance now in spite of the fact that the Civil Rights Act of 1964 required all corporations that employ 15 or more persons and engage in interstate commerce to be equal employment opportunities employers. Each must report to one or another federal regulatory agency. In spite of the law, I do not believe that widespread compliance exists. What we do have is the ability to make reports.

Q: *If this pattern doesn't really produce significant change, what do you suggest as a remedy?*

A: The federal government has a plethora of regulatory agencies allegedly dealing with this problem of affirmative action or equality of opportunity. In addition to the Equal Employment Opportunity Commission (EEOC) and the Office of Federal Contract Compliance (OFCC), there are the civil rights division of HEW and the Justice Department. . . . This is really a hodge-podge. Some of my clients tell me, and I think with justification, that they have had audits with quite contradictory conclusions from different regulatory agencies. The amount of red tape involved and the time that's required to comply with the statistical records for one or more federal agencies are tremendous.

Q: *Do you see signs of retreat in affirmative action in higher education or in business or industry in the wake of growing charges of "reverse discrimination" against white males?*

A: My answer is quite simple, maybe too simple: historically the inequity was perpetrated against blacks and women; the civil rights movement, the cases that were brought before the federal courts, and the Civil Rights Act were attempts to remedy these past inequities. If it is true that affirmative action is now judged as imposing discrimination upon those who benefited from such discrimination in the past, then one has no remedy. One has to accept the fact that the consequences of past discrimination will have to continue into the present and into the future. This to me makes a mockery of the possibility of extending democracy to those who had previously been denied its benefits. So far, American minorities have made gains through democratic government. This must continue or we will have subtle and flagrant anarchy.

Q: *Many opponents of affirmative action programs, such as quotas, say that they will dilute efficiency and productivity. Is social justice a relevant issue to economists or business leaders?*

A: First, let me talk about quotas. This is another example of what I call the "semantic diversion." Traditionally, quotas were used and had a meaning as exclusion. Justifiably there was an argument against quotas where the term was practically synonymous with arbitrary exclusion of certain groups of human beings. It seems to me to be a strain on the logic and reason inherent in language to use the same term with the same negative meaning when you are dealing with a process of *inclusion*.

Q: *I suppose one of the arguments has been that people are qualified for jobs at higher levels only after many years of experience, and because*

blacks and women haven't had that degree of experience, they can't expect
to move up for some years.

A: Yes, I've heard that argument, but I've also seen that many corporations do bring in young white males who do not have experience right out of business school or other forms of training. They are given the experience, they are trained, they are made protégés and sometimes if they are successful, bright, and charming, they quickly become competitors of their more experienced superiors. This belief that all minorities are inadequate and in need of special training and that all white males are adequate and ready to move in and function efficiently in any position which their status, club membership, or as Dean Rusk said in 1963, "Their membership in the circle of gossip," would prepare them for is a fascinating and, I think, new kind of stereotype—based upon the older stereotype of course. (Clark, "The Costs of Discrimination," *Challenge* [May–June 1977]: 33–36.)

The business of improving demonstrably the educational efficiency of urban public schools must be a matter of the highest priority for socially responsible private corporations. This is now clearly a hard matter of self-interest. The involvement of private corporations in this complex and difficult social and economic problem must be carefully planned and staffed by individuals of competence and courage and rigorously implemented. It will not be easy to overcome the formidable barriers to the improvement of the quality of education in urban public schools. (Clark, "The Core Problem" [memorandum to the General Motors Public Policy Committee on Urban Crisis and Public Education, April 15, 1977], 12–13.)

America and its working force are staring squarely in the face of the phenomenon of *under*employment, a problem that not only is widespread and growing but also a problem accompanied by far-reaching, rippling effects. Very few are unaffected.

Who are the underemployed? They are the unemployed, those so often counted in an attempt to judge a country's economic health. But they also are household heads under retirement age, who earn less than sixty-five dollars weekly; those holding temporary or part-time employment but seeking permanent, full-time work. In the telecommunications industry, an installer who holds an engineering degree would be considered underemployed. So is the clerk who is qualified to work as an installer but accepts a part-time assignment because the "overqualified" installer is on the payroll. Underemployed, too, is the out-of-work man or woman who could have filled the clerical job. (Clark, "Underemployment—a Postgraduate Nightmare," *Bell Telephone Magazine* 59.1–2 [1980]: 36.)

I would like to share some of my observations and experiences as a member of a minority who sought to develop his own business. Nearly 10 years ago I retired from academic life. I wanted to try my hand and test my ability in another area, a second career. In 1975, I founded Clark, Phipps, Clark & Harris, Inc. I had a small working capital. My first hurdle was the problem of seeking adequate capital: facing the banks' realistic approach, which is detrimental to inexperienced minority members—and others. Caught in the double bind, Small Business Administration questioned whether I was economically "disadvantaged" while the banks questioned my lack of experience. My second hurdle was that marketing and promotional skills were invisible as I had come from academia and my associates were professors. It was difficult to finance and pay for individuals with marketing and promotional skills. My third hurdle was inadequate political support or clout; a hard lesson to learn: the political reality of our developing proposals were frustrated—although they were excellent and were later seen to be the basis of those presented by other firms. (Clark, "The Minority Member as Entrepreneur" [address, Minority Enterprise Development, Minority Business Development Agency, New York, October 7, 1983].)

COMMENTARY

Herbert Hill

I first met Kenneth Clark in 1948, the year that I joined the NAACP staff, when Roy Wilkins introduced me to him. As the years went by, the warmth of Ken's personal friendship, his integrity, and his sharp mind had become increasingly evident to me. I was struck by his commitment to the highest standards of scholarship and his devotion to the civil rights struggle.

Ken's impact was primarily behind the scenes, and this was perhaps especially true in the labor context. In his book *Dark Ghetto*, he wrote that the International Ladies' Garment Workers Union (ILGWU)—one of the most powerful and politically important unions with a liberal reputation—was together with employers responsible for discriminatory practices in the garment industry. He frequently referred in his speeches and writings to the fact that his mother was a garment worker and a member of the ILGWU. And he said that he remembers his mother coming home and telling him, even as a child, of the terrible discriminatory pattern that existed in the New York garment industry and about her frustration with the union. He never forgot that, and in his interviews and in his writings, he often described his mother's painful experiences with the ILGWU, and he encouraged the workers within the union as they struggled for racial justice.

Kenneth Clark is a visionary in the civil rights movement, and he wanted verifiable social science data applied to the struggle for equality. He learned from W.E.B. Du Bois the importance of using empirical data in a disciplined, conceptual way to serve the needs of a civil rights movement now functioning in a sophisticated, new world. One of his most important contributions was the work he did in Harlem where he established a research program that led to wide-ranging consequences. Among these was the publication of a detailed community action study that was designed to help troubled youth in Harlem, using data that teenagers themselves had collected through thousands of street interviews.

In all of the years that he taught, gave speeches, and in his extensive writing, Ken provided valuable leadership skills for the national movement struggling for equal job opportunity and school integration. His statement in 1993, in the book *Race In America: The Struggle for Equality*, which I edited with James E. Jones, Jr., sums up how many of us who spent our lives in the civil rights movement now feel.

Ken Clark was aware of the lack of critical self-analysis by the movement's leaders. He urged a reexamination of programs and priorities, and he wanted to apply useful social science insights into planning for the next stage of struggle. Ken wanted to know where the movement was going, but while almost everyone involved agreed, his approach was not acted upon. For him this was a great disappointment, as was the failure of the Kennedy administration to use his talents. Nevertheless, his legacy as activist and scholar remain the standard by which future leaders of the civil rights movement will be judged.

Kenneth Clark with his wife, Mamie, at her family's home in Hot Springs, Arkansas, 1941. Courtesy of Kenneth B. Clark Archives.

Kenneth Clark with his friend and mentor, Swedish Nobel Prize–winner and economist Gunnar Myrdal, author of *An American Dilemma*, 1944. Courtesy of Kenneth B. Clark Archives.

Kenneth Clark (lower right) with New York Mayor John V. Lindsay (lower left) and other unidentified New York City leaders, circa 1960s. Courtesy of Kenneth B. Clark Archives.

Kenneth Clark (left) with unidentified clergyman and New York Governor Nelson
A. Rockefeller, circa 1960s. Courtesy of Kenneth B. Clark Archives.

Kenneth Clark with President Richard M. Nixon, circa late 1960s. White House Photo.

Kenneth Clark with Washington, DC Mayor Walter Washington, 1969.
Photo by Fletcher Drake.

Kenneth Clark with his son, Hilton, his wife, Mamie, and his daughter,
Kate, at home at Hastings-on-Hudson, New York, circa 1970s. Courtesy
of Kenneth B. Clark Archives.

From left: Muhammad Ali, unidentified woman, Mamie Clark, and Kenneth Clark. © 1976, The Washington Post. Photo by Ellsworth Davis. Reprinted with permission.

Mamie and Kenneth Clark at home, circa 1970s. Courtesy of Kenneth B. Clark Archives.

Kenneth Clark with Vice President Walter F. Mondale, the White House, 1979. Courtesy of Kenneth B. Clark Archives.

President Jimmy Carter congratulates Kenneth Clark during a visit to the White House in the spring of 1979 (see text of President Carter's letter at right) on his award from the Washington, DC–based Joint Center for Political and Economic Studies, headed by Eddie N. Williams (see text of tribute below). Photo courtesy of the Jimmy Carter Library.

JOINT
CENTER
— FOR —
POLITICAL
AND ECONOMIC
STUDIES

*Empowering People Through
Information and Technology*

A TRIBUTE
March 6, 1979

"Dr. Clark has been acclaimed around the world as a distinguished scholar and author. He has also been a courageous leader in the struggle for human dignity and a fighter for the rights of all children to an education that will enrich their lives, a passionate advocate of racial justice in the United States and around the world, and as a wise and sophisticated practitioner of the art of the possible."

Eddie N. Williams
President
Joint Center for Political
and Economic Studies

THE WHITE HOUSE
WASHINGTON, D.C.

March 1, 1979

To Kenneth Clark

Psychologist, educator, business executive and
tireless public servant, you have earned the
respect and enduring gratitude of all Americans.

I welcome the opportunity to share in the senti-
ments of this tribute to you by the Joint Center
for Political Studies. As founding father and
guiding force of this fine organization, you
have made it an important vehicle for advancing
human rights and furthering sensitivity and
responsiveness in government.

I applaud your enduring accomplishments and hope
you will continue to give me and my Administration
the benefit of your wisdom and experience.

Sincerely,

Jimmy Carter

Kenneth Clark with his colleague, Professor Otto Klineberg of Columbia University, at the annual convention of the American Psychological Association, New York, 1979. Courtesy of Kenneth B. Clark Archives.

Kenneth Clark with Professor John Hope Franklin and unidentified woman, circa 1970s. Courtesy of Kenneth B. Clark Archives.

Entertainer and good friend Bill Cosby helps celebrate Dr. Clark's eight-
ieth birthday at his home in Hastings-on-Hudson, New York, in 1994.
Courtesy of Kenneth B. Clark Archives.

Kenneth Clark with his dog, Penn, on Cape Cod, Massachusetts, circa late
1990s. Courtesy of Kenneth B. Clark Archives.

PART III

Race Relations: The Ongoing Struggle

Gary Orfield

Kenneth Clark's work and eloquence were key elements in the background for *Brown* and in explaining the harm of segregation and the possibilities of integration in the country. The social service evidence provided by Clark and the other researchers cited by the Court provided an essential premise for the Court's conclusions about the irreversible harm inherent in segregation. Equally important, Clark's persistence in raising the issue when it went out of style was very important in keeping the issue alive.

CHAPTER 15

Race Relations and the Media

There are many positive and encouraging things in the school desegregation picture. The press, including outstanding southern newspapers, has played a most objective and positive role in presenting news and opinion on this important issue of the desegregation of the schools. (Clark, White Paper, Clark Archives, Hastings-on-Hudson, NY, October 28, 1954.)

In seeking to understand the origin and source of racial attitudes in children, one should not ignore the role of the mass media of communications. Until recently, the treatment of Negro characters in the movies, over the radio, and on television has contributed to the perpetuation of stereotypes. This treatment has labeled the Negro as either comic, menial, or inferior. But it is possible to overemphasize the role of even the powerful instruments of mass communications. It is doubtful that television, the radio, and the movies can be held totally responsible for the racial attitudes of American children. Rather, the treatment of racial groups by these media reflects the prevailing racial attitudes in the larger culture. The media are mirrors of society. (Clark, *Prejudice and Your Child* [Boston: Beacon Press, 1955], 28.)

The metropolitan press, national magazines, radio, and television have given considerable attention to the activities, ideology, and demonstrations of Black Nationalist groups. These black nationalists, who have been accurately described as the contemporary descendants of the Garvey movement of the 1920's, are, like the Garvey movement, predominantly, if not exclusively, a northern urban social phenomenon. (Clark, "The New Negro in the North," in Mathew A. Ahmann, ed., *The New Negro* [Notre Dame, IN: Fides Publishers, 1961], 31.)

Those of us who are struggling to strengthen and reinforce the more positive potentials of man have a more difficult task. It is not easy for us to dramatize it. If you look, for example, at our newspapers, newspaper headlines are clear indications of the fact that it is easier to dramatize the negative. There are many communities in America, interestingly enough, where the arguments of the segregationists are belied in terms of workable patterns of non-segregated residential patterns. Believe it or not, there are many communities in America, north and south, where Negroes and whites do live in peace side by side, are such good neighbors that they can fight without regard to color. (Clark, "The Role of Whites in the Civil Rights Struggle" [address given at the World Affairs Conference, Mills College, December 4, 1963].)

The counteracting forces of the cycle of negatives within the social and personal aspects of the ghetto stem from the fact that the ghetto is not ever totally isolated. And I think in this fact may be the essence of the horror and the cruelty that is in the American ghetto. It is not totally isolated. It cannot be. The mass media, the radio, television, moving pictures, magazines and the press penetrate, in fact they invade, the values and the aspirations, the manners, the style and some of the techniques of the larger middle class–dominated society. As a consequence of this continuous and inevitable communication which largely is one way, the individuals actually and psychologically confined within the ghetto are influenced in some ways by the values of the larger society. They unquestionably share the aspirations of the slick magazine versions of a desirable standard of living at the same time that they are required to function within the realities and the conditions of life imposed upon them, or found around them within the ghetto. They would like homes in the suburbs, scrubbed, antiseptic, empty and despairing; they would like to share the American suburban emptiness and confusion, but they know they cannot. (Clark, address to a Symposium on School Integration, Michigan State University, May 8, 1964.)

The Negro press is, in character, very different from the white-owned press, but it also has power. If a Negro newspaper is to be successful it must reflect the atmosphere of the ghetto it serves and at the same time express both aspiration and protest. These goals have often been at odds with each other; and as a result the Negro newspaper, like Harlem's *Amsterdam News*, may contain bizarre inconsistencies. The *Amsterdam News* has to make money like any other paper to survive, and therefore addresses itself, through flamboyant headlines, makeup, and front-page articles on crime and scandal, to those it considers its audience, thereby ironically reinforcing the white stereotype of the Negro, against which it argues vehemently on its editorial page. Many of its local advertisements are devoted to fortune telling, the sale of dream books and skin bleaches, exploiting the misery and fantasy of ghetto life. The editor defends the paper by pointing to its editorial support of racial militancy, arguing that in its news stories and advertising the paper must serve the people. He does not wrestle with the implications of contradiction implicit in his stand. And by exaggerating the importance of Negro successes—the first Negro newspaper to do this—the paper contributes to the fantasy of denial that tends to refute the need for militancy at all.

Though the Negro press has articulated the Negro's demands for social change, by its stand for uncompromising militancy, it may contribute to fantasy as surely as it does in its hawking of dream books; for militancy that allows for no rational assessment of strategies may deceive the Negro into believing that the potential effectiveness of a plan is to be judged by one standard—absolutism. It tends to ally itself with or support the more sensational leaders and to give excessive coverage in its news columns to the [Adam Clayton] Powell-type of extremist leadership. It tends to use as its barometer the prevailing white view on any issue and to support whatever irritates whites. Its reaction to militant proposals is generally uncritical; it saves its most caustic barbs for the more judicious, hardheaded strategies, thereby oversimplifying the issues of civil rights for masses of Negroes. Most attempts to think reasonably about Negro problems are greeted as "Uncle Tomism."

Some of the more obvious deficiencies of the Negro press seem to be absent in the national magazines which are devoted to Negro news, aspirations, and achievements. The most successful of these magazines are published by John H. Johnson of Chicago. Johnson is a shrewd man, one of the few Negroes who has succeeded in breaking out of the constricted standards of the ghetto. His magazines are significant not only because of their nationwide circulation, which for the first time demonstrates that Negroes can sustain a national press, but because they show that publications controlled by Negroes can meet the competitive, aesthetic standards of the "larger," i.e., the white, society.

The Johnson publications provide for Negroes concrete images of middle-class success in their stories and pictures of Negro doctors, teachers, businessmen, and others. While there is some exaggeration in the implication that Negro achievement is more prevalent than it is, thereby reinforcing the Negro's fantasies about himself, these are fantasies of affirmation, and if they encourage in the Negro the motivation to seek achievements of his own, they may eventually be translated into reality. . . . The middle-class image is further projected in the magazines' pages in even more discreet ways, with emphasis on quiet, tasteful language, dress and grooming, design, and interior decoration. The ostentatious is muted;

the attractive but restrained is approved. The names of the magazines themselves are a subtle endorsement of a positive Negro image: The names *Ebony* and *Jet* and *Tan* are fashionable synonyms for the colors "black" and "brown" in the white world.

Because the Johnson publications, unlike the Negro newspapers on the whole, are directed toward the middle-class and upward-striving Negro on whom the Negro community must depend for leadership, they may well prove to have a more powerful impact on the civil rights movement in the long run than all of the Negro newspapers combined. (Clark, "The Power of the Press," in *Dark Ghetto: Dilemmas of Social Power* [New York: Harper & Row, 1965], 168–169, 172.)

The slogan, "Black Power," has been widely discussed in the press, magazines, on radio, and on television. I must confess that I personally felt that there was something a little obscene about the tremendous amount of attention which seemingly intelligent and serious people were giving to a slogan in the face of the fact—and I may have distorted this, it may be that my memory has been affected by my own biases—that similar attention was not given to a situation in which four youngsters were killed by the bombing of a church or to the frequent unpunished assaults and murders of civil rights workers or their allies in the South. (Clark, "Social Power and Social Change in Contemporary America" [address before an audience of summer interns working in the Department of State, the Agency for International Development, and the United States Information Agency, July 18, 1966].)

If I were a broadcaster I would show the evidence—show people the bad education their children are getting and shock their sensibilities. Arouse their sense of outrage. (Clark, quoted in "A Report and Summary of the Philadelphia Conference on Local Public Service Programming" [from a conference titled The Unfinished American Revolution, an Examination of the Problems of Urban America, sponsored by Group W, Westinghouse Broadcasting Company, Inc., at Syracuse University, October 25, 1966], 29.)

There is a role for the mass media in dealing with this present [educational] catastrophe. . . . I would like to make the following suggestions—again from my role of expert as defined in terms of practical ignorance. First, develop a parallel educational program on television. And, I'm suggesting, outside of the control of the present educational bureaucracy. A parallel educational program in basic skills of reading, arithmetic, communication—oral and written—because the public schools have totally given up in the area of oral communication for underprivileged children. In fact, they have come up with such nonsense as a "second language" for these youngsters.

Which to me is the most preposterous and condescending approach—you wonder how intelligent people could dare to state this. But here, then, is a vacuum in which I think a concerned (and I am presuming concern on your part) educational television could play an effective role by actually teaching the skills on which the public schools have defaulted and now alibi that they cannot teach reading, arithmetic, communication. And teaching them in rated terms.

I believe that television—a relevant, and rational, morally responsive educational television—has the opportunity to make a major contribution to the education of the general public. A contribution, again, which our educational institutions have failed to make. That is, in teaching social sensitivity, in teaching social responsibility, fulfilling the goals of education in general—which our traditional educational institutions have run away from, mainly—the goals of freeing the human mind from shackling, inhibiting, irrational fears and hatreds; from primitive ignorance; from magical superstitions; and from the inhibitions of petty provincialism. I think educational television can perform a significant function for our society as a whole. (Clark, "New Relationships in TV" [address to a conference jointly sponsored by The Education Section of the Electronic Industries Association and The Instructional Division of the National Association of Educational Broadcasters in Cooperation with the Educational Media Council, The Educational Media Council, Washington, DC, April 18–20, 1967].)

General indoctrination in unworthiness has transcended even the barriers of racially segregated schools; it is reinforced by the development of the mass media in this century. (Clark, "The Present Dilemma of the Negro" [address to the annual meeting of the Southern Regional Council, Atlanta, GA, November 2, 1967], 4.)

The emotional appeals of the Black Power rhetoric attracted a variety of followers, would-be leaders and competitors for TV exposure. It soon became apparent that the more outrageous, aggressive, defiant or violent the demand or comment the greater the number of TV cameras and avid reporters an aspiring Black Power leader could attract. (Clark, "The Trained Negro and the Present Racial Polarization in America" [address to Delta Pi Phi, Philadelphia, PA, July 29, 1968].)

The black press has been a part of the experiences of blacks and an important weapon in the struggle for social justice since Emancipation. Within recent decades, magazines owned and published by blacks have become an important factor in projecting the aspirations and achievements of blacks. There are reasons to believe that these black magazines are contributing and will contribute to the development of a positive self-image among blacks. They can counter the negative stereotypes which bombard blacks and their children from the traditional and institutional racism of the larger society. (Mamie P. Clark and Kenneth B. Clark, "What Do Blacks Think of Themselves?" *Ebony* [November 1980]: 82.)

The approach to social science research that makes it a media event—the converting of social scientists to the status of celebrities—also makes suspect valid and important social research findings. Journalists must be sensitive to the current social and political fashions. They must be able to write about those events and ideas in ways that catch and hold the immediate interest of their readers. Journalists are not primarily educators, and they are certainly not social scientists. Traditionally, social science is an intellectual discipline, seeking answers to social problems by methods and critical thought designed to minimize the effects of bias and dogma. When social scientists become the willing creatures of the media, becoming primarily responsive to the imperatives of journalism, they are no longer social scientists; they become politicians or tools of politicians. In order to be effective in contributing to social progress and moral stability among human beings, total critical independence is as essential to social science as oxygen is to life. (Clark, "Scholarship and Politics in Education," *Social Policy* [September–October 1981]: 23.)

It has become increasingly clear that social science findings and social scientists can be manipulated; that social scientists can become self-conscious newsmakers, public personages and sought-after celebrities. Through control of the extent of coverage, the press and the media now have the power to determine what findings and which scientists are to be granted the power to be accepted by the public as opinion makers. This media's manipulative approach to the role of social scientists and the importance of social science findings has obvious political and social policy implications. (Clark, "Politics and Social Science," White Paper, Clark Archives, Hastings-on-Hudson, NY, June 1981.)

Problems of urban violence within the past few decades have been highlighted and dramatized by the media, particularly the electronic media. Television and radio can directly present the more dramatic crimes and their perpetrators as new and marginal forms of celebrities. What this new and intense form of presentation of urban violence does not disclose to the public is an understanding of the context within which these crimes occur. Unless you know and attempt to correct the causes, dramatizable forms of urban violence will continue to occur, if not increase. As seen from the TV news pictures and the printed media's racial identification of the suspects, the overwhelming majority of alleged crimes, and actual ones, are committed by blacks or Hispanics. Yet, there is no discussion of the racial, ethnic, social, class, and educational determinants of the crimes. (Clark, quoted in "The Study of Urban Violence: Some Reflections," Center on Violence and Human Survival, John Jay College of Criminal Justice, New York, October 2, 1989.)

COMMENTARY

Clarence Page

As I read Clark's 1965 comments on the press,[1] I am taken with the broad and objective clarity of his vision. His assessment of black ambivalence and contradictions regarding integration versus separatism— just before the rise of the black power movement—sound prophetic today. His assessment of [John H.] Johnson's impact on young blacks with *Ebony*'s portrayals of middle-class black success rings true to me, too, as someone who was just graduating from high school in 1965 and finding the "fantasy" in *Ebony*'s pages to be very important in helping me to visualize future success.

NOTE

1. [*Editor's Note*: See Kenneth B. Clark, "The Power of the Press," in *Dark Ghetto: Dilemmas of Social Power* (New York: Harper & Row, 1965), 168–173.]

CHAPTER 16

On Leaders, Philosophy, and Issues

My respect for Dean Rusk, the Secretary of State, reached practically unlimited levels when he spoke to a small group of us in August 1964 and said in so many words, "Look, we need more Negroes in the Foreign Service of the United States Government, not because of sentimental, ethical, moral reasons, no matter how important they are. We must do whatever is necessary to overcome these forces in the past which precluded the involvement of Negroes in this." I respected the clarity, the honesty, the hard, tough focus on the reality of the contemporary aspect of the problem of education for Negroes which his words indicated. I have never forgotten them because I think they tell us the story of the demands of the present and, hopefully, the direction of the future. (Clark, "Social and Economic Implications of Integration in the Public Schools" [seminar address, U.S. Department of Labor, Manpower Administration, Office of Manpower, Automation and Training, November 12, 1964].)

President Johnson stated the goals of a non-segregated and racially democratic America in his famous Howard University speech on June 4, 1965, with an eloquence and directness matched only by the historic significance and majesty of the *Brown* decision. (Clark, "American Race Relations Today—A Role for Group Service Agencies" [address, The National Association of Social Workers, Cleveland, OH, November 30, 1965].)

[*Editor's Note*: *The Library Journal* asked 130 well-known New Yorkers to share their favorite spots in New York. Following is Dr. Clark's reply:]

I am one of those provincial New Yorkers who respond with positive emotions to all of New York. I know its problems. Many times I become exasperated with its noise, its dirt, its over overcrowdedness, and its generally hectic nature, but in spite of all these things, I believe it is one of the most exciting and challenging cities in the world. The place I like best in New York is the whole Hudson River area. The drive down to the Henry Hudson Parkway from the tip of Manhattan to the Battery presents one with a combination of natural beauty and man-made grandeur which result in a sense of awe. I cannot decide whether the George Washington Bridge is more beautiful with its lights at night or with its stark simplicity during the day. Whenever I see it, it is my favorite view. Once I thought that I would settle for the Cloisters as my single most favorite spot in New York, but as I thought about what I liked about the Cloisters, I knew that it was not just the beauty of the buildings, the serenity of the grounds or the medieval art and music which it contained, but all of these things were made more magnificent by the fact that the Cloisters overlooked the Hudson River. When one visits the Cloisters, one becomes possessed by the timelessness of the river, the beauty of the George Washington Bridge, and the total fascination and promise that could be New York City. (Clark, quoted in *The Library Journal* 91.12 [June 15, 1966]: 3085.)

In the belief no doubt that this was a statement of compassion, one white opponent of New York's school integration plan said: "If I were God, what would I do to improve the lot of the Negro? If I were God, I'd make everybody white." To sensitive Negroes, this betrays the ultimate condescension—the belief that to *be* Negro means irrevocable rejection. (Clark, quoted in Peter I. Rose, ed., *The Study of Society: An Integrated Anthology* [New York: Random House, 1967], 508.)

Man has the intellect and the capacity to develop cities of the future which are responsive to, monuments of, and continuous stimulants to the soaring human spirit and the empathic quests for human communication, interaction, and love. The cities of the future can be so beautiful that they bring out the beauty in man. They can be so imaginative as to inspire and sustain the limitless creativity within man. Man can transform his chaotic or lawless or indifferent environment into the truly rich communities that reflect man's respect for himself, his fellow man, and his God. Those men who have not already been irrevocably constricted by greed, or damaged by the squalor of neglect or blind privilege, or desensitized by the monotony and chronic inefficient efficiency of our cities are obligated to dream and construct the humane cities for the future. Only this type of community—only this city of beauty and poetry and justice and love—will be worthy of the beauty and poetry and love which are the potential within each human child. The only realities of the human experience are the boldest dreams.

Given the interdependence of man with his environment and man with man, these are our only hope for richness of a real community—our basis for survival. (Clark, "Cities for Man—Man's Hope for Richness of Real Community" [address sponsored by The Graduate School of the U.S. Department of Agriculture, Washington, DC, November 1967].)

Q: *How would you describe you as other than a sincere scholar and a national leader in solid social action?*

A: Do you know what I am? I am a bewildered, concerned man.

(Clark, quoted in Mary Harrington Hall, "A Conversation with Kenneth B. Clark," *Psychology Today* 2.1 [1968]: 21.)

List of greatest men? I would start with Socrates, with his indomitable belief in freedom and humanity. Then I would go to Christ, with His strong belief in the properties of man. I would include John Locke as father of Jeffersonian democracy, a great mind and a great spirit. I couldn't include any of the founding fathers. They were caught up in their own contradiction, and they were pragmatic men. The next man on my list would be Gandhi. He faced everything in the tradition of poverty. Again, my standard is total commitment, not just a verbal commitment. From Gandhi I would go to Einstein, the great, beautiful total person. He was not just a mind, but his mind unfortunately overshadows the greatness of the total man. And the last is Bertrand Russell. The greatness of Russell lies in the fact that Russell transcended his high-born British origins. All the other men we have considered come from relatively humble origins. One could almost theorize that it is relatively easy to be great and compassionate and full of love when you are disadvantaged. (Clark, quoted in Mary Harrington Hall, "A Conversation with Kenneth B. Clark," *Psychology Today* 2.1 [1968]: 23.)

Bertrand Russell once said that the trouble with the world was that the ignorant are cocksure and the intelligent full of doubt. (Clark, quoted in "Civil Liberties and Confrontation Politics," White Paper, Clark Archives, Hastings-on-Hudson, NY, April 21, 1969.)

Landing a man on the moon [July 20, 1969] is the latest and the most dramatic example of the awesome complexity that is man. With the success of Apollo 11 we are once again presented with the evidence that the human mind is extraordinary; that man's flair for the dramatic gesture and his need to transform his ideas of grandeur into concrete symbols and acts persists and that one success demands more and more successes. (Clark, "Some Would Forge Ahead in Space, Others Would Turn to Earth's Affairs," *New York Times*, July 21, 1969, 7.)

Earl Warren is a model of what it means to be a human being. He is an example of the fact that human beings must be concerned, and must seek to protect the rights and humanity of others. Specifically, Earl Warren has brought greatness to the office of the Chief Justice of the United States because he brought compassion and humanity to that office. He could do this because he is a person who has the courage required of greatness—the courage to believe in, to insist upon and to act in terms of the constructive potentials of man. He dared to use his office and the discipline of the law as instruments in reinforcing the best within man, thereby giving depth to the meaning of being human. In doing so, he taught us that the law is not merely a device for the regulation and control of human behavior, that the law can be a powerful instrument for the implementation of love and kindness and empathy among men. He has extended the traditional boundaries of the legal and judicial process—he has transcended the distinctions between law on the one hand and social ethics and religion on the other. (Clark, "The Meaning of Earl Warren—a Tribute" [address at the Lincoln Memorial, Washington, DC, June 29, 1969].)

One of the most important problems posed for an individual who seeks to live in terms of the Socratic dictum that "the unexamined life is not worth living" is that of justifying life once it is examined. For myself there is the recurrent temptation to deal with the problems of social injustices; the problems of man's inhumanity to man; the problems of seemingly compulsive hostility and aggression among men; and the problems of irrationality, insensitivity, and a jungle-type barbarity which seems to dominate so much of what passes for human civilization.

I have often wished that I were free of the necessity to examine life and the requirement to act upon the basis of the examination. I must confess also that I have frequently wished for the apparent bliss of insensitivity; and I have flirted with the notion that it is the examined life that is difficult to live even if the unexamined life is not worth living. As I have flirted on the brink of a sense of total personal futility and despair and entertained the notion that the human species is tragically incapable of mobilizing the moral and ethical resources necessary for its survival, I have been saved from the personal philosophical disasters of cynicism and immobilizing pessimism by the examples of more wise and mature human beings. These are the human beings who have been able to demonstrate by their lives—by their being—that it is possible for the individual human being to live a life of realistic assessment of the problems of man; to live a life of social sensitivity and personal responsibility. These individuals give meaning and substance to their lives through their persistence in seeking and identifying with the goals and programs based upon the hope of controlling the more primitive forces in man and reinforcing the more positive potentials of the human being. These individuals face the difficulties and the challenges of life with admirable zest, courage, and compassion. They assume the obligation of improving the conditions of their fellow human beings not as if this were a burden, but as if it were the essence of their own reason for being.

I have known in my lifetime a few such individuals. Some have been relatives, some have been friends and some I have known from a distance. They come in different colors and from different classes and backgrounds. Some are male and some female. Some of these individuals, without knowing it, saved me from wallowing in the mire of hopelessness and self-righteous passivity. (Clark, "An Open Letter to Nanny Pollitzer on the Occasion of Her 100th Birthday," Clark Archives, Hastings-on-Hudson, NY, May 18, 1970.)[1]

Of all the compensatory protective agents invented or created by the human brain as a cushion against the intolerable realities of human flimsiness, probably the most flexible and effective has been the idea of God. Man has invested God with both omnipotence and permanence. An analysis of the characteristics of God, the powers and functions of God, betrays the pathos and the vulnerability of man. One of the most important functions of God is that of protecting man against accepting and coming to terms with the realities of human limitations. In a most literal and basic psychological sense, God is the primary source of power for man. Man created God to create man with introspective strengths, with solidity, and with purpose and substance. To perform this awesome and important task there must be an ideationally literal God. If for no other reason, therefore, God is not only not dead, man cannot permit God to die. If God were to die, human beings would have to die psychologically, even though alive as organisms. (Clark, "The Pathos of Power: A Psychological Perspective" [address to the American Psychological Association, Washington, DC, September 4, 1971].)

In recent pre-nuclear history, at least two powerful national leaders have been described and analyzed in terms of their emotional instability. In the cases of both Hitler and Stalin one is confronted with the disturbing possibility that the very nature and pattern of their symptoms of instability reinforced rather than reduced or controlled their power and determined the quality, style and consequences of their leadership. The enormity of the problem now confronting mankind can probably be most clearly and dramatically understood if one dares to think about what would have happened if either Stalin or Hitler had been in possession of nuclear weapons. It is even more disturbing now to face the stark fact that there are no absolute safeguards against a Hitler or a Stalin-type leader coming to power in either an "authoritarian" or a "democratic" nation now or in the foreseeable future. (Clark, "A Fail-Safe Plan" (My Turn), *Newsweek*, February 23, 1973.)

One of my favorite human beings was Bertrand Russell. I've kept some of my heroes, as if I were an adolescent—Einstein is one, Russell is another. In 1963, my wife and I spent a whole day with him [Russell]. I've read practically every word he's written. But one little essay . . . stands out in my mind. The essay was devoted to problems and conflicts among human beings, interpersonal, intergroup, international problems; and near the end he says: "I've been asked, is there a solution to the fundamental problems of human cruelty and conflict—and I believe there is. Well, I'm somewhat embarrassed. It isn't sophistication, it isn't complicated, it is not a brilliant philosophical analysis, it's very simple. If we could find some way in which human beings could have kindness as the essence of their relationship with their fellow human beings, this would be the answer." I've never forgotten that. And all the damned things I've ever written about education and teachers and society, I suppose they get down to that. (Clark, "Kenneth Clark's Revolutionary Slogan: Just Teach Them to Read," *New York Times Magazine*, March 18, 1973, 63.)

A few weeks ago I read a commentary on the ubiquitous Watergate affair by Billy Graham which was published on the Op-Ed page of the Sunday issue of *The New York Times*. When I finished reading the Billy Graham apologia, I had a strange feeling of intellectual and emotional nausea. I was particularly disturbed at my inability to understand my amorphous revulsion of what I had just read. I had never been a fan of Billy Graham. I have always suspected the professional, evangelical moralist who had a shrewd ability to balance a selective approach to morality with the maintenance of close personal relations with the leaders of political power without regard to party, ideology or morality. I therefore should not have been particularly surprised or disturbed at his equivocating, somewhat incoherent attempts at explaining political venality. (Clark, "De Facto Segregation in the North—Pious Lawlessness and Insidious Defiance" [address delivered at a dinner of the NAACP Legal Defense Fund, New York, May 17, 1973].)

The Negro intellectual must clearly differentiate his role from the equally important roles of others. He cannot confuse his role with that of the politician or the mass leader. He cannot hope to be successful by imitating or adopting their techniques or their slogans. He certainly cannot appeal to the man in the street through the uncritical use of slogans, emotional phrases, and other devices which have been found effective in arousing the emotions and allegiances of the crowd. On the contrary, he is obligated to scrutinize the ideology, the motivation, and the methods of the popular leaders. He must interpret them and repudiate or accept them when the evidence so demands. The Negro intellectual would reduce his effectiveness if he sought to compete with others more competent and more suited in temperament and background for the status of popular leader. His role is to interpret, supplement, and give substance to the work of these leaders. He must content himself with the limited role of speaking to a minority at any given point in history. This, however, does not mean that the Negro intellectual can use this required division of labor as an excuse for withdrawal from social action. The dangers and imperatives of our times require that thought and responsible action merge into a single pattern of commitment. It is the fate of the Negro intellectual that he has no choice but to accept the challenge of trying to help America survive. (Clark, "The Duty of the Intellectual," in *The Pathos of Power* [New York: Harper & Row, 1974], 27, 29.)

The value of the WASPs [white Anglo-Saxon Protestants] in America is that, whether they like it or not, they represent the standard against which all other groups measure themselves. The WASPs fulfill a role that is the opposite of the role of blacks, who represent the negative standard by which mobility of the other ethnic groups can be measured. About 25 years ago I pointed out that the rate of Americanization of ethnic groups can be measured in terms of the increase in their anti-black attitudes. In the past, the status of the blacks was held constant. They were not permitted the same access to mobility as European immigrants. WASPs are the positive constant. Ethnic groups measure the degree of their assimilation in American society by the extent to which they are permitted participation in WASP clubs or WASP power or economic groups. (Clark, quoted in *The Study of Society: Sociology* [Guilford, CT: Dushkin Publishing Group, 1974], 249.)

Realism to me is that I can't accept things, which for some reason I find unacceptable. I don't know what good fighting against something which you feel you should be against does. Are you going to win? I don't know. Have you won? No. But that's what I believe. I would rather die actively than die passively. I would rather live a life of strident desperation than the life of quiet desperation. Even if the end is the same. (Clark, from a transcript of a Clark interview with Larry Nyman at City College of New York, Clark Archives, Hastings-on-Hudson, NY, June 19, 1975.)

The 50s were an exciting period. It was the McCarthy period, for one. [Sen. Joseph R.] McCarthy had an effect on the College—a demoralizing effect, I think. The red hunts almost decimated City College. It placed a pall over things. Let me tell you how I reacted to McCarthyism. In my typical defiant way, I practically said, "To hell with him." I assumed in every class there were agents and I operated on the assumption by saying, "Look, here is what I think, and here is when I think it. Now report the hell out of me if you want." I was probably overreacting. It was during that period that a few students protested that I was Godless. I think what I really was doing was testing the limits. I was deliberately daring the reactionary climate to zero in on me. And they disappointed me and never did. I got away with everything. I never belonged to any Communist Party or any Communist front organizations. I didn't like organizations. I didn't like anybody—right, left, middle—telling me what to think, so I guess because I knew that I didn't have anything that they could really pillar me on, I could say, "Oh, screw you." (Clark, from a transcript of a Clark interview with Larry Nyman at City College of New York, Clark Archives, Hastings-on-Hudson, NY, June 19, 1975.)

What came out in the [John F.] Kennedy years was the anti-poverty programs, the report, "Youth in the Ghetto," and my book, *Dark Ghetto*. It was the excitement of the 60s, which culminated in the urban riots, which I studied. These events really led to the disillusionment of the 70s, and my not even being able to pretend surprise at Watergate. (Clark, from a transcript of a Clark interview with Larry Nyman at City College of New York, Clark Archives, Hastings-on-Hudson, NY, June 19, 1975.)

What are the criteria which the truly great American leader must meet?

First, I think, he must meet the test of a disciplined and trained mind—a disciplined and trained mind which makes impossible his resort to the easy temptation of demagoguery and the exploitation of the irrational and emotional forces which may be so easily aroused in men.

Second, he must demonstrate his capacity to work with others and to understand the points of view of others, the limitations, the conflicts, the anxieties and the impatience, blending these into an effective force for good.

Third, he must show humility—a humility which reflects a balanced perspective. This means recognition of the fact that the opportunity for leadership is often not a result of personal assets but may often be determined by accidental circumstance which places a particular individual at a particular time in a position to exert leadership.

Fourth, he must show the capacity for fundamental courage—not just verbal bravado but courage where it is difficult to be courageous.

Fifth, he must show in his every behavior clarity of values and the primacy of human, moral and ethical values over the values of expediency and power. And he must show also the capacity to translate these values into social action.

Finally, he must at all times reveal by his every word and deed that his fundamental concern is not himself but the concern for the welfare of mankind.

It is a distinct privilege and honor for me to have the opportunity to introduce to you this afternoon, the Reverend Martin Luther King Jr. He is a young man. But the characteristics which I have enumerated are not relevant to age. I believe that he has within him the potential for truly great leadership. (Clark, Excerpt of text of Clark introduction of Dr. Martin Luther King on December 21, 1956, to the National Committee for the Rural Schools in New York, in *Tech Talk* [MIT News Office] 25.21 [January 12, 1981]: 2.)

The most frequent criticism I receive from colleagues is that I am not sufficiently balanced when I discuss what is happening in the schools. That I am too emotional. I admit it. I am emotional. I am deeply disturbed, because I identify with the children who are being destroyed in those schools. But most middle-class educators are indeed balanced and cautious as they keep finding excuses for not educating these children. I have a hope that eventually our educational institutions will see as one of their responsibilities the training of human beings to be sensitive to what is done to human beings who are not like themselves. Until this happens, we will have one damn seminar like this after another, with no change in the status quo. I am sorry to have to say that it is really *not* a pleasure to be here. (Clark, quoted in Nat Hentoff, "Profiles: The Integrationist," *The New Yorker*, August 23, 1982, 38.)

During the [Franklin Delano] Roosevelt New Deal era, race relations and racial problems seemed to have been subordinated to the pervasive economic factors of the Great Depression affecting all Americans. . . . We look upon the Roosevelt Administration as a model in liberalism, but the liberalism of the Roosevelt era did not concern itself with racial matters. During the Roosevelt administration, racial segregation prevailed. There was segregation in public accommodations, in transportation, in professional sports, in education, and in the armed forces. President Roosevelt did nothing to alleviate flagrant examples of racial inequities. In fact, he had to be coerced by A. Philip Randolph. In a confrontation with F.D.R., Randolph threatened to stage a massive March on Washington in order to get a reluctant F.D.R. to appoint a Fair Employment Practices Commission. Eleanor Roosevelt helped Randolph bring to F.D.R.'s attention the importance of racial problems. (Clark, "Contemporary Realities in American Race Relations," White Paper, Clark Archives, Hastings-on-Hudson, NY, 1983.)

It was not until the [Harry S] Truman Administration that the executive branch of the federal government began to concern itself with race. President Truman made a major contribution to racial equality in the United States when he appointed a Commission on Civil Rights to look into the problems of how the United States could become democratic in the area of race. The report, entitled, "To Secure These Rights," prepared by the Commission can be considered a design for the federal government's involvement in racial problems in the United States. It is difficult to understand why this important contribution of Harry Truman's has been consistently ignored. In addition, President Truman desegregated the United States armed forces. (Clark, "Contemporary Realities in American Race Relations," White Paper, Clark Archives, Hastings-on-Hudson, NY, 1983.)

President Eisenhower did not make a direct contribution to racial progress, but he made an important indirect contribution in his appointment of [former California Governor] Earl Warren as Chief Justice of the United States Supreme Court. Eisenhower did not expect Earl Warren to fulfill a major historic role by getting a unanimous decision in the *Brown v. Board of Education of Topeka* on May 17, 1954. Eisenhower did not believe the United States Supreme Court should rule that racial integration in public schools violated the Fourteenth Amendment of the United States Constitution, and he said so. He believed that racial justice could not be brought about by laws or by court decisions, and frequently said that the only way change could be brought about was by changing the hearts and minds of the American people. However, when confronted with Governor [Orville] Faubus' resistance to the desegregation of the public schools in Little Rock, Arkansas, President Eisenhower, in spite of his personal disagreement with the *Brown* decision, sent the Federal troops into Little Rock to desegregate Central High School. He would not allow the law and authority of the federal government to be flouted. (Clark, "Contemporary Realities in American Race Relations," White Paper, Clark Archives, Hastings-on-Hudson, NY, 1983.)

The Kennedy Administration was apparently not in power long enough to make any major contributions to racial progress. Although the civil rights movement seemed to have built up steam during the Kennedy Administration, it received no direct support from the White House. When the nonviolent disobedience in the South, led so well by Martin Luther King Jr., became a major method for seeking social justice, neither Jack nor Bobby Kennedy lent any direct help. In the March on Washington when Martin Luther King made his famous "I Have a Dream" speech, neither of the Kennedys participated. In fact, they deliberately kept their distance. (Clark, "Contemporary Realities in American Race Relations," White Paper, Clark Archives, Hastings-on-Hudson, NY, 1983.)

The president who made a major contribution to racial justice in the United States in the last 50 years was Lyndon B. Johnson. Were it not for the tragedy of his being entrapped in the Vietnam War, history would reveal that of all the presidents of the United States, Lyndon Johnson made the most important contribution to the attainment of racial justice since Lincoln. Johnson was genuinely concerned with the attainment of racial justice in the United States. Probably one of the most important civil rights speeches made by either a black or white was made by Johnson in his Howard University speech when he described specific goals for social justice. It was also under Lyndon Johnson's shrewd direction that the Congress of the United States passed the Civil Rights Act of 1964 which prohibited discrimination on the basis of race, sex, or national origin in public accommodations, in federally assisted programs, and in employment; and the Voting Rights Act of 1965 which authorized the Attorney General to appoint federal examiners to register voters in certain areas, thereby enabling disenfranchised citizens the opportunity to vote. (Clark, "Contemporary Realities in American Race Relations," White Paper, Clark Archives, Hastings-on-Hudson, NY, 1983.)

To evaluate Richard Nixon on the basis of the contemporary realities of race relations in the United States is difficult. On the one hand Nixon rather obviously pandered to the latent racial prejudices of Middle America. He certainly exploited the anti-busing issue for personal and party political gains. On the other hand, there is more actual desegregation of schools in the southern states under the Nixon administration than under the administrations of either Kennedy or Johnson. This inconsistency, his pandering to the prejudices of northerners while permitting the desegregation of southern public schools, remains a confusing factor. What emerged during the Nixon Administration was this regional division. In the northern urban centers, such as New York City, Chicago, Cleveland, Philadelphia, Detroit, Los Angeles, more black and white children are attending segregated schools than at the time of the *Brown* decision. A contemporary reality in American race relations is now clear that racism is more deeply embedded in northern urban centers than we had thought when we were fighting for racial justice in the southern states. (Clark, "Contemporary Realities in American Race Relations," White Paper, Clark Archives, Hastings-on-Hudson, NY, 1983.)

The Carter administration seemed to have been the beginning of a clear, quiet battle fatigue in race relations—the becalming of the civil rights movement. White and black liberals in the civil rights movement seemed to believe that the battle had been won. They seemed willing to accept the rhetoric of racial progress without examining its substance and foundation. The perception of this passive aspect of the Carter Administration may have been obscured by the dramatic role of Andy Young as our ambassador to the United Nations. Whatever the cause, there was a quietus on civil rights progress during this period. To me, the Carter administration became the symbol of passivity, the beginning of a marking time and of confusion, if not an outright retreat in civil rights. (Clark, "Contemporary Complexities in American Race Relations" [address given at The City Club, Cleveland, OH, February 1983].)

Long before we had laws or even a court decision dealing with the problem of trying to make justice literally color blind, Algernon Black [a leader of the Ethical Culture Schools] was laboring in the vineyards of Harlem. I recall that he was constantly dragging me to meetings for bettering conditions in Harlem, for better housing for the people. There is no question in my mind that Algernon Black is the sort of permanent symbol of the ongoing struggle for decency and justice in our society. (Clark, "The Civil Rights Act—20th Anniversary" [address given at the New York Society for Ethical Culture, New York, NY, November 17, 1984].)

It is a clear fact that the Reagan Administration has sought to reverse the positive goals and procedures for remedying past racial discrimination in employment. While the executive branch of the Federal government, including the Civil Rights Division of the Department of Justice and the U.S. Civil Rights Commission, consistently seek to dilute the positives of affirmative action, it is significant that—so far—the United States Supreme Court and the Federal courts have not followed this trend. (Clark, "Affirmative Action at the Crossroads: A Manifest for Change" [address sponsored by the Board of Governors, California Community Colleges, San Jose City College, September 26, 1986].)

[*Editor's Note*: Following, an excerpt from a 1995 interview with Dr. Clark by Sam Roberts of the *New York Times*].

Q: *Professor John Hope Franklin suggests that some victories now seem counterproductive. The desegregation decision in the* Brown *case wasn't counterproductive, was it?*

A: But what has happened to *Brown*? I mean I had to fight like hell for decent race relations in New York City public schools after *Brown*. And where am I now with race? If color were not as obvious a barrier as it is, I could say that the civil rights movement was helping us to move toward a positive cycle. I'm not so sure that that is happening with blacks like it happened with the Irish or Italians. Because you can see blacks—there they are. You can put them in jail, put them in certain schools. I'm not going to write, "Dark Ghetto" again. But if I look at the prisons, would it be the same? If I looked at delinquency, would it be the same?

Q: *So it would be worse?*

A: Shhh.

Q: *If color is too decisive, is anything short of generations of intermarriage going to improve things?*

A: Ah. What do you think white males are going to do about that?

Q: *As whites become a minority, won't they see it's in their interest that blacks succeed?*

A: They're not that bright. I don't think you can expect whites to understand the effects of prejudice and discrimination against blacks affecting them. If whites really understood, they would do something about it.

Q: *Don't dashed hopes breed frustration?*

A: Well, it won't be that they'll be frustrated generation after generation. Each generation will, I hope, have some hope.

Q: *You've seen the evolution from Negro to black to African-American? What is the best thing for blacks to call themselves?*

A: White. (Clark, quoted in Sam Roberts, "Conversation/Kenneth Clark," *New York Times*, sec. 4, May 7, 1995.)

I am forced to agree with James Baldwin that so far as the Negro is concerned, liberalism as it is practiced—I am not talking of it as it is verbalized—is an affliction. It is an insidious type of affliction because it attempts to impose guilt upon the Negro when he has to face the hypocrisy of the liberal. (Clark, quoted in Carol Polsgrove, *Divided Minds: Intellectuals and the Civil Rights Movement* [New York: W.W. Norton, 2001], 204–205.)

Racial separation is a blind alley. It means the abandonment of hope. Furthermore, just as there are white idiots, so there are black idiots. (Clark, quoted in Nat Hentoff, *The Nat Hentoff Reader* [Cambridge, MA: Da Capo Press, Perseus Books Group, 2001], 203.)

COMMENTARY

Vernon E. Jordan, Jr.[2]

Kenneth Clark was an extraordinarily able man. He cared deeply and passionately about equal opportunity in America. He took a special interest in the leadership of the movement, and he made it a point to be close, to be involved, and to be helpful to the leadership.

NOTES

1. [*Editor's Note*: Alice K. "Nanny" Pollitzer, a graduate of Barnard College who died at the age of 102 in 1973, was a devoted member of the Ethical Culture Movement. She was the wife of Dr. Sigmund Pollitzer. Her interest in children led her to become secretary of the Vocational Advisory Service for Youth and later secretary of the Walden School. She worked with the Child Study Association and the magazine *Story Parade*. An early activist, she marched for the women's vote

before World War I. In the 1930s, she talked in the streets and made speeches in the campaigns for Franklin Delano Roosevelt. She also marched for peace in support of the League of Nations and the United Nations. In 1946, at the age of 75, she helped found the Encampment for Citizenship and became the chair of its board of directors, a position she held for almost 20 years.]

2. [*Editor's Note*: In his autobiography (with Annette Gordon-Reed) *Vernon Can Read!* (New York: Public Affairs, of Perseus Books Group, 2001), Mr. Jordan refers to Kenneth B. Clark as "my friend and mentor" and credits Dr. Clark with playing a key role in his being offered the position as executive of the National Urban League (331).]

CHAPTER 17

Beyond America

The values and attitudes of a given human being are a consequence of the stimuli, experiences and culture to which he has been subjected. An enlightened approach to society, an understanding of the fact that human society can exist with stability only in terms of the dominance of a basic humanism in the attitude toward people, should no longer be the personal philosophy of a few advanced social philosophers or sensitive academicians, but should become, and can become, the basic determining attitude of the peoples of the world. (Clark, interview with Georgene H. Seward, quoted in Gardner Murphy, ed., *Human Nature and Enduring Peace* [New York: Houghton Mifflin, 1945], 337–338.)

With the American victory against the oppressive Nazi forces and with the Nuremberg convictions and execution of those judged chiefly responsible for the hate and death, America has emerged from World War II not only in the role of one of the most powerful nations the world has known but also has assumed the role of a great moral force. It now seeks to lead the peoples of the world away from another form of totalitarianism toward its concept of individual freedom and democratic society. In view of the fact that the majority of the peoples in the world are colored, the success of America in its present role may well be determined by its ability to solve its indigenous "racial" problem. In its competition for power, Russia has been most successful in the area of propaganda, which gives wide publicity to the many incidents of racial injustice in America. The effect of this propaganda and the general knowledge of American racism have weakened the moral foundations of American democratic appeals and tend to mock our pleas for freedom and justice for the peoples of the world. It is mandatory, therefore, that the problem of intergroup prejudices in America be solved unless we assume that the American position and power will and can be maintained exclusively by economic and military force. Without an understanding of the nature of such prejudice and the ability and desire to control them, America necessarily must forfeit its claim to world leadership in terms of moral force. (Clark, 1st Draft: "The Effects of Prejudice and Discrimination on Personality Development," Fact-Finding Report, Mid-Century White House Conference on Children and Youth, Children's Bureau, Federal Security Agency, 1950 [mimeographed], "Kenneth Bancroft Clark, A Register of His Papers in the Library of Congress," Professional File, Box 104, January 25, 1950.)

I believe that Nehru and some of the younger leaders in Africa and Asia are showing, in their own way, what the future solution to man's political and intellectual dilemma might be. Nehru particularly is attempting to show that man may obtain the advantages of modern industrialization without becoming its slave; of modern political organization without being tyrants or abject subjects; the advantages of intelligence without loss of spirit.

Can we as American Negroes serve our country in this epoch struggle? We can if we are not content merely to imitate the white American's worship of power, technology, materialism and soulless efficiency. We can if we do not just blindly imitate his facts and his errors—if we do not merely accept his educational theories and rigidly seek to conform to the world which he has cast for himself. The advantage of the meeting of diverse people is that each gives to and receives from the other with the resulting product being better than that which was brought by each. The American Negro is obligated, therefore, to create and contribute to the growth and solidity of American and world culture. (Clark, "Dilemma of Intelligence in the Contemporary World," White Paper, Clark Archives, Hastings-on-Hudson, NY., n.d. [1950s].)

The present international picture, for obvious reasons, must be recognized as favorable for changes in race relations in America. From a humanitarian point of view it would be preferable to ignore or reject international power competition as a factor in the resolution of a domestic problem of social ethics. We nonetheless live in a real world in which sometimes, or maybe too often, humanitarian and ethical considerations are subordinated to more "practical" determinants of social progress. (Clark, "A Struggle for Complete Human Dignity," *The Christian Register* [Massachusetts Universalist Association] [July 1956]: 37.)

There is probably no more ominous and pervasive issue facing America and the world today than the problems involved in the rapidly changing status of nonwhite groups in their relationship to the previously dominant Europeans. The delicacy of the relationship between China and the Soviet Union, the seething surge toward independent nationalism on the part of the peoples of Asia and Africa, and the reorganization of the British Empire into a multi-racial Commonwealth of equal status partners are some of the contemporary manifestations of the profound social and psychological revolution precipitated by the infectiousness of the democratic idea. Racial desegregation in the United States must be seen as a crucial aspect of this world pattern of democratic social change. (Clark, "The Role of the Social Sciences," *Teachers College Record* 62.1 [October 1960]: 1.)

[*Editor's Note*: Dr. Clark delivered the following comments at the time of the Cuban Missile Crisis in October 1961.]

The present moral crisis which threatens mankind reveals the many other problems which remain unsolved. It is now possible to see that the problems of international tensions and the problems of racial justice are not separate problems. It is now ironically clear that if human intelligence had in the past been more successful in its quest for effective answers to problems of human justice, compassion, kindness, and the control of greed and hostility, we might not now be confronted with the possibility of the ultimate catastrophe.

Paradoxically, however, we must proceed as if there is still time to discuss and seek solutions to the fundamental problems involved in man's relationship to his fellow man. (Clark, "Interracial Justice—Our Common Task" [address given at the James J. Hoey Awards luncheon, New York, October 29, 1961].)

There is no doubt that a new image of the Negro has emerged in the years following World War II. Among the factors are the participation of Negroes in two major World Wars for democracy within this generation and their unwillingness to give their lives for democracy elsewhere while they are denied the benefits of democracy in their own land. (Clark, quoted in Mathew A. Ahmann, ed., *The New Negro* [Notre Dame, IN: Fides Publishers, 1961], 37.)

I am optimistic not because I believe that there has been any moral awakening or conversion among the American people, but because I believe the present international political, economic and industrial manpower realities make racial democracy in America mandatory. (Clark, "What the Marchers Really Want," *New York Times Magazine*, August 25, 1963, 57.)

Another factor affecting the present momentum in the use of federal power for positive change toward racial justice is the rise of nationalism in Asia and Africa. The whole world, in fact, has been undergoing a racial revolution, a breakdown in imperialism and a change in the relationship between white Europeans and the colored peoples of the world. White and Negro Americans could not escape the impact of this worldwide racial revolution. (Clark, "The Dilemma of Power," in Talcott Parsons and Kenneth B. Clark, eds., *The Negro American* [Boston: Beacon Press, 1965], xv.)

The world has changed. The United States in order to survive must change. America's posture of the democratic leader of the world together with the challenge of Soviet Communism and the more ominous racially toned challenge of Chinese Communism demands honest examination of the unfinished business of democracy in America and the development of programs designed to implement social and racial justice. The realistic hope for the attainment of these goals is to be found in Gunnar Myrdal's observation that never in the history of America has there been a greater and more complete identity between the ideals of social justice and the requirements of economic progress. (Clark, "Brown v. Board of Education" [address, Sidney Hillman Lecture, University of Rochester, May 16, 1966].)

During the decades since World War II, the idea of democracy has infected more and more peoples throughout the world as previously subjugated darker peoples have taken seriously the semantics of political, economic, and spiritual equality.

The essence of worldwide and American forms of social turbulence—the movement from the status of colonials to that of independent peoples and the persistent conflicts and rebellion in South America, Africa, Asia and the ghettos of American cities—are identical, namely, a seemingly irresistible thrust on the part of the previously exploited and neglected for food, freedom and dignity and the countervailing restraints and barriers imposed by their exploiters to restrict quality, or control the rate of or block the attainment of these goals. The power and force demanding changes come in conflict with the power and force resisting change. (Clark, "Learning from Students" [commencement address, Antioch College, June 22, 1968].)

It must be obvious to the most patriotic of Americans that as long as any observable proportion of our citizens are imprisoned in poverty, slums and ghettoes, and are victims of the total pathology inherent in these prisons, America cannot be taken seriously as the nation which brings hope in the form of genuine respect for man to the underdeveloped nations of the world. As long as these manifestations of disrespect for the humanity of man are permitted to prevail, are subordinated to our military adventures, and are considered of lesser priority to our exploration of space, then it follows that there must be dangers, tensions, disruptions and other manifestations of disunity within our nation and throughout the world.

The determinants of national and international disunity are all the more intolerable and unacceptable because they are remediable. If I had any doubts about the possibility for remedying these indications of disrespect by man of man, all such doubts were removed this past summer through a visit to Scandinavia. My observations of the social, economic and political systems of Norway, Sweden and Denmark resulted in the conclusion that it is possible to demonstrate concern for human beings by building into the social, political and economic system of a modern industrial nation, the demonstrations of humanity, sensitivity and concern. One searches in vain for slums in Scandinavia. The direct observation of the operation of the medical and welfare system reveals that human beings are respected for their humanity. They are treated as if they were a precious commodity. Evidence of respect is found in the fact that, as far as I was able to determine, no human being is permitted to be hungry, or required to live below a certain economic level inconsistent with human dignity or is required to go without medical care for economic reasons. . . . This quiet civilized interaction among human beings must enhance the effectiveness of the services offered and accepted with mutual dignity. If this can be true in Scandinavia it can be true also in America. (Clark, "Respect for Man—The Unqualifiable Basis for Unity" [address to the Conference on National Unity, Sterling Forest Gardens, NY, November 19, 1969], 12, 13.)

International politics played a strong role in the struggle for justice. With the overthrow of colonial domination in the postwar decade, white Europeans and Americans could no longer sustain their political dominance over the nonwhite peoples of Asia and Africa. The increasing dignity associated with the independence of these colored peoples provided a new source of strength for the American Negro. And one should not underestimate the role of the Communist ideology as an aggressive world adversary of the American and Western concept of democracy. . . . The competitive struggle between world Communism and the American concept of democracy demanded an American response to this embarrassing and easily exploited violation of democratic ideals. America risked standing before the world as a hypocrite or resting its claims for leadership on might alone, subordinating any democratic ideological basis of appeal. (Clark, "The History of the Civil Rights Movement," *The Negro American* [June 1969]: 595.)

With the end of World War II and throughout the Cold War there have been increasing tensions, sporadic rebellions and seething discontent among the darker peoples of the world, among young people and women who have developed a variety of techniques to challenge, confront and seek to remedy the remaining vestiges of human cruelty, injustice and the varieties of subtle and flagrant forms of oppression.

Minorities in America have stepped up their insistence for unqualified racial justice. The peoples of Asia, Africa and South America have demanded an end to all forms of European imperialism and insist upon their rights to control their own destiny. A worldwide youth movement is challenging the institutions of their nation and demanding reforms in education, the economy and the political process. Organizations of women have raised the question of sexism—the institutional oppression of females by males. Even within the church the demands for structural and power reforms have been raised and could not be ignored. (Clark, "Psychology and Social Responsibility: Toward a Scientific Social Ethics," White Paper for discussion with the American Psychological Association board, Clark Archives, Hastings-on-Hudson, NY, December 15, 1970.)

I think the United States has a wonderful opportunity to take its racial homogeneity, its ethnic homogeneity, and turn it into a social, economic, educational, and, if you will, international asset. (Clark, from testimony before Senator Walter Mondale's Select Committee on Equal Educational Opportunity, *South Today* 2.5 [December 15, 1970]: 27.)

The present generation of Americans and Europeans, Asians, Russians, and Africans—all of these young people must accept the challenge of believing that nuclear warfare can be made anachronistic by realistic and serious disarmament and that nothing is any more important than that. And if they don't, they will be the last generation. (Clark, transcript, *Voice of America*, June 10, 1975.)

I recall that after World War II we . . . developed quite effective [Marshall Plan] programs to stimulate and raise the economies of Europe, including those of some of our enemies. . . . Now America itself has a group of people within the nation that is, in effect, an economically underdeveloped group. . . . I can't understand why the rationale of, say, the Marshall Plan and our aid program, does not operate here. (Clark, "The Costs of Discrimination," *Challenge* [May–June 1977]: 38–39.)

In many respects, American racism is unique. Unlike British colonial racism which not only permitted, but trained non-whites to enter the upper and governing class in many of the former colonies, American racism was and remains, for the most part, "democratic" in that all blacks were perceived and treated alike. In American racism, class and race tended to be used and reacted to interchangeably. Traditionally, American whites tended to react to a person of color as if he were automatically lower class. This was and continues to be generally true without regard to distinctions among individual blacks in terms of education, economic status, and other generally accepted class symbols. Racial stereotypes were applied to all blacks. Exceptional blacks were and are grudgingly accepted as "different." (Clark, address at a symposium on "The Declining Significance of Race," University of Pennsylvania, under the sponsorship of the Afro-American Studies Program, March 1979.)

When the Russians sent the first Sputnik [October 4, 1957] into orbit we became excited and concerned about the need to improve the quality of American education. The goals of education were then defined to ensure that American students become more proficient in math and those sciences which would make our nation more competitive and overtake the Russians in the space age. Educators and educational institutions accepted uncritically this competitive power, these military objectives, this purpose of education. The dominance of the computer age and its technology has become incorporated into the educational process and is resulting in the increasing mechanization of education and social interaction.

As we approach the twenty-first century, therefore, the processes and goals of education become more restricted. Education and educators appear to be less and less concerned with human values such as justice, equality, morality, and empathy. This narrowly defined form of education, no matter how successful it is in exploring space and increasing the effectiveness of nuclear missiles, will be the chief threat to human survival. This type of education will not be a positive force; it will be destructive, as it will harness human intelligence in the service of man's irrational, primitive, and egocentric impulses in his blind quest for power and status. In a pre-nuclear age this would have been dangerous. In a nuclear age it is catastrophic. (Clark, "Crossroads to the 21st Century: Changing Curriculum for Changing Times" [address, Bowling Green State University, Bowling Green, OH, November 21, 1985].)

One of the greatest minds of the twentieth century, Albert Einstein, once stated: "The splitting of the atom has changed everything save our mode of thinking, and thus we drift toward unparalleled catastrophe." This prophetic observation has not been generally quoted. I have carried it around in my pocketbook and have referred to it many times as I tried to understand the complexities of international affairs, dehumanization conflicts, and regional wars which have dominated the pattern of world events since the onset of the atomic and nuclear age.

Mankind, in this latter part of the twentieth century, is still thinking and functioning within the residues of a pre-atomic age. We do not seem to see that this pre-atomic residual thinking is in fact drifting us toward unparalleled catastrophe. Domestic policies and approaches to social and human problems remain mired in the dilemmas of the pre-atomic past. The most serious threat which all human beings throughout the world face is the development and training of human intelligence devoid of moral, ethical, and empathic concerns. Disciplined intelligence is a social trust which must be conserved and enhanced through education for the benefit of all mankind. (Clark, "Education for the Present and the Future" [convocation address, Lehman College–City University of New York, October 5, 1988].)

For his personal commitment, Martin Luther King received the Nobel Peace Prize at a time when conflicts were dominating Europe, Asia, and Africa. . . . It is not enough to bemoan the fact that the education in our public schools is inferior to that in other advanced countries, such as Japan, Germany, Britain. These results are based upon the traditional educational indicators, such as reading and math. We can make a real contribution by developing a more inclusive definition of education. We can do that by having our children learn cooperation and sensitivity as a way of increasing their skills in reading and math. If it were understood and incorporated by educational institutions, rather than merely verbalized, it would be the educational and human contribution of Martin Luther King. (Clark, "Martin Luther King Jr.: The Humanist" [address before the Coordinating Council for Minority Issues, University of Chicago, January 18, 1993], 1, 4.)

COMMENTARY

Franklin A. Thomas

Ken Clark is a scholar and teacher with a powerful commitment to racial justice and understanding. Early on, he saw and understood the capacity of racial discrimination to scar the minds and souls of its victims and of the society that permitted its practice; and he worked hard to bring this to public attention. Ken is an emotional man who tempers that emotion so that the force of his ideas can be heard by all audiences, understood by them, and acted upon. Ken is a true patriot who wants America to live up to its ideals and potential as a great nation. He has been a mentor to many of us, and I'm proud to be his friend.

CHAPTER 18

"Racial Progress and Retreat: A Personal Memoir," by Kenneth B. Clark[1]

When I was about six years old, my mother told me we were going to Childs restaurant for lunch. It was located on 125th Street and Seventh Avenue in what was, at that time, the commercial center of developing Harlem. Needless to say, I was excited and looked forward to what for me was an adventure. I remember we sat at a table and waited for the waitress to come to take our order. We waited and waited and waited. When the waitress did come, instead of having a smile on her face, she had a frown. My mother started to give our order, but the waitress stopped her by saying in a matter-of-fact manner, "We don't serve you here."

My mother reacted with verbal hostility. I don't remember exactly what she said to the waitress. What I do remember was that my mother threw a dish on the floor. I remember the shattering of the dish. My mother took me by the hand and we walked out of Childs restaurant. I knew the adventure was over. I must confess that I did not associate this clearly hostile experience with racial rejection. I knew my mother was angry and outraged, but I didn't know exactly why; nor did my mother explain it to me. What I do know, however, is that from that time on, I associated Childs restaurants with my mother's anger, and with her shattering of the dish; and I don't remember where we had lunch that day.

The schools in Harlem at that time, in the early 1920s, were well integrated. My classmates were Irish, Italian, and Jewish. The Jewish children came down from the Jewish orphan asylum at the top of St. Nicholas Hill. Color and ethnic differences did not seem at all important in our relationships. Our teachers, who were all white, seemed more concerned with our ability to read and with our penmanship than with other matters. My mother had enrolled me in the first grade when I was five years old by saying I was six. She had taught me to read at home when I was three and four. She kept cookies on the shelf, I remember, and I was given the treat when my lesson was over.

I recall my first-grade teacher made it clear that I was the best reader in the class. Whenever the principal brought a visitor to our classroom, my teacher would call on me to demonstrate my reading ability. Even at that time, I was aware that she was giving the impression that my ability to read was due to her teaching skills. This demonstration of my reading ability did not endear me to all the members of my class. I particularly remember that one classmate who was Irish waited after school to engage me in a fight. I did not associate his grudge with color. I thought his problem was that he had not yet learned to read, and would have been angry and jealous of any other member of the class who was being favorably noticed by the teacher. Nor was my color a factor in the teacher's giving the impression that my reading ability was a product of her teaching skills.

I had friends across racial, color, and ethnic lines. As a matter of fact, one of my closest friends was Harry Moore, also Irish. We would walk home from school together. He lived on Eighth Avenue and 138th Street, which was predominantly white. Harry did not walk to my house, on 140th Street and Seventh Avenue, which was becoming a black street. I remember when Harry told me his family was moving away. We were in the fourth grade, I believe. He was sorry and I was sorry. I never saw or heard from Harry after his family moved. I learned later that this move was a part of the exodus of whites from that area of Harlem. By the time I reached the end of the sixth grade, the classes were predominantly black.

In the seventh grade at junior high school, there was only one white student in the class. He was Italian, and also a close friend of mine. His family moved at the end of the eighth grade. After that, all classes consisted of only black students.

During junior high school, my teachers held all of the students to high academic standards. My English teacher, Mr. Mitchell, taught us Shakespeare. We had reading assignments and discussed our work in class. Mr. Mitchell, to my recollection, never once mentioned race or color in those discussions, even when we discussed *Othello*. Another English teacher, Miss McGuire, insisted upon our understanding and using the logic of grammar. She would diagram sentences on the board to illustrate the relationship between nouns and verbs. I found this challenging and intriguing. Mr. Ruprecht, a mathematics teacher, was most demanding. He refused to accept any excuse whatever for our not having our algebra homework ready. Again, I do not recall any of these teachers using our color, or our economic status, or our family background as a basis for our not meeting their standards. In spite of the academic requirements placed on us, there was also room for graphic arts and music.

Mr. Dixon was in charge of speech and orchestra. He refused to assign me to the chair of first violinist in the orchestra, in spite of my desire to have that position. It would have pleased my mother. My classmate, William Collymore, was without question more talented. I had to accept Mr. Dixon's decision. However, he did encourage me to speak and to write. Periodically we were required to prepare and present a three-minute speech to the class, and the class reacted to our presentation. One day he asked me to stay after class. He told me that the Bond Bread Company was conducting an essay contest. He suggested that I contribute to it. I was surprised and pleased that he thought I was able to compete in the contest. I was even more pleased when I won a gold medal. Mr. Dixon and I were very proud when the medal was presented to me at the school assembly.

In those early school years, race was not a factor in my interaction with my teachers. I do not recall any teacher communicating, directly or indirectly, the factor of my color, or the fact that I came from a single-parent family. It was not until the eighth grade that I had a black teacher. Miss Thomas taught Spanish. Again, I respected her methods, her standards, and her insistence that the class fulfill her requirements.

Some teachers did not expect high standards. I did not admire them and I have forgotten their names. Those who were willing to accept inferior or mediocre performance from their students seemed to me to be lazy, or indifferent.

In the ninth grade, a very important decision had to be made. Each student had to choose and be recommended to a high school. I was called to the guidance counselor's office to discuss my decision. The guidance counselor was white. She told me that I should choose a vocational high school. When I went home and told my mother about the guidance counselor's suggestion, I again saw the anger on my mother's face that I had seen at Childs restaurant. She said, "You will not go to a vocational high school. You are going to go to an academic high school, and you will do well."

The next day my mother got me out of my classroom and took me with her to the guidance counselor's office. I will never forget the scene; I was so embarrassed by my mother's confrontation with the guidance counselor. She said, "I don't care where you send your child. You can send him to a vocational school if you want to, but my son is going to go to George Washington High School." My mother had attended night classes at George Washington High School and she knew where she wanted her son to go. Soon after that meeting with the guidance counselor, I was told that I had been assigned to George Washington High School.

There were not many minority students at George Washington High School, yet I still did not sense race or color as negative factors. There were a number of teachers I respected. Again, I was impressed with an English teacher, Miss Chapin. She taught us literature and grammar, without regard to race. In her class, we dramatized our reading assignments. I recall she once had me take the part of *Macbeth*. I also looked forward to my history class with Miss O'Ryan, who made history exciting.

In my senior year, economics was probably my most stimulating class. Mr. Gottesman, the teacher, used the Socratic method in teaching his subject. I took every opportunity to answer questions and problems he raised. My classmates were convinced that I would receive the economics prize Mr. Gottesman gave each year. One of my classmates, Howard Fast, congratulated me before the announcement was made. I was shocked when one of my classmates, not an outstanding student, received the prize. This was the first time I felt that my race was a critical and destructive factor. My respect for Mr. Gottesman crumbled, and I decided never again to take a course in economics.

At this point in my life, at age 16, 1 saw clearly that race could be an unfair component in judging the performance of human beings. My art teacher at George Washington High School was the opposite of Mr. Gottesman: while he underestimated my performance, she overestimated my talent. She wanted me to become a sculptor.

At this stage, something was happening in the area of insight and understanding that had not happened before. I was beginning to see that race played a role in the way society functioned. I began to evaluate myself, and the small percentage of minority students at George Washington High School, in terms of an inferior status. I began to see white students, rightly or wrongly, as having special advantages which they appeared to enjoy. Looking back on that stage of my social awareness, I was already determined that I would not permit my color to determine my goals and performance. I began to better understand what my mother felt. I shared her insistence that I go to college, and I knew why I should.

About this time I met and got to know a young woman who was a second year medical student at Howard University. She told me about her experiences at an all-black school. I became very interested in having for the first time the opportunity to observe and to participate in an all-black educational institution. I began to see that race could be an important part of an educational process. I wanted to see how it worked. This woman talked of an all-black faculty, which I had not experienced, nor even imagined. I told my mother I wanted to apply to Howard University. She did not know about the school, but she agreed that if that was what I wanted, she would help me financially.

This greatly impressed me. My mother was a worker in the garment district and it was the depth of the Depression. She had been subjected to discrimination on the job, and by the International Ladies Garment Workers Union. In fact, I was very pleased years later when the NAACP exposed the discriminatory pattern in New York's garment industry and attacked the racial practices of the ILGWU. Fortunately, my mother had the courage and vision to pledge her support and affirmation for my future. Although

I was able to receive a scholarship to Howard, I was fully aware of the financial burden that my education placed on her.

I felt very comfortable at Howard. I intruded myself among the faculty. I talked with them out of class. By my sophomore year, I had learned why these professors were at Howard. It was because of their race that Ralph Bunche, Alain Locke, Sterling Brown, Abraham Harris, and other outstanding scholars were concentrated at this one institution. I developed a curious and pervasive relationship with these people I so highly respected. I got to know how they felt. I learned more about racism in academia than I had been aware of before. Howard University was the beginning of the persistent preoccupation I have had with American racial injustice.

At this stage in my personal development, I became engrossed in the contradictions which exist: the eloquence of American "democracy" and academic hypocrisy. These members of the Howard faculty I respected all became my mentors against American racism. My life became dominated by an ongoing struggle against racial injustice. I do not believe this would have happened if I had attended an integrated institution. These outstanding professors made it very clear to me that under no circumstances should I ever accept racial injustice. They advised me to go to graduate school and get my Ph.D. They further warned me against ever teaching in a segregated college if at all possible. They believed I should pursue the goal of knocking down racial barriers in institutions of higher education.

During the Christmas holiday that first year at Howard, I was able to obtain a job at the main post office in Washington, D.C. It was a boring job, sorting mail during the graveyard shift, from 12 midnight to 8 A.M. My first night at work, I went with a fellow-classmate worker during the meal break to a White Tower eating-house across the street. When we walked in, I saw two vacant seats. I went and sat in one. My companion did not take the second seat. I soon found out why. The counterman came over, shouting that I was to get up. I could buy food to take out, but I was not allowed to sit and eat it. I asked him, "Why not?" He became even more angry and shouted louder that I would not be served because I was a Negro. I, too, became angry and did not want to leave. I felt the outrage that my mother expressed at the Childs restaurant many years before. My companion came over and said, "Let's get out of here." He escorted me out. At that time I was taking democracy seriously. A few blocks away the Capitol of the United States was visible and illuminated. As I was leaving, I looked at the building and cursed. I do not believe I have ever again entered a White Tower eating-house since that time.

This was another experience in hypocrisy in America. I learned in Washington, D.C., in the shadow of the Capitol, that democracy was not to be taken seriously. This lesson stayed with me throughout my college days at Howard University.

In my senior year I was part of a group of students who demonstrated inside the Capitol building. At that time, 1935, they did not serve Negroes in the restaurant. We marched into the building with signs protesting this racial exclusion. I shall not forget that a Negro attendant came up and started pushing some of us out. He punched a few of us. Even though this was long before the Martin Luther King Jr. training in nonviolent protest, we did not punch him back. I felt sorry and somewhat contemptuous of him.

Meanwhile, a cadre of white policemen came and arrested a number of us. We were taken to the nearest police station in a paddy wagon. When we got to the desk, we were told to remove our ties and belts. The desk sergeant asked the arresting policemen what the charges were. He was told, "Guilty of disorderly conduct." As the sergeant was taking our names, the captain of the precinct came out of his office and asked why we were there. The policemen and the desk sergeant repeated the charge against us. The captain became red in the face and ordered, "Take their names off the books. These young men should be praised, not arrested. Let them go. Let them go." I was fascinated by his anger, by the fact that he was white, and by his identification with the issues and goals.

The press carried the story. The *New York Times* carried it on the front page. When we returned to the campus the following Monday, we were brought up on discipline charges. The president of the university and the disciplinary committee made it clear that by our actions we were threatening the security of the university (Howard University received funds from Congress). The disciplinary committee said we would be suspended or expelled for our actions. While they decided which punishment to impose, we were asked to step outside. We could hear the debate going on in the conference room. I recognized the voice and passionate insistence of Ralph Bunche. He maintained that the disciplinary committee must not even consider suspending or expelling us. He argued that what we were doing was not only courageous, but essential in dealing with America's racial injustice. He maintained that Howard University would be embarrassed if it took any negative action against us. The implications were that if the disciplinary committee took such action against us, he would resign. After a prolonged discussion, we were brought back into the conference room and the disciplinary committee told us they had decided against punishing us.

I was then the editor of the college newspaper. I wrote an editorial to the effect that my fellow students and I were saved from being expelled by Ralph Bunche. His unmistakable position was that verbal expressions and concerns about racial injustice were not enough. It is important that those concerns go hand in hand with rational and courageous actions. I don't know how I would have managed at this stage of my life in dealing with those aspects of the racial injustice that impinged on me without the kind, considerate, generous, wise support I received from my good friends on the faculty.

Ralph Bunche and the other Howard professors I had come to know well encouraged me to go to Columbia University for graduate work. They maintained that it was essential to combine academic credentials with the capacity and qualifications for activism. They led me to believe that I was to be a part of the ongoing struggle for social justice. And I was naive and confident enough to believe I could do it. I received encouragement and support in my decision to pursue a Ph.D. in psychology at Columbia University.

Around 1936, Professor Otto Klineberg of Columbia University came to Howard University to give a talk on social psychology, with particular emphasis on his research on racial differences. I was impressed with the sagacity, humanity, and objectivity of his ideas. I decided I would like to study with him while working on my Ph.D. at Columbia. I told my major psychology professor at Howard, Dr. Francis Cecil Sumner, of this goal. He encouraged me to apply and assured me I would have no difficulty in being admitted for graduate work at Columbia. He was practical, however, and advised me to apply to at least two or three other universities as well. He wrote strong letters of recommendation for me. We agreed that I should apply to Columbia and to Cornell. We felt sure that on the basis of my academic record and his recommendations, I would be admitted to both universities.

Within a month after submitting my application, I received a letter from Cornell informing me that my credentials and recommendations were most acceptable. However, they had decided, after serious consideration, that it would not be wise to admit me to their Ph.D. program. They stated that the small number of doctoral students worked very closely with the faculty in laboratories, in classrooms, and in seminars, and that they worked socially with each other. For that reason, they did not believe I would be happy in their doctoral department. I was irritated and affronted by this decision. I shared with Dr. Sumner the letter I wrote in response assuring Cornell that I had not applied to the university to be "happy." Rather, I was seeking to meet the requirements for my Ph.D.

Soon after this disturbing conflict with Cornell, I received a letter from Columbia University saying that on the basis of my academic record and the letters of recommendation from my major professors at Howard, they were pleased to admit me to the Ph.D. program in psychology. No mention of my race or my personal desire to be "happy" was made. Ironically, I was in fact happy because Columbia had been my number one choice, and I had looked forward to working with Otto Klineberg in social psychology.

My experience at Columbia was most stimulating. Most of my professors held high standards which they expected their graduate students to meet and maintain. Before being accepted into the final stage of the Ph.D. program, the graduate students were required to take and pass the Ph.D. general matriculation examination. I accepted this challenge without anxiety.

I later learned from Professor Klineberg that I had passed that exam at the highest level. After the members of the department evaluated the students' performance on this exam, it was agreed that the quality of my response was outstanding, and superior to that of the other students who took the exam at that time. Needless to say, I was "happy" when I heard this.

Professor Robert Woodworth, dean of American psychologists, and retired chairman of the Department of Psychology, invited me to visit him in his office. He asked me a number of questions about my academic background. He wanted to know about Professor Sumner and other professors at Howard University. It was clear to me that he had not expected a Negro student from a traditional black university to meet and surpass the Ph.D. standards of the Department of Psychology at Columbia University. I tried to explain to him, and to other professors who raised these questions directly or indirectly, that Professor Sumner and the other professors at Howard had prepared me to meet the standards and requirements for a Ph.D. at any first-rate American university. From this point on, the question of my race and the nature of the psychology program at Howard became secondary. My performance in seminars, my papers, and my contributions to general discussions concerning research projects which were part of the Ph.D. plan dominated my involvement in and enjoyment of the Ph.D. process.

My work with Otto Klineberg and, to a lesser extent, with Gardner Murphy formed the basis of my continued interest in social psychology. When it became evident that I was interested in the development and complexities of racial attitudes, I was gently advised by Gardner Murphy [author of *Human Nature and Enduring Peace*] and, to my surprise, even by Otto Klineberg, that I should not concentrate my research interest on specific racial problems. Subtly they suggested that this focus would raise political academic problems. I accepted their advice and concentrated my research on the effects of social attitudes on remembering. This dissertation research problem was accepted by the department without question and I was invited to join Sigma Xi, the national scientific honorary society. In spite of the fact that I was the only black student in the Ph.D. program and thus the first black to be granted a Ph.D. in psychology at Columbia University, I was personally and academically "happy" in pursuing the process and attaining the goal.

By the time I had received my Ph.D., I was confident that I would be invited by the psychology faculty at Columbia to assume a junior faculty position, which I believed was the usual route for Ph.D.'s. That was not so. Apparently my Columbia professors assumed that I would return to teach at a traditionally black college. They did not take seriously my previous indications that I wanted to teach psychology at one of the academic institutions where my Columbia classmates had been hired. I persisted and continued to inquire about the possibilities of obtaining a nonracial opportunity.

At this time, Columbia University Professor Gardner Murphy accepted the position of chairman of the Department of Psychology at the College of the City of New York. I was aware that there were no blacks as regular faculty members in any department at CCNY. Nevertheless, I spoke with Professor Murphy of my desire to be appointed to the CCNY Psychology Department. Soon after our discussions, I received an invitation to become an instructor. As part of the usual process of evaluation and promotion, senior members of the department visited my classes and observed my teaching methods and style. I received their approval. I felt comfortable with the members of the department. I felt even more accepted when Gardner Murphy invited me to contribute a chapter to a book he was editing, entitled *Human Nature and Enduring Peace*. He accepted and published my chapter with professional and personal praise. Each year it became increasingly apparent that I was being seriously considered for tenure and promotion.

One day I received a visit from the academic dean of Hampton Institute, who informed me that he and the president of Hampton were inviting me to build a psychology department from scratch. I was promised freedom and the necessary resources toward this goal. In spite of my earlier desire not to return to a traditionally black college, and after discussions with my wife, with Dr. Sumner, with Dr. Bunche, and probably my ego and greed for the increased salary also played a part—I accepted the invitation.

My early months at Hampton Institute were challenging. I tried to stimulate my students by combining social psychology concepts with American racial attitudes and realities. For the most part, my students understood and responded positively to this approach. Then I received an invitation to dinner from President McLean. He was white, and had formerly been the chairman of President Franklin Roosevelt's Committee on Fair Employment Practice. He was generally respected as a racial liberal. This reputation was one of the reasons I had accepted the Hampton invitation. During the early part of the evening, President McLean was most affable and gracious. I thought our discussion pleasant. To my surprise, during after-dinner drinks, the quality of his conversation shifted. It was then that I found that his agenda was to communicate to me his displeasure with the fact that I was agitating my students by introducing racial problems in class discussions. He stated unequivocally that the purpose of Hampton Institute was not to disturb students and to create racial conflicts in them, but to help them adjust to and accept the realities of American life. I was shocked. I remembered the promise of freedom which was part of the Hampton invitation. I recall almost verbatim President McLean's final remarks to me. "Kenneth," he said, "I want you to understand how important it is for you to cooperate with me. If you understand our goals at Hampton, and prepare our students for our world of reality, I could make you the best-known black psychologist in America."

I don't remember what I said, but I knew then I was going to leave Hampton as soon as possible. When I told Dr. Sumner and Ralph Bunche of this surprising turn of events at Hampton and my desire to resign, they both agreed with me that I should. Very soon afterwards, on December 7, 1941, the bombing of Pearl Harbor projected the United States into World War II. Ralph Bunche advised me that this was the most appropriate time to leave Hampton and accept a position with the government. He arranged to have me placed with the Office of War Information.

At OWI, I was put in charge of a group of distinguished social psychologists. Our assignment was to study the state of morale among Negro civilians and their opinions about race and the war. The group was made up of black and white interviewers who were required to travel together throughout the country. As head of the group, it was my responsibility to inform the appropriate government officials in each community that we planned to work there.

Because we were working on an important war-related government assignment, my associates and I did not expect any difficulties. We certainly did not expect any racial problems. We soon learned, however, that the fact that I was black and head of a mixed group of black and white interviewers, both male and female, created difficulties everywhere. It was particularly troublesome in the southern communities. We could not meet in hotels where white members of the group could stay and black members could not. We had to meet in hotels where black members of the group could stay. Thus the white interviewers had to travel separately from the black and attend meetings in black hotels. We discovered that the local police were following the white members of the group, and remaining outside the hotels during our meetings. This obviously interfered with the performance of our work.

I called the top OWI administrator in Washington and was advised to inform the FBI of this infringement on our research. The FBI officials with whom I spoke had been aware of our problems. They knew that we were being followed by local police cars, but they were clearly indifferent. They stated that they were unable to be of any help. Given the dangers involved and the lack of support from the law enforcement officials, I felt there was little if anything I could do except to write up my reports and submit my resignation. I returned to my faculty position at CCNY.

These experiences made me increasingly cynical and bitter about the irrationality of American racism. Looking back on this stage of my life, I am surprised that my racial hostility did not spill over into my relationship with my colleagues at City College. They encouraged me to share with them some of my concerns and experiences, and they continued to be emphatic in their support. I was granted tenure and was promoted at appropriate times. I concentrated on my teaching and on the research I had undertaken in collaboration with my wife.

The specific research on the effects of racial prejudice on personality development and self-image of Negro children was originally Mamie Phipps's master's thesis research study. After receiving my B.S. at Howard University in 1935, I had stayed on to work on my master's degree. I was then invited to teach an introductory psychology course to the freshman class. In my class was Mamie Phipps, an outstanding student, of unusual poise, purpose, and intellectual ability. Mamie Phipps had come to Washington, D.C., from Hot Springs, Arkansas. She intended to major in mathematics. However, after being in my class, and consistently subject to my advice, she agreed to change her major from math to psychology. She graduated *magna cum laude* in 1938.

She continued at Howard for the next year, working on her master's degree. Initially her research was concerned with the general problem of the development of the self-image in children. At first this was not related to race. However, as her research was to be done in the segregated Washington, D.C., public schools, her subjects were restricted to Negro children because of her own race. Ironically, the racism of the school system made it possible to discover that race and color were key factors in the development of the sense of self in these children. When the significance of this factor of race became apparent to both of us, we decided to collaborate and conduct a more extensive study of the problem.

We were married in 1938, and I went to Columbia University to work on my Ph.D. After receiving her M.A. in 1939, Mamie was also admitted to Columbia University, seeking her Ph.D., which she received in 1944. We were then granted a postdoctoral Rosenwald Fellowship to continue our research. Using the larger number of children in both nonsegregated schools in northern states and segregated schools in southern states as the basis for our study, together with the development of an extensive methodology, we confirmed our earlier findings. It became even more clear that the majority of Negro children we studied incorporated into their developing self-image feelings of racial inferiority. Mamie and I were so disturbed by these results and their implications that we were reluctant to publish them. Otto Klineberg thought differently. Finally, in 1958, we agreed to publish our findings as a chapter in a book entitled *Readings in Social Psychology*, edited by Theodore M. Newcomb and Eugene L. Hartley.

In 1950 there was a conference held in Washington, D.C., known as the Mid-Century White House Conference on Children and Youth. Its theme was the personality development of American children. On its national advisory committee were two of my former professors, Alain Locke (Howard University) and Otto Klineberg (Columbia University). As they participated in the preliminary discussions and plans, they became increasingly troubled by the fact that none of the seminars, studies, and research being conducted for the conference included an examination of the effect of racial discrimination on the personality of American children. They finally persuaded their colleagues to invite me to prepare a summary report of the available and relevant psychological studies of this problem for the conference. The report I submitted was entitled "The Effects of Prejudice and Discrimination on Personality Development." This fact-finding report [see Appendix 2, this volume] was one of the documents made available for discussions, conclusions, and recommendations at the conference.

About a year after the Mid-Century White House Conference, around 1951, I received a visit from Robert L. Carter. He was an associate of Thurgood Marshall, the chief lawyer of the Legal Defense Fund of the NAACP. Carter informed me that the lawyers of the NAACP were engaged in litigation in the federal courts. They were seeking the repeal of the *Plessy v. Ferguson* doctrine of "separate but equal" which required or permitted racial segregation in the public schools. They were seeking to demonstrate to the courts that even if the conditions were adequate, racially separate schools could never be equal.

The lawyers for the cases asked Otto Klineberg for advice and help in demonstrating before the federal courts the inequality and damage inherent in segregated schools. The lawyers of the NAACP stated that they knew they could not show that school segregation resulted in physical or medical damage. They, therefore, had to prove the psychological damage inherent in racial segregation. They sought to argue that, as educational segregation was psychologically damaging to Negro children, this was in violation of the equal protection clause of the Fourteenth Amendment to the United States Constitution.

Otto Klineberg told them of the report which I had prepared and submitted to the Mid-Century White House Conference. He suggested that they discuss that document with me to determine whether it was relevant. Robert Carter visited my office to discuss with me the possibility of correlating the legal and psychological problems.

When Robert Carter described the problem to me, I found it more challenging. I told him I did not know if my report was relevant to the lawyers' objectives. I gave him a copy for their examination and analysis. I said that if Thurgood Marshall and his legal colleagues felt that it was useful, I would participate to the extent required. Within three weeks after receiving the report, Robert Carter returned to my office and stated that the report could not have been more relevant to their legal goals if it had been specially prepared for them. He then asked me to suggest possible roles for psychologists and social scientists in the trial level of the cases. I was to designate which of the scholars who had conducted research and published papers on the nature and effect of racial prejudice and segregation would be available to assume the role of expert witnesses at the trial level before the federal courts. I was asked to serve as liaison between the NAACP lawyers and the psychologists and social scientists.

There was a broad positive reaction when the Supreme Court handed down its decision on *Brown v. Board of Education.* A general optimism prevailed that at long last the United States was removing legal support from racial restrictions, rejections, and oppression. However, this euphoria was eclipsed by two realities. First, as might be expected, some major southern political officials decided to resist compliance under the guise of states' rights and southern autonomy. Second, the Supreme Court itself vitiated the protective constitutional power of the May 17, 1954, decision by the ambiguous "deliberate speed" clause of the May 31, 1955, administrative decision. This later decision was employed by opponents of racial justice as an invitation to procrastinate in implementing *Brown* and to retain segregated schools.

The complexity and depth of American racism were reflected in the fact that, even while the *Brown* decision was opening the doors to the civil rights movement, the seeds of racial backlash were being sown. Even among some social scientists there was disagreement and discord. A number of social scientists at the conclusion of the trial level of school segregation cases had submitted, at the request of the NAACP lawyers, the *Social Science Appendix to the Legal Brief,* which was a summary of the trial level testimony [see Appendix 3, this volume]. This was accepted by the Supreme Court and noted in Footnote 11 [see Appendix 5, this volume] of the *Brown* decision. Following this, some social scientists were critical of the psychological findings, asserting that racial segregation was not damaging to children.

Attempts to desegregate northern public schools elicited an intense and sustained antibusing campaign in deference to *de facto* segregated schools. Curiously, after the *Brown* decision more students were attending segregated schools in northern cities, such as New York City, Chicago, Los Angeles, and Detroit, than in many southern communities. The educational and psychological damage inflicted upon the children in northern *de facto* segregated schools was as great as that in *de jure* segregated schools cited by the Supreme Court. Political and educational officials flagrantly ignored this fact. The *Brown* decision seemed to have had minimal effect on public education in northern communities.

Probably the most important consequence of *Brown,* however, was the increase of morale among blacks. It motivated them to seek and obtain equality in other areas of society: racial segregation and discrimination in public facilities, accommodations, and transportation were ruled unconstitutional by federal courts.

The nonviolent tactics and methods organized under the leadership of Martin Luther King Jr., greatly enhanced the strategy and increased the success of the civil rights movement. In 1964 and 1965, a coalition of black leaders—A. Philip Randolph, Roy Wilkins, Whitney Young, and others working together—prevailed upon the legislative and executive branches of the federal government to reinforce the Supreme Court decision by passage of the Civil Rights Act of 1964 and the Voting Rights Act of 1965. These two acts appeared to propel the nation toward racial justice. In spite of the continued resistance and the white backlash against desegregation and affirmative action, racial progress persisted. The United States Supreme Court remained firm in its insistence that the Constitution was essentially color-blind.

At the same time that progress in economic, political, and social equality was being observed, there were clues that racism was not being easily eradicated. One of the first tangible signs that the Supreme Court was tempering its previous approach toward racial equality came in the *Bakke* case in 1978. Ironically, the majority of the justices of the Court used the Civil Rights Act as the rationale for reducing the number of blacks to be admitted to the University of California medical school. This decision was made in spite of Justice Harry Blackmun's admonition:

In order to get beyond racism, we must first take account of race. . . . And in order to treat some persons equally, we must treat them differently. We cannot—we dare not—let the Equal Protection Clause perpetuate racial supremacy.

In spite of Justice Blackmun's insight, the civil rights process was being reduced by the subtle attitude and, at times, obvious arguments of "reverse discrimination." Some whites argued that the process of social justice for blacks resulted in injustice for whites. They maintained that obtaining equality for blacks could only be done at the expense of whites—especially white males. This mode of thinking persisted in spite of the evidence of past and continuing racial injustices.

At the time that this form of reasoning by white supremacists was gaining favor with decision makers, it was being paralleled by complex psychological reasoning on the part of black separatists. These black nationalists openly renounced racial desegregation, arguing that racial justice could be obtained only by their form of isolation and inverse racism. They received a disproportionate amount of attention from the press. One can assume that white supremacists and conservatives saw these black separatists as allies against the positive goals of the civil rights movement.

The steady progress of blacks in the political arena made possible by the implementation of the Voting Rights Act seemed to have reduced the influence of the black separatists. In communities with a high proportion of blacks, some succeeded in obtaining political office, and their success precluded an adherence to a Black Nationalist position.

The number of black elected officials has increased in the years since the Voting Rights Act. In 1970 there were 1,469 black elected officials in the

United States; in 1980 there were 4,912; in 1990, 7,370. The effect the increased number of black political officials has had on the status of blacks in general remains to be determined. Has it resulted in greater justice for blacks? Have economic opportunities for blacks demonstrably increased with political success? Has the educational system served black youth better?

Consistent indications suggest that the status of inner-city blacks has deteriorated. A small number of blacks have benefited from affirmative action and have moved into the middle class. But an increasing number have remained in the inner-city underclass. These serve as the symptom and the reality of current racism.

During the years before *Brown*, racial injustice was perceived in its southern manifestations. In the southern states, racism was direct, overt, and supported by law. Many northern-based civil rights institutions and individuals found this conduct offensive. They joined blacks and the NAACP lawyers in seeking the repeal of the *Plessy v. Ferguson*, the "separate but equal," doctrine.

When the historic 1954 *Brown* decision pronounced racial segregation illegal, it inspired an optimistic outlook tantamount to euphoria. I felt then that this was the beginning of major positive changes in American race relations. In spite of continued resistance by some southern politicians, the momentum of the civil rights movement and the nonviolent leadership of Martin Luther King gave hope for eventual racial justice.

In the enthusiasm of the period, it was not clear to many of us that racism was not limited to its flagrant forms found in the southern states where the glaring abuses could be remedied by litigation. We soon found that there were deeper, more profound forms of racial injustice to be found in northern states. In such large urban communities as Los Angeles, Boston, Chicago, Detroit, Philadelphia, and New York City, patterns of racial injustice were deeply imbedded in the social structure, and whites bitterly resisted change.

In spite of the clarity of the *Brown* decision, segregated schools not only continued, but in some cases actually increased as white parents moved away from inner cities toward suburbs. The antibusing movement was fundamentally a northern urban phenomenon. Of course, there have been some gains as a result of the civil rights laws of the 1960s. Yet, the resentment against affirmative action has been found more in northern than in southern communities. The optimism elicited by the *Brown* decision and the momentum of the civil rights movement did not last and the initial thrust has been retarded by the deep-seated forms of northern racism.

The existing total pattern and the cycle of pathology now inflicted upon the nonwhite underclass in our deteriorating inner cities are found in the buildings that are abandoned and in the human beings who are also abandoned. These are the symptoms of a deep and pervasive racism. Apparently the methods of previous civil rights struggles have not redressed that racism. Even the increased number of black elected officials are unable to increase justice and humanity for those who have been forgotten in the inner cities. More appropriate and effective methods must now be developed and used to obtain observable progress at this stage of the continuing struggle for racial justice. If this is not done, the civil rights movement will remain stagnant and the quest for racial justice will regress.

I write these words in my seventy-sixth year. My beloved wife is dead and my career is nearing an end. Reluctantly, I am forced to face the likely possibility that the United States will never rid itself of racism and reach true integration. I look back and I shudder at how naive we all were in our belief in the steady progress racial minorities would make through programs of litigation and education, and while I very much hope for the emergence of a revived civil rights movement with innovative programs and dedicated leaders, I am forced to recognize that my life has, in fact, been a series of glorious defeats.

NOTE

1. [*Editor's Note*: From Kenneth B. Clark, "Racial Progress and Retreat: A Personal Memoir," in Herbert Hill and James E. Jones, Jr., eds., *Race in America: The Struggle for Equality* (Madison: University of Wisconsin Press, 1993), 3–18. Reprinted by permission of the University of Wisconsin Press.]

CHAPTER 19

Afterword: An Academician and an Activist

Hilton B. Clark

My father's major contribution to this nation's dialogue on civil rights was adding substance to the debate.[1] Getting people to look at things rationally, objectively, and using hard data to substantiate opinions, direction, and action—not just shooting from the hip. He had a brilliant and involved career. His concern was people, and he demonstrated that by his consistency, perseverance, and longevity. Although he was an academic, I was not surprised when he became involved in the political process. He always dealt with the issues, and part of that was talking with allies and associates, as well as dealing with those with differing opinions. It was creative conflict, and he was very good at it.

I am not the most objective observer, but I believe his writings, speeches, and interviews in the mass media all contributed a kind of substance and documentation to issues and situations that had not really been a part of the civil rights conversation before he spoke out. There had been goals and objectives, but he added an academic emphasis, which was important. He was a prodigious writer and lecturer. He used to write three, four, or five drafts. He was rarely satisfied with the finished product. He was satisfied with the concepts, but it was the form he tried to get just right. He would show his drafts to my mother, and occasionally I would look at them. He was a superlative writer. His writings came from his teaching. He used tape recorders and dictation, and he wrote out his thoughts by hand. It was all one thing—the writing and the teaching. That is what he was, in essence, a college professor.

Kenneth Clark bridged the gap between academicians and activists in the streets because he was able to communicate plainly. He had the ability to go to the core of issues. He was not swayed when black power became popular but was able to examine the concept objectively. His concentration on hard facts and data kept him away from trends and what was merely popular. He was an academician to the core. People may not have liked what he said, but they had a hard time challenging it in terms of its validity. If you wanted to attack what he said, you had to get your facts together.

When I was growing up in Harlem, he was "Dad" at home and "Professor Clark" when he left the house. There was not an intermingling of the two people. It was not often that my mother and father would talk business at the dinner table. After my sister and I went to bed, we could sometimes hear them discussing issues, but the professional work was kept separate from the family. Still, to me he was the greatest dad in the world. We did things together, we went for drives, and we went to baseball games. He was an avid Brooklyn Dodger and Jackie Robinson fan. We went on vacations together as a family. We would go with our parents to Hyannis, Massachusetts; we drove across the country together, when my father taught a semester at Stanford; and we always celebrated the holidays together. He had a separate family life. For recreation, he barbecued and loved to entertain. He was loquacious, very much a social animal. He loved people, especially loved his children.

Attending elementary school in Hastings-on-Hudson, I experienced the more subtle forms of prejudice. At an early age I had the benefit of reading my father's book *Prejudice and Your Child*. It gave me a lot of insight into white people, actually, the development and impact of prejudice. I learned a lot from my father. I recall vividly attending many of my father's classes at City College. I had the opportunity to discuss his lectures with him afterward. One of the most incisive things my father said—it was during a small luncheon discussion—was: "How ironic it is that the increased level of our education is directly responsible for the increase in our ability to destroy ourselves." Another thing he said that I thought was brilliant is that our educational system did not teach us about character and morality and that was its major failing. I still believe that to this day. In fact, they are now talking about high schools introducing character courses. He suggested that many years ago.

Of all the activities in which he participated, the U.S. Supreme Court decision of 1954 was the one that most impacted our family. I was aware that he was involved in some very serious business. I didn't understand it, but it was clear from the radio and other sources that something big was going on, and there were a lot of expectations in terms of awaiting the May 17, 1954, decisions. But I was eleven years old, so I did not fully understand all of it.

It was during that exciting time that I met Bob Carter and Thurgood Marshall [the attorneys representing the NAACP before the United States Supreme Court]. My father felt good when Carter and Marshall asked him to provide evidence that "separate but equal" schools were injurious to black children. My father knew that his work—the so-called "doll study"—was relevant. I met many of the people working on that case.

My father and I have worked closely together. He has been supportive of me all of my life, no matter what I did, no matter how much I messed up. He was always there for me. I would say 90 percent of the time we have spent together has been very positive. Obviously, we have had our differences, but never on any major issues of principle. We ran a consultant human relations firm working with corporations, governmental agencies, and educational institutions dealing with affirmative action and equal employment opportunity laws that were developing at the time in our legal system.

I believe my father's work will be seen in the long view by historians as a pioneering effort. He was a professor, an academician; he brought those academic and professorial traits to social issues. He pioneered the concept of working as a participant observer, someone who was both researching and involved in the situation. He was a social activist. That will be his legacy.

NOTE

1. [*Editor's Note*: Hilton B. Clark has worked with his father for three decades. Dr. Clark sent his son to the private Kent School in Connecticut after the eighth grade, and then to Columbia University Law School. "I wanted him to understand the power and training of people who wield power," Dr. Clark once said. From Walter Goodman, interview in the *New York Times*, March 17, 1983, 14.]

CHAPTER 20

Epilogue

The problem of the twenty-first century will be the problem of the color line. . . . By any standard of measurement or evaluation the problem has not been solved in the twentieth century and thus becomes a part of the legacy and burden of the next century. (John Hope Franklin, *The Color Line: Legacy for the Twenty-first Century* [Columbia: University of Missouri Press, 1993], 5.)

Appendixes

Biography of Kenneth B. Clark[1]

Woody Klein

Dr. Kenneth B. Clark, one of America's most distinguished social scientists, has contributed a valuable body of work for more than half a century to the cause of improving race relations in America. A noted educator, psychologist, scholar, author, and civil rights advocate, he is best known for his key role in the landmark *Brown v. Board of Education* desegregation decision of the U.S. Supreme Court in 1954. Dr. Clark contributed an extraordinary study to the National Association for the Advancement of Colored People's brief in *Brown*, an appendix that contained data showing the damaging psychological effects of segregation on black children. The NAACP legal team, headed by Thurgood Marshall—who later became a U.S. Supreme Court justice—based its decision, in large part, on Dr. Clark's study.

Born in the Panama Canal Zone on July 24, 1914, and raised in the New York Harlem ghetto, Dr. Clark has devoted a lifetime to the eradication of institutionalized racism and to improving the quality of education in our nation's schools. He has had a profound effect on public policy and public education in America. He is a Phi Beta Kappa graduate from Howard University where he received his bachelor's and master's degrees. He was soon to join the company of many distinguished social scientists who had come before him when he then became the first black Ph.D. in psychology at Columbia University.[2] He taught for a while at Hampton Institute in Virginia, worked as chief research assistant to Swedish Nobel Prize winner Gunnar Myrdal on his epic *An American Dilemma*, volunteered to work in the Office of War Information, where in 1941–1942 he did a study of the morale of Negroes on the home front during World Wars I and II. In 1942, he joined the City College (now City University) of New York, where he served for thirty-three years and eventually retired as a Distinguished University Professor Emeritus in 1975. During his tenure there, he also was director of the Dynamics Research Institute of the City College. He served as a visiting professor at Columbia and Harvard Universities and at the University of California, Berkeley, Brooklyn College, and Queens College in New York.

He served as a member of the Board of Regents of the State of New York for twenty years and as a member of the Board of Trustees of the Woodrow Wilson International Center for Scholars at Princeton, as well as Antioch College. Among his many awards are the Spingarn Medal from the NAACP, the Kurt Lewin Memorial in 1966, and the Sidney Hillman Peace Prize Book Award in 1965. In 1985, he was awarded an honorary Doctor of Laws by Georgetown University for his "intellectual integrity and lifelong dedication on behalf of racial justice and civil rights," and in 1979, he was honored by the Joint Center for Political Studies in Washington, DC, an organization he helped to create. In addition, he supervised projects for the Commonwealth of Massachusetts and the State of New York, the Rockefeller Foundation, and the cities of Newark, New Jersey, and White Plains, New York, and the Washington, DC public schools system.

In 1946, he founded—together with his wife, Dr. Mamie Phipps Clark— the Northside Center for Child Development to assist emotionally disturbed Harlem children. In 1964, he founded Harlem Youth Opportunities Unlimited (HARYOU), dedicated to making a better life for black youth and overcoming the pathology of the ghetto. In 1967, he formed the consulting firm of Clark, Phipps, Clark and Harris, and subsequently the Metropolitan Applied Research Center in New York City, in which he served as a consultant on race relations and affirmative action programs to numerous organizations, among them Princeton University, Massachusetts Institute of Technology, Western Electric, The Chase Manhattan Bank, Seagram's, the Rand Corporation, the government of Bermuda, American Telephone and Telegraph, Con Edison, IBM, and Chemical Bank Corporation. He also served as a consultant to the Personnel Division of the U.S. Department of State; as a member of the board of directors of Harper & Row, the Lincoln Savings Bank, the University of Chicago, and the Woodrow Wilson International Center for Scholars; chairman of the Affirmative Action Committee of the Urban Development Corporation; and as president of the American Psychological Association, which honored him with the first annual "Award for Distinguished Contributions to Psychology in the Public Interest" in 1978, which read:

A pioneer in the Civil Rights Movement and in the continuing fight for equality and justice for all individuals, Professor Kenneth B. Clark has expertly translated fundamental principles of human behavior—many of which he discovered and formulated during his brilliant career as a scholar—into politics and programs that have deepened the sense of self-respect and raised the hopes and expectations of countless individuals of every age, race, and creed. He has unselfishly served federal, state, and local governments; public and private education; community agencies; and, of course, the profession of psychology. But perhaps his most enduring contribution is the brilliance and clarity with which he has demonstrated that the social sciences—and, in particular the field of psychology—can contribute to—and have responsibility to contribute to—determining the quality of life we experience and provide for others.

Dr. Clark is the author of fifteen books, including *Prejudice and Your Child* (1955), *The Negro Protest: Interviews with James Baldwin, Malcolm X, and Martin Luther King, Jr.* (1963), *Dark Ghetto: Dilemmas of Social Power* (1965), *The Negro American* with co-editor Talcott Parsons (1966), *A Relevant War against Poverty*, co-authored with Jeanette Hopkins (1969), and *Pathos of Power* (1974). In 2000, Dr. Clark's lifetime achievements were honored with the opening of The Kenneth B. Clark Center at the University of Illinois at Chicago (UIC) campus, a research institution in UIC's Criminal Justice Department. The Clark Center's stated purpose is to use social research to help poor communities share in the benefits of the new information economy. Dr. Clark resides in Hastings-on-Hudson, New York.

NOTES

1. Adapted by the author from material in the Clark Archives.
2. Dr. Clark graduated from Howard University in 1938 with a master's degree and registered at Columbia University, where highly respected psychologists Otto Klineberg and Gardner Murphy and famed anthropologists Margaret Mead, Franz Boaz, and Ruth Benedict had created the beginnings of the social sciences.

APPENDIX 2

Mid-Century White House Conference on Children and Youth: Paper, "The Effects of Prejudice and Discrimination on Personality Development," by Kenneth B. Clark

[*Editor's Note*: This research paper served as the basis of the U.S. Supreme Court's *Brown v. Board of Education* decision. The following are excerpts from that paper.][1]

Prejudice may be seen as one of the many ways in which man has attempted to understand and manipulate his environment and his fellow human beings. The growth and development of crystallized prejudices would seem to be part of the general pattern of growth and expression of the discriminative and evaluative powers of man—the development of increasingly complex cultures. Other aspects of this same pattern are: all rules and rituals which govern those aspects of human behavior which are not biologically imperative; culturally supported or transmitted myths, taboos, beliefs; dietary regulations and religious and mystical concepts; the society-defined status of women in relation to men; and the myriad of individual preferences, aversions and irritations.

Racial and religious prejudices, like other forms of prejudices, may be seen as a form of thinking characterized by (1) the recognition or creation of differences; (2) the emphasizing and evaluation of these differences; (3) the ascribing of differential status through the exercise of preference rejection or exclusion; and (4) the simplification of experience and meaning and the development of a pattern of generalization which leads to an apparent increase in the efficiency with which the individual copes with relevant social experiences.

A discussion of the nature of prejudice without including a discussion of overt cruelty (as one of its essential ingredients) would be meaningless academic abstraction having little or no relation to social reality. It may well be that the problem of human prejudices may in the long run be better understood through the study of the more basic problems of the nature and determinants of cruelty—the expression of non-rational, non-adaptive hostility and aggression—in man.

It seems clear that each society seeks to enforce its system of values, ideas, beliefs and patterns of behavior upon each individual who seeks adjustment within it. The usual positive determinants of socialization of the individual are almost always supplemented, either actually or potentially, by some negative means of social control; e.g., ridicule, name calling, threat of ostracism, physical punishment, and in extreme cases, death. The threat which the non-conformist presents to the subjective security of the given society seems directly proportional to the intensity of the methods used against him. It appears that this is one of the lessons, which each individual must learn—consciously or unconsciously—during the process of his socialization. A further hypothesis might be stated as follows: The apparent ease with which an individual accepts and practices prejudice might be a function of his desire to escape the probability of his being the object of the punishment and cruelty ordinarily directed toward the out-group member; or to avoid the hostile methods used by the society to compel conformity from its in-group members.

The inferior status of the American Negro—and presumably overt manifestations of prejudice toward any religious, ethnic or national minority—are seen from this point of view as a patent contradiction of the American Creed: "... of the essential dignity of the individual human being, of the fundamental equality of all men, and of certain inalienable rights to freedom, justice, and a fair opportunity."

A motivational approach to the understanding of this apparent contradiction would start with an attempt to understand the basic factors at work in the colonization, development, and the eventual emergence of America as a world power. One clear fact emerges; namely, that all Americans (save Indians) were at one time immigrants or the descendents of immigrants. Each wave of newcomers had in common the fact that the group was feeling either economic hardships, religious or political persecution or social humiliation. The people who were to make up this new nation, therefore, were driven by some form of basic and immediate personal and/or group *insecurity*. This insecurity must have been strong enough to compensate for the disadvantages and discomforts involved in leaving their homeland and migrating to a new world to form a new nation. In time America became the land of opportunity—the land which promised a security which was denied the marginal or non-conforming men of the old world.

If one accepts the assumption that inherent in the very formation of the American nation was this basic *insecurity* motivation, then it is possible to understand the pattern of American civilization and culture in terms of a basic internal consistency. It would seem that the initial insecurity of the American "character structure" did not only result in a systematic exploitation of the natural resources of the new land, a pushing back of the frontiers, a glorification of work, and the rise of a technology which has practically dominated the culture; but also resulted in a fundamental concern with the ideas and practices of general equalitarianism and political democracy. The entrenchment in the culture of the verbalized ideals of the "American Creed" can be seen as determined by the insecurity motives—the past inferiority status—which made their native land no longer tolerable. It seems reasonable to assume that the "American Creed," like American technology, was another technique accepted and sustained in order to obtain a security and integrity, which had been previously denied. If this be true, it may offer us an explanation of the relationship between American protestations of brotherhood and equality and the American form of social and racial prejudices. It is conceivable from a psychological, if not from a rational, point of view that an insecure individual in quest of security and status may seek to obtain it not only through positive objective methods: e.g., work and personal achievement, but may attempt to enhance his personal status by denying security to another person or group. The ability to exercise this power over another may bring with it a subjective security and status feeling, which equal in degree of satisfaction that received by actual concrete effort. The white American's espousal of the American Creed is real and meaningful for him. It is the expressing of *his* desire for equality, status and security. His denial of these to the Negro is a manifestation of this same desire for status and an enhancement of his subjective feelings of having obtained a superior status. From this dynamics level the American Creed and American racism are not contradictory but compatible ingredients of the American pattern. Each has the same motivation: an intense drive for status and security, which the white American can back with power. Seen within this framework, prejudice appears as a recurrent feature of American life and history.

It would appear, therefore, that if the resolution of the American dilemma is in the direction of realization of the American Creed it will not be because of the power of ideals, themselves, or because of the apparent contradiction, but because the pressure of economic, social, and political events within the national scene and in the area of international relations would have forced America to adhere to these ideals as the most effective and realistic weapon of defensive and offensive competition with opposing ideologies and power structures.

It is only within a moral framework that science can evaluate the effects of prejudices and discrimination upon human personalities and seek to determine methods for bringing about desirable social changes. The imperativeness of a moral framework in social science does not relieve the social scientist in his quest for facts of the responsibility for maintaining a tough-minded attitude, free from stultifying dogmatic preconceptions. In fact, it imposes upon him greater responsibilities to obtain the freedom necessary to search for his facts unfettered by biases, myths, mysticism and the pleadings of special privilege. He must be guided by his intelligence, integrity and dedication to the quest for truth so far as it is available to man even though in his interpretation of the meaning of these facts he is required to evaluate in terms of moral standards.

Nor does the moral framework of social science give to the social scientist the license to impose upon social reality his own moral concepts, which the realities may or may not have. A clear concept of the nature of the actual reality seems essential to the ability to interpret or evaluate it. When one examines the statistics in the area of indices of social disorganization in America in terms of racial breakdown, one consistently finds that the Negro in general is found in a more disadvantaged position compared to the general norms of the white American. Statistics in the following areas confirm this: (1) housing standards, slums, population density in northern urban Negro ghettoes; (2) family stability patterns, broken homes, deserted and working mothers; (3) families on public charity, aid to dependent children; (4) maternal and infant mortality statistics, childhood diseases, deficiency diseases and diseases indicative of malnutrition and generally low environmental conditions; (5) quality of schooling, amount of schooling, dropouts; (6) discrepancy in job opportunities, evidence on types of jobs obtained by Negro youth; (7) delinquency rates in urban areas; (8) incidence of institutionalization in correctional institutions and northern hospitals for mentally disturbed.

The positive findings in these areas must be seen in terms of the detrimental effects of racial prejudice not only upon the Negro youth but also as a threat to the very foundations of the society as a whole. The alternative to this interpretation is that these are indications of the inherent inferiority of the Negro people which is not only reflected in the indices of social disorganization among them but is also a prime cause of prejudice and discrimination. In the light of the more recent findings in anthropology, psychology, and sociology, this latter hypothesis seems no longer tenable.

To discuss intergroup prejudices in children in terms of whether these prejudices are inborn or instinctive is, at the present stage of psychology, a spurious statement of the issue. The evidence from recent researches in

social psychology strongly indicates that prejudices are learned by children—that children acquire the social antipathies which are prevalent in
that particular culture.

It would seem a mistake, however, to conclude that because children
acquire their prejudices toward people of different colors, religion or nationality, that these acquired prejudices are any less fundamentally a part
of the individual, any less intense, complex or detrimental in effect than if
they were inborn. It is also true that children are not born with the ability
to speak any specific human language. In the course of their development
and socialization normal children acquire the ability to speak fluently and
efficiently the particular language of their social environment. This language then becomes an intrinsic aspect of their own person.

In a similar manner they learn the social language, status symbols, roles
and norms. The acquisition of intergroup prejudices by children is an integral aspect of their socialization within those cultures, in which these
prejudices exist. If this be true then the issue can be more effectively stated
in the following terms: How do children acquire their prejudices? What are
the conditions which facilitate the acquisition and intensification of antipathies toward different groups of people? What can be done to prevent the
development of stultifying and detrimental prejudices in children?

NOTE

1. [*Editor's Note*: From Kenneth B. Clark, 1st Draft: "The Effects of Prejudice
and Discrimination on Personality Development," Fact-Finding Report, Mid-
Century White House Conference on Children and Youth, Children's Bureau, Federal Security Agency, 1950 (mimeographed). "Kenneth Bancroft Clark, A Register
of His Papers in the Library of Congress," Professional File, Box 104, January 25,
1950, The Library of Congress, Manuscript Division, Washington, DC.]

"Appendix to Appellant's Briefs—The Effects of Segregation and the Consequences of Desegregation: A Social Science Statement," by Kenneth B. Clark, Principal Author

[*Editor's Note*: Dr. Clark was the principal author in drafting the "Social Science Statement" signed in 1952 by thirty-five psychologists and medical doctors that was submitted to the Court as an Appendix to Appellant's Briefs, the NAACP's brief that brought him to the attention of the legal and social science communities. Excerpts from that work follow.][1]

I THE PROBLEM

The problem of the segregation of racial and ethnic groups constitutes one of the major problems facing the American people today. It seems desirable, therefore, to summarize the contributions which contemporary social science can make toward its resolution. There are, of course, moral and legal issues involved with respect to which the signers of the present statement cannot speak with any special authority and which must be taken into account in the solution of the problem. There are, however, also factual issues involved with respect to which certain conclusions seem to be justified on the basis of the available scientific evidence. It is with these issues only that this paper is concerned. Some of the issues have to do with the consequences of segregation, some with the problems of changing from segregated to unsegregated practices. These two groups of issues will be dealt with in separate sections below. It is necessary, first, however, to define and delimit the problem to be discussed. For purposes of the present statement, *segregation* refers to that restriction of opportunities for different types of associations between the members of one racial, religious, national or geographic origin, or linguistic group and those of other groups, which results from or is supported by the action of any official body or agency, representing some branch of government. We are not here concerned with such segregation as arises from the free movements of individuals which are neither enforced nor supported by official bodies, nor with the segregation of criminals or of individuals with communicable diseases which aims at protecting society from those who might harm it.

Where the action takes place in a social milieu in which the groups involved do not enjoy equal social status, the group that is of lesser social status will be referred to as the *segregated* group. In dealing with the question of the effects of segregation, it must be recognized that these effects do not take place in a vacuum, but in a social context. The segregation of Negroes and of other groups in the United States takes place in a social milieu in which "race" prejudice and discrimination exist. It is questionable in the view of some students of the problem whether it is possible to have segregation without substantial discrimination. Myrdal states: "Segregation is financially possible and, indeed, a device of economy only as it is combined with substantial discrimination" (p. 629). The imbeddedness of segregation in such a context makes it difficult to disentangle the effects of segregation per se from the effects of the context. Similarly, it is difficult to disentangle the effects of segregation from the effects of a pattern of social disorganization commonly associated with it; and reflected in high disease and mortality rates, crime and delinquency, poor housing, disrupted family life and general substandard living conditions. We shall, however, return to this problem after consideration of the observable effects of the total social complex in which segregation is a major component.

II FACT-FINDING REPORT

At the recent Mid-Century White House Conference on Children and Youth, a fact-finding report on the effects of prejudice, discrimination and segregation on the personality development of children was prepared as a basis for some of the deliberations. This report brought together the available social science and psychological studies which were related to the problem of how racial and religious prejudices influenced the development of a healthy personality. It highlighted the fact that segregation, prejudices and discriminations, and their social concomitants potentially damage the personality of all children—the children of the majority group in a somewhat different way than the more obviously damaged children of the minority group.

The report indicates that as minority group children learn the inferior status to which they are assigned—as they observe the fact that they are almost always segregated and kept apart from others who are treated with more respect by the society as a whole—they often react with feelings of inferiority and a sense of personal humiliation. Many of them become confused about their own personal worth. On the one hand, like all other human beings they require a sense of personal dignity; on the other hand, almost nowhere in the larger society do they find their dignity as human beings respected by others. Under these conditions, the minority group child is thrown into a conflict with regard to his feelings about himself and his group. He wonders whether his group and he himself are worthy of no more respect than they receive. This conflict and confusion leads to self-hatred and rejection of his own group.

The report goes on to point out that these children must find ways with which to cope with this conflict. Not every child, of course, reacts with the same patterns of behavior. The particular pattern depends upon many interrelated factors, among which are the stability and quality of his family relations; the social and economic class to which he belongs; the cultural and educational background of his parents; the particular minority group to which he belongs; his personal characteristics, intelligence, special talents, and personality pattern.

Some children, usually of the lower socio-economic classes, may react by overt aggressions and hostility directed toward their own group or members of the dominant group. Anti-social and delinquent behavior may often be interpreted as reactions to these racial frustrations. These reactions are self-destructive in that the larger society not only punishes those who commit them, but often interprets such aggressive and anti-social behavior as justification for continuing prejudice and segregation.

Middle class and upper class minority group children are likely to react to their racial frustrations and conflicts by withdrawal and submissive behavior. Or, they may react with compensatory and rigid conformity to the prevailing middle class values and standards and an aggressive determination to succeed in these terms in spite of the handicap of their minority status.

The report indicates that minority group children of all social and economic classes often react with a generally defeatist attitude and a lowering of personal ambitions. This, for example, is reflected in a lowering of pupil morale and a depression of the educational aspiration even among minority group children in segregated schools. In producing such effects, segregated schools impair the ability of the child to profit from the educational opportunities provided him.

Many minority group children of all classes also tend to be hypersensitive and anxious about their relation with the larger society. They tend to see hostility and rejection even in those areas where these might not actually exist.

The report concludes that while the range of individual differences among members of a rejected minority group is as wide as among other peoples, the evidence suggests that all of these children are unnecessarily encumbered in some ways by segregation and its concomitants.

With reference to the impact of segregation and its concomitants on chil-

dren of the majority group, the report indicates that the effects are somewhat more obscure. Those children who learn the prejudices of our society
are also being taught to gain personal status in an unrealistic and non-
adaptive way. When comparing themselves to members of the minority
group, they are not required to evaluate themselves in terms of the more
basic standards of actual personal ability and achievement. The culture
permits and, at times, encourages them to direct their feelings of hostility
and aggression against whole groups of people; the members of which are
perceived as weaker than themselves. They often develop patterns of guilt
feelings, rationalizations and other mechanisms which they must use in an
attempt to protect themselves from recognizing the essential injustice of
their unrealistic fears and hatreds of minority groups.

The report indicates further that confusion, conflict, moral cynicism, and
disrespect for authority may arise in majority group children as a consequence of being taught the moral, religious and democratic principles of
the brotherhood of man and the importance of justice and fair play by the
same persons and institutions who, in their support of racial segregation
and related practices, seem to be acting in a prejudiced and discriminatory
manner. Some individuals may attempt to resolve this conflict by intensifying their hostility toward the minority group. Others may react by guilt
feelings which are not necessarily reflected in more humane attitudes toward the minority group. Still others react by developing an unwholesome,
rigid, and uncritical idealization of all authority figures—their parents,
strong political and economic leaders. As described in *The Authoritarian
Personality*, they despise the weak, while they obsequiously and unquestioningly conform to the demands of the strong whom they also, paradoxically, subconsciously hate.

With respect to the setting in which these difficulties develop, the report
emphasized the role of the home, school, and other social institutions. Studies have shown that from the earliest school years children are not only
aware of the status differences among different groups in the society but
begin to react with the patterns described above.

This seems to be true for the following reasons among others: (1) because
enforced segregation results from the decision of the majority group without the consent of the segregated and is commonly so perceived; and (2)
because historically segregation patterns in the United States were developed on the assumption of the inferiority of the segregated.

In addition, enforced segregation gives official recognition and sanction
to these other factors of the social complex, and thereby enhances the effects of the latter in creating the awareness of social status differences and
feelings of inferiority. The child who, for example, is compelled to attend
a segregated school may be able to cope with ordinary expressions of prejudice by regarding the prejudiced person as evil or misguided; but he can-

not readily cope with symbols of authority, the full force of the authority of the State—the school or the school board, in this instance—in the same manner. Given both the ordinary expression of prejudice and the school's policy of segregation, the former takes on greater force and seemingly becomes an official expression of the latter.

Not all of the psychological traits which are commonly observed in the social complex under discussion can be related so directly to the awareness of status differences—which in turn is, as we have already noted, materially contributed to by the practices of segregation. Thus, the low level of aspiration and defeatism so commonly observed in segregated groups is undoubtedly related to the level of self-evaluation; but it is also, in some measure, related among other things to one's expectations with regard to opportunities for achievement, and, having achieved, to the opportunities for making use of these achievements. Similarly, the hypersensitivity and anxiety displayed by many minority group children about their relations with the larger society probably reflects their awareness of status differences; but it may also be influenced by the relative absence of opportunities for equal status contact which would provide correctives for prevailing unrealistic stereotypes.

The preceding view is consistent with the opinion stated by a large majority (90 percent) of social scientists who replied to a questionnaire concerning the probable effects of enforced segregation under conditions of equal facilities. This opinion was that, regardless of the facilities which are provided, enforced segregation is psychologically detrimental to the members of the segregated group.

Similar considerations apply to the question of what features of the social complex of which segregation is a part contribute to the development of the traits which have been observed in majority group members. Some of these are probably quite closely related to the awareness of status differences to which, as has already been pointed out, segregation makes a material contribution. Others have a more complicated relationship to the total social setting. Thus, the acquisition of an unrealistic basis for self-evaluation as a consequence of majority group membership probably reflects fairly closely the awareness of status differences. On the other hand, unrealistic fears and hatreds of minority groups, as in the case of the converse phenomenon among minority group members, are probably significantly influenced as well by the lack of opportunities for equal status contact.

With reference to the probable effects of segregation under conditions of equal facilities on majority group members, many of the social scientists who responded to the poll in the survey cited above felt that the evidence is less convincing than with regard to the probable effects of such segregation on minority group members, and the effects are possibly less widespread. Nonetheless, more than 80 percent stated it as their opinion that the effects of such segregation are psychologically detrimental to the majority group members.

It may be noted that many of these social scientists supported their opinions on the effects of segregation on both majority and minority groups by reference to one or another or to several of the following four lines of published and unpublished evidence. First, studies of children throw light on the relative priority of the awareness of status differentials in facilities. On this basis, it is possible to infer some of the consequences of segregation as distinct from the influence of inequalities of facilities. Second, clinical studies and depth interviews throw light on the genetic sources and causal sequences of various patterns of psychological reaction; and, again, certain inferences are possible with respect to the effects of segregation per se. Third, there actually are some relevant but relatively rare instances of segregation with equal or even superior facilities, as in the cases of certain Indian reservations. Fourth, since there are inequalities of facilities in racially and ethnically homogeneous groups, it is possible to infer the kinds of effects attributable to such inequalities in the absence of effects of segregation and, by a kind of subtraction to estimate the effects of segregation *per se* in situations where one finds both segregation and unequal facilities.

III INTELLECTUAL QUALITY

One such question asks whether the inclusion of an intellectually inferior group may jeopardize the education of the more intelligent group by lowering educational standards or damage the less intelligent group by placing it in a situation where it is at a marked, competitive disadvantage. Behind this question is the assumption, which is examined below, that the presently segregated groups actually are inferior intellectually.

The available scientific evidence indicates that much, perhaps all, of the observable differences among various racial and national groups can be adequately explained in terms of environmental differences. It has been found, for instance, that the differences between the average intelligence test scores of Negro and white children decrease, and the overlap of the distributions increases, proportionately to the number of years that the Negro children have lived in the north. Related studies have shown that this change cannot be explained by the hypothesis of selective migration. It seems clear, therefore, that fears based on the assumption of innate racial differences in intelligence are not well founded.

It may also be noted in passing that the argument regarding the intellectual inferiority of one group as compared to another is, as applied to schools, essentially an argument for homogeneous groupings of children by intelligence rather than by race. Since even those who believe that there are innate differences between Negroes and whites in America in average intelligence grant that considerable overlap between the two groups exists, it would follow that it may be expedient to group together the superior whites and Negroes, the average whites and Negroes, and so on. Actually, many educators have come to doubt the wisdom of class groupings made homogeneous solely on the basis of intelligence. Those who are opposed to such homogeneous grouping believe that this type of segregation, too, appears to create generalized feelings of inferiority in the child who attends a below average class, leads to undesirable emotional consequences in the education of the gifted child, and reduces learning opportunities which result from the interaction of individuals with varied gifts.

A second problem that comes up in an evaluation of the possible consequences of desegregation involves the question of whether segregation prevents or stimulates interracial tension and conflict and the corollary question of whether desegregation has one or the other effect.

The most direct evidence available on this problem comes from observations and systematic study of instances in which desegregation has occurred. Comprehensive reviews of such instances clearly establish the fact that desegregation has been carried out successfully in a variety of situations although outbreaks of violence had been commonly predicted. Extensive desegregation has taken place without major incidents in the armed services both in Northern and Southern installations and involving officers and enlisted men from all parts of the country, including the South. Similar changes have been noted in housing and industry. During the last war, many factories both in the North and South hired Negroes on a non-segregated, non-discriminatory basis; while a few strikes occurred, refusal by management and unions to yield quelled all strikes within a few days.

Relevant to this general problem is a comprehensive study of urban race riots which found that race riots occurred in segregated neighborhoods, whereas there was no violence in sections of the city where the two races lived, worked and attended school together.

Under certain circumstances desegregation not only proceeds without major difficulties, but has been observed to lead to the emergence of more favorable attitudes and friendlier relations between races. Relevant studies may be cited with respect to housing, employment, the armed services and the merchant marines, recreation agency, and general community life.

Much depends, however, on the circumstances under which members of previously segregated groups first come in contact with others in unsegregated situations. Available evidence suggests, first, that there is less likelihood of unfriendly relations when the change is simultaneously introduced into all units of a social institution to which it is applicable—e.g. all of the schools in a school system or all of the shops in a given factory. When factories introduced Negroes in only some shops but not in the others the prejudiced workers tended to classify the desegregated shops as inferior, "Negro work." Such objections were not raised when complete integration was introduced.

The available evidence also suggests the importance of consistent and firm enforcement of the new policy by those in authority. It indicates also the importance of such factors as: the absence of competition for a limited number of facilities or benefits; the possibility of contacts which permit individuals to learn about one another as individuals; and the possibility of equivalence of positions and functions among all of the participants within the unsegregated situation. These conditions can generally be satisfied in a number of situations, as in the armed services, public housing developments, and public schools.

IV AN AGREEMENT

The problem with which we have here attempted to deal is admittedly on the frontiers of scientific knowledge. Inevitably, there must be some differences of opinion among us concerning the conclusiveness of certain items of evidence, and concerning the particular choice of words and placement of emphasis in the preceding statement. We are nonetheless in agreement that this statement is substantially correct and justified by the evidence, and the differences among us, if any, are of a relatively minor order and would not materially influence the preceding conclusions.

(Signed by)
Floyd H. Allport, Syracuse, New York; Gordon W. Allport, Cambridge, Massachusetts; Charlotte Babcock, M.D., Chicago, Illinois; Viola Bernard, M.D., New York, New York; Jerome S. Bruner, Cambridge, Massachusetts; Hadley Cantril, Princeton, New Jersey; Isidor Chein, New York, New York; Kenneth B. Clark, New York, New York; Mamie P. Clark, New York, New York; Stuart W. Cook, New York, New York; Bingham Dai, Durham, North Carolina; Allison Davis, Chicago, Illinois; Else Frenkel-Brunswik, Berkeley, California; Noel P. Gist, Columbia, Missouri; Charles S. Johnson, Nashville, Tennessee; Daniel Katz, Ann Arbor, Michigan; Otto Klineberg, New York, New York; David Krech, Berkeley, California; Paul F. Lazarsfeld, New York, New York; Alfred McClung Lee, Brooklyn, New York; R.M. MacIver, New York, New York; Robert K. Merton, New York, New York; Gardner Murphy, Topeka, Kansas; Theodore M. Newcomb, Ann Arbor, Michigan; Robert Redfield, Chicago, Illinois; Ira DeA. Reid, Haverford, Pennsylvania; Arnold M. Rose, Minneapolis, Minnesota; Gerhart Saenger, New York, New York; R. Nevitt Sanford, Poughkeepsie, New York; S. Stanfield Sargent, New York, New York; M. Brewster Smith, New York, New York; Samuel A. Stouffer, Cambridge, Massachusetts; Wellman Warner, New York, New York; Goodwin Watson, New York, New York; Robin M. Williams, Ithaca, New York.

—Dated: September 22, 1952.

NOTE

1. [*Editor's Note*: From Kenneth B. Clark, "Appendix to Appellant's Briefs—The Effects of Segregation and the Consequences of Desegregation: A Social Science Statement," Library of Congress, Clark Archives, Hastings-on-Hudson, NY, 1952, 1–12.]

APPENDIX 4

"Desegregation: An Appraisal of the Evidence," by Kenneth B. Clark

[*Editor's Note*: Following are excerpts of a paper by Dr. Kenneth B. Clark published in the *Journal of Social Issues* in 1953.[1] It was written in four parts: Part I. The Background: The Role of Social Scientists; Part II. The Question Posed and the Strategy of the Reply; Part III. Findings; and Part IV. Some Implications for a Theory of Social Change.]

PREFACE
BY M. BREWSTER SMITH, GENERAL EDITOR

Readers of this issue can rightly feel themselves to be participating in a momentous development of current history. As it [this issue] goes to press, the question pends before the United States Supreme Court of whether segregation by law of facilities for Negro and white children in the public schools shall be ruled unconstitutional, regardless of purported "equality." The case in terms of which the Court has accepted the burden of responsible decision represents the culmination of a long series, in which the legal staff of the NAACP has steadily widened the breach in the tight system of Jim Crow that was consolidated in the south by the turn of the century. What, the court asked in effect, is known about the social outcome of sudden or gradual desegregation? Here is the evidence.

In evaluating the experience to date with instances of desegregation, Dr. Clark took on a Herculean task. This summary of instances was available in the social science literature. The inventory of instances was at hand. . . . Entirely as a volunteer, though with the help of the NAACP staff, Dr. Clark has combed reports published in the most scattered quarters, corresponded, traveled, and interviewed to assemble a record that will be new to most of us. And he has drawn from this record a number of principles that summarizes the burden of this evidence.

So as to increase its value as a primary source, the issue presents *facts* and documentation in detail unusual for this Journal. The implications of the evidence for psychological and social scientists are drawn in the list of principles and in the concluding chapter, which must be regarded as significant contributions to social psychology.

But the importance of the issue is not merely historical and theoretical. Whatever the Court decides, the evidence presented here will in one way or another be an important resource for guiding enlightened decisions and practice in this critical realm of social policy.

PART I. THE BACKGROUND: THE ROLE OF SOCIAL SCIENTISTS BY DR. KENNETH B. CLARK

Proof of the arguments that segregation itself inflicts injuries upon the Negro had to come from the social psychologists and other social scientists.[2] Because of this fact it was necessary in the trying of these public school cases to develop an extensive collaboration between social psychologists and the legal profession, particularly the legal staff of the NAACP. This collaboration began before the trial of the first case in Federal District Court level and continued through the argument (December 1952) and reargument (December 1953) before the United States Supreme Court. The details and extent of this collaboration are presented here for the record and in order to serve as a guide for future collaboration between social psychologists and other social scientists and the legal profession.

In their work with the lawyers, the social psychologists assumed the following responsibilities:

(1) They testified in the Federal District Courts and in one State Court as expert witnesses on the effects of segregation on personality development, the effects of school segregation in lowering the motivation and impairing ability to learn, the social and psychological significance of a state-imposed racially segregated society, the consequences of desegregation, and the relationship between desegregation on the graduate and professional school level and the possibilities of desegregating the elementary and high schools. One social psychologist examined the Negro children involved in three of these cases with appropriate projective techniques and interviews in order to determine whether they showed evidence of personality distortions related to racial discrimination and segregation.

(2) They prepared *Appendix to Appellant's Briefs* entitled "The Effects of Segregation and the Consequences of Desegregation: A Social Science Statement." [See Appendix 3, this volume.] This appendix was submitted to and accepted by the United States Supreme Court during the October term, 1952, and was considered in conjunction with the legal briefs sub-

mitted in the South Carolina (*Briggs v. Elliott*), Kansas (*Brown v. Board of Education of Topeka*), and the Virginia (*Davis v. County School Board*) cases in the first argument before the U.S. Supreme Court in December 1952.

(3) They collected and analyzed relevant data on actual incidents of racial desegregation. This material was made available to the lawyers for their use in answering one of the five questions which the U.S. Supreme Court posed as the basis for the reargument in December 1953.

(4) One social psychologist, the present author [Dr. Clark], acted as general social science consultant to the Legal Staff of the NAACP. In this capacity, he served as liaison between the lawyers and the social psychologists who participated in these cases whether as expert witnesses or in helping to prepare the social science brief or both. It was his responsibility, further, to advise the lawyers on such matters as the special areas of competence of prospective expert witnesses; to suggest competent individuals who might accept the responsibility of testifying as expert witnesses; to approach such individuals when so directed by the legal staff; to attend certain conferences of the legal staff of the NAACP in order to become familiar with the legal issues, arguments, and terminology involved in these cases and in order to offer suggestions concerning the limits and scope of available and relevant social psychological data. He and others aided in the preparation of these cases for presentation both at the trial and at the appellate level; and in the Virginia case he and others helped in analyzing the testimony of expert social science witnesses called by the defendants so that inconsistencies and weaknesses in their testimony could be brought up in cross examination.

The original draft of the Social Science Brief was prepared by a special committee of SPSSI (The Society for the Psychological Study of Social Issues) under the chairmanship of Gerhart Saenger, which collected and analyzed the available data and theory on the effects of segregation on personality development.

The specific responsibility for preparing a preliminary draft of the report was given to Gerhart Saenger, Isidor Chein and Kenneth B. Clark. The final form of this report which was printed as the Appendix to Appellant's Briefs—The Effects of Segregation and the Consequences of Desegregation: A Social Science Statement resulted from the collaboration of Isidor Chein, Stuart Cook and Kenneth B. Clark in revising and rewriting the preliminary draft. Thirty-two social scientists, psychologists, and psychiatrists endorsed this statement which was submitted to the United States Supreme Court over their signatures.

In preparation for the reargument before the United States Supreme Court it was necessary to continue and broaden the scope of social science collaboration with the Legal Staff of the NAACP. This was so since the five questions posed by the Court as the basis for this reargument seemed primarily social science rather than legal questions. . . .

The first three questions were clearly within the province of those historians who were specialists in the post–Civil War period of American history and constitutional and legal history.

. . . An attempt was made to answer Question IV collecting and analyzing instances of change from a segregated to a nonsegregated situation. It was decided that this task was primarily the responsibility of social psychologists. The author [Dr. Clark] of this issue of the *Journal of Social Sciences* developed a research plan within the limits of the available time and budget in order to obtain empirical answers to this question.

PART II. THE QUESTION POSED AND THE STRATEGY OF THE REPLY

Among the questions posed[3] by the United States Supreme Court as the basis for the reargument of the five cases which challenge the constitutionality of state-imposed racial segregation in public elementary and high schools was the following:

(Question IV). Assuming it is decided that segregation in public schools violates the Fourteenth Amendment,

(a) Would a decree necessarily follow providing that, within the limits set by normal geographic school districting, Negro children should forthwith be admitted to schools of their choice, or

(b) May this court, in the exercise of its equity powers, permit an effective gradual adjustment to be brought about from existing systems to a system not based on color distinctions?

In attempting to answer this question [Question IV], it is necessary to make certain assumptions concerning the intent of the Court in asking it. A basic assumption which must be made is that this question suggests a concern that there might be important social problems which would arise if the Court were to decide that segregation in public schools is unconstitutional and on the basis of this finding were to issue a decree requiring that "within the limits set by normal geographic school districting, Negro children should forthwith be admitted to schools of their choice."

Part (b) of the question, therefore, may be seen as an attempt on the part of the Court to reconcile the legal and constitutional rights of Negroes with some "effective gradual adjustment" from the "existing segregated systems to a system not based on color distinctions." Implicitly this part of the question suggests that this approach is less likely to lead to social disruptions and, therefore, would be more socially desirable, provided it is possible to reconcile it with judicial powers, precedence, and procedures.

Although the specific legal issues inherent in this question are outside of the province of social science, the social scientists may provide the facts which would contribute answers to the above question and its implications.

The following are some of the questions which social scientists may seek to answer in light of the empirical evidence:

1. In what areas of American life have there been significant recent changes from racially segregated to unsegregated patterns?

   (a) How were these changes brought about? What were the actual mechanics of change? What type of preparation was made for the change?

   (b) What were some of the problems which arose in the transition from segregated to unsegregated systems?

   (c) How were these problems effectively dealt with?

   (d) What were the immediate and long range consequences of the change?

2. Does a direct and immediate order to change from a segregated to a nonsegregated situation in itself lead to major social disruptions?

3. Is a "gradual adjustment" or change from "segregated systems" "to a system not based on color distinctions" likely to be more "effective" than a direct and immediate change?

4. What are the conditions which determine the effectiveness of a change from racially segregated to nonsegregated systems?

The task of the social scientists in this phase of the litigations was (1) to attempt to answer the above questions through collecting and analyzing all of the available evidence, particularly in the south, as to whether and how a change from a segregated to nonsegregated situation can be smoothly and effectively accomplished; and (2) to present this evidence in a specific and concrete way in order to make clear the conditions under which nonsegregation has been and, therefore, can be, accomplished without severe or permanent disruption of a community.

Relevant information was obtained in the following ways: (1) examining of the available literature in social science journals, general periodicals, and newspapers which described or analyzed specific examples of changes in patterns of American race relations; (2) obtaining direct reports from individuals who observed directly or participated in situations which changed or were changing from a segregated to a racially nonsegregated pattern; (3) reading of relevant unpublished research manuscripts and unpublished research data.

In the *Appendix to Appellant's Briefs—the Effects of Segregation and the Consequences of Desegregation: A Social Science Statement,*[4] a summary of the contributions of contemporary social science on the consequences of segregation and some of the factors involved in changing from segregated to nonsegregated practices were presented. Upon the basis of the studies examined, the following conclusions are stated:

... desegregation has been carried out successfully in a variety of situations although outbreaks of violence had been predicted. Under certain circumstances, desegregation not only proceeds without major difficulties, but has been observed to lead to the emergence of more favorable attitudes and friendlier relations between the races.

The term *desegregation* is used in this report to describe the process of change in social situations or institutions from a system of organization in terms of separate facilities for whites and Negroes, exclusion of Negroes, or a deliberate restriction of the extent or area of participation of Negroes to a system wherein distinctions, exclusion, or restriction of participation based upon race no longer prevail. Desegregation seems a more descriptive term for the actual process which this report is concerned with than is the term racial integration. Desegregation is a more objective and empirical term and does not imply the complexity of social and individual adjustments and attitudinal factors which are inherent in the more evaluative term integration. Desegregation is also preferable to nonsegregation in that it connotes a process rather than a single act. Desegregation is considered *effective* in this report if it fulfills the following conditions: (a) was accomplished; (b) there was relative ease in overcoming initial resistance; (c) there was no loss, or there was an increase, in the general efficiency of functioning of the institution involved; (d) or any initial disruption or loss in efficiency was overcome as the desegregation process continued.

NOTES

1. [*Editor's Note*: From Kenneth B. Clark, "Desegregation: An Appraisal of the Evidence," *Journal of Social Issues* 9 (1953): 1–12.]

2. [*Editor's Note*: For a preliminary discussion of the role of social scientists as expert witnesses in these public school segregation cases and a consideration of some of the general problems that social scientists must solve as they seek to function in this area, see Kenneth B. Clark, "The Social Scientist as an Expert Witness in Civil Rights Litigation," *Social Problems* 1.1 (1953): 5–10. See Appendix 5, this volume.]

3. Otto Klineberg and Robert K. Merton of Columbia University aided in the development of the plan and were consulted by the author [Dr. Clark] during the early stages of the actual collection of data. Many other outstanding social scientists contributed to the collection of data in this research. All of the individuals who signed the Social Science *Appendix to Appellant's Briefs* were sent letters requesting help in the search for specific instances of desegregation. The majority responded immediately. Many of those who did not respond at that time could not do so because they were out of the country. It is not possible to list the many individuals who helped in the collection of data for this monograph. In many cases the cited references to unpublished memoranda, reports, and letters in the body of this report reflect those who have helped us in the collection of this data.

It is necessary to express my gratitude to my wife, Mamie P. Clark. Her constant encouragement and her practical help contributed significantly in the compilation and publication of this issue.

The major credit for the collection and use of these and other relevant data must go to Thurgood Marshall and Robert L. Carter and the other lawyers on the Legal Staff of the NAACP for having the foresight to recognize the need for this type of evidence and testimony, for making the decision to obtain it, and above all, for having the courage to push forward the frontiers of constitutional law and legal precedence by using this testimony at the trial and appellate level of these cases. In doing so, these lawyers made it possible for social science to have a more direct contact with this immediate practical problem of society.

4. [*Editor's Note*: Some 113 footnotes in this document list the sources of information, most of them psychologists, answering the questions.]

APPENDIX 5

"The Social Scientist as an Expert Witness in Civil Rights Litigation," by Kenneth B. Clark

[*Editor's Note*: Following are excerpts from a paper delivered by Dr. Kenneth B. Clark at a joint meeting of the Society for the Study of Social Problems and the Society for the Psychological Study of Social Issues, New York, February 14–15, 1953.][1]

During the last three years, the Legal Division of the National Association for the Advancement of Colored People has been making a frontal attack on state laws which require racially segregated elementary and high schools. For the first time these lawyers have extensively used expert social science testimony.[2]

In evaluating the testimony of the witnesses who were called by both sides in the school cases, it is clear that there were no essential differences among these social scientists on the crucial issue of the detrimental effects of segregation. Now that the precedent of admitting social science testimony has been established, it is certain that social scientists will be used in similar cases in the future.

The future uses of expert social science witnesses in civil rights litigation, however, raises some fundamental questions concerning the objectivity of testimony, the basis of testimony (research data, theoretical considerations, or personal opinion), and complex ethical considerations. As the gap between social science and legal considerations narrows, it becomes increasingly necessary for the social scientist to deal effectively with the responsibilities which accompany his activities in this area. This is particularly true since the present school cases may be viewed as merely the beginning of this type of social science—legal collaboration.

This additional role of the social scientist places upon him at least the following burdens: the social scientist who participates in civil rights or civil liberties litigation as an expert witness must exercise the maximum degree of care and objectivity in the collection and interpretation of the relevant data.

The social science testimony in the public schools segregation cases has opened the door of the courts to the social sciences. This now makes possible the direct use of social science findings in the process of social change.

NOTES

1. [*Editor's Note*: From Kenneth B. Clark, "The Social Scientist as an Expert Witness in Civil Rights Litigation," *Social Problems* 1.1 (1953): 5–10.]

2. See Thurgood Marshall, "An Evaluation of Recent Efforts to Achieve Racial Integration in Education through Resort to the Court," *Journal of Negro Education* (Summer 1952): 315–325.

U.S. Supreme Court: *Brown v. Board of Education* (Excerpts)[1]

Argued December 9, 1952, Reargued December 8, 1953, Decided May 17, 1954

MR. CHIEF JUSTICE WARREN delivered the unanimous opinion of the Court:

These cases come to us from the States of Kansas, South Carolina, Virginia, and Delaware. They are premised on different facts and different local conditions, but a common legal question justifies their consideration together in this consolidated opinion.

In each of the cases, minors of the Negro race, through their legal representatives, seek the aid of the courts in obtaining admission to the public schools of their community on a nonsegregated basis. In each instance, they had been denied admission to schools attended by white children under laws requiring or permitting segregation according to race. This segregation was alleged to deprive the plaintiffs of the equal protection of the laws under the Fourteenth Amendment.

The plaintiffs contend that segregated public schools are not "equal" and cannot be made "equal," and that hence they are deprived of the equal protection of the laws. Because of the obvious importance of the question presented, the Court took jurisdiction. Argument was heard in the 1952 Term, and reargument was heard this Term on certain questions propounded by the Court.

Today, education is perhaps the most important function of state and local governments. Compulsory school attendance laws and the great expenditures for education both demonstrate our recognition of the importance of education to our democratic society. It is required in the performance of our most basic public responsibilities, even service in the armed forces. It is the very foundation of good citizenship. Today it is a principal instrument in awakening the child to cultural values, in preparing him for later professional training, and in helping him to adjust normally to his environment. In these days, it is doubtful that any child may reasonably be expected to succeed in life if he is denied the opportunity of an education. Such an opportunity, where the state has undertaken to provide it, is a right which must be made available to all on equal terms.

We come then to the question presented: Does segregation of children in public schools solely on the basis of race, even though the physical facilities and other "tangible" factors may be equal, deprive the children of the minority group of equal educational opportunities? We believe that it does.

Segregation of white and colored children in public schools has a detrimental effect upon the colored children. The impact is greater when it has the sanction of the law, for the policy of separating the races is usually interpreted as denoting the inferiority of the Negro group. A sense of inferiority affects the motivation of a child to learn. Segregation with the sanction of law, therefore, has a tendency to [retard] the educational and mental development of Negro children and to deprive them of some of the benefits they would receive in a racially integrated school system.

Whatever may have been the extent of psychological knowledge at the time of *Plessy v. Ferguson* [1896], this finding is amply supported by modern authority.[2] Any language in *Plessy v. Ferguson* contrary to this finding is rejected.

We conclude that, in the field of public education, the doctrine of "separate but equal" has no place. Separate educational facilities are inherently unequal. Therefore, we hold that the plaintiffs and others similarly situated for whom the actions have been brought are, by reason of the segregation complained of, deprived of the equal protection of the laws guaranteed by the Fourteenth Amendment. This disposition makes unnecessary any discussion whether such segregation also violates the Due Process Clause of the Fourteenth Amendment.

NOTES

1. [*Editor's Note*: *Brown v. Board of Education*, 347 U.S. 483 (1954); Argued December 9, 1952; Reargued December 8, 1953; Decided May 17, 1954. Courtesy of the Library of Congress.]

2. [*Editor's Note*: The Court is referring to Footnote 11, the study by Kenneth B. Clark, 1st Draft: "The Effects of Prejudice and Discrimination on Personality Development," Fact-Finding Report, Mid-Century White House Conference on

Children and Youth, Children's Bureau, Federal Security Agency, 1950 (mimeo-graphed). "Kenneth Bancroft Clark, A Register of His Papers in the Library of Congress," Professional File, Box 104, January 25, 1950, The Library of Congress, Manuscript Division, Washington, DC.]

1955 *Annual Survey of American Law*: Part Five—"Legal Philosophy and Reform," by Edmond Cahn (Excerpts)[1]

We may be moving into a new phase of the relations between law and the social sciences. If recent experience with the testimony of social psychologists is typical, the several elements of the American bar are facing unaccustomed challenges. For a generation or more, liberal lawyers had regarded the claims of social scientists with cordiality and encouragement. Then in 1954, when the Supreme Court decided the *School Segregation* cases, Chief Justice Warren devoted a footnote to citing certain works written by social psychologists. Thereupon the impression rose, and was ardently fostered, that it was their testimony and scientific findings that had won the victory. Seconding this impression, Senators Strom Thurmond of South Carolina and James O. Eastland of Mississippi publicly charged the Court with following the social psychologists instead of the law.

Last year, in an article [1954, *Annual Survey of American Law*, 809), analyzing the most conspicuous "proof" offered by the social psychologists in the *School Segregation* cases, I submitted that (1) neither the testimony nor the cited publications of the social psychologists determined the outcome of the *School Segregation* cases; (2) their testimony and cited publications had only reiterated facts of common knowledge; (3) the purported demonstration in Professor Kenneth Clark's highly publicized "doll test" did not approach the level of scientific proof; and (4) it would be dangerous for constitutional law to drift away from the established doctrine that discrimination is itself an injury (*injuria*) regardless of psychological or other kinds of damage (*damnum*). While uttering these warnings, the article endeavored to make clear that the outcome of the cases was entirely right, that the attorneys who offered the social psychologists' testimony were justified in doing so, and that the trial courts had acted properly in admitting the testimony for whatever it might be worth. All in all, the attitude I favored toward social psychology would express receptivity seasoned with critical judgment.

[Other experts] contend that everyone knows that expert witnesses are partisan and biased, that everyone discounts expert testimony to a great extent (even to the extent of not crediting it at all), and that the courts' daily experiences with, say, medical experts shows that the process does not cause any extraneous social harm. We do not worry, they say, about lawyers corrupting the medical profession or the doctors corrupting the lawyers with regard to objectivity and scientific truth. Why then feel concern about the reciprocal influence of social psychologists and lawyers?

There are several reasons. The dangers to both law and social psychology seem quite different in degree when compared with the possibe influence of medical testimony. For one thing, the court testimony of social psychologists is concerned not so much with individual as with public issues. Hence if accepted uncritically, it can cause immense public harm. Moreover, the dangers to the progress of psychological science are more serious. The medical profession does not owe its prestige and social importance to appearances in court but to the theoretical and practical achievements in laboratories and hospitals. There is no significant hazard that, however physicians might testify in court, they could impair the general objectivity or impede the beneficent advance of medical science. By way of contrast, social psychology, a young profession, has not enjoyed the prestige which the American public accords to medicine, engineering, and even to economics. To some social psychologists, the new wine of public attention and influence seems quite heady. The temptations are not trivial. If a social psychologist finds it hard to prove his assertions, will not anyone else find it still harder to disprove them? With the most idealistic motives he may come to acquiesce in compromises that physicians or engineers would not dare consider.

Most of us would agree that, if there is any single quality distinguishing the policy judgments of lawyers from those of the general community, it could to be the quality of responsibility. Our daily experience prepares us and our millennial tradition admonishes us to maintain a posture of deliberation amid the currents and blasts of public enthusiasm. Society looks to us for the jural development of its values, trusting we will not revolve with every passing ideological fad.

If the testimony of the social scientists seems vulnerable on inspection, then it is our professional duty to point out the shortcomings and advocate the use of better methods and standards. We ought no longer debate the general admissibility of testimony from authentic social science sources; on the contrary, we ought to welcome and encourage evidence of this kind.

Our studies and criticisms should be addressed rather to consideration of weight and materiality. While we ought to keep our minds receptive and open, open minds need not be drafty. Being servants of justice and officers of the court we have an obligation to consider the quality and propriety of expert evidence before we offer it. In many instances, lawyers participate in projecting, planning, and assembling polls and studies and other items of social-science evidence. By doing so, we do not become sureties for the logical or scientific validity of the evidence; nevertheless at some point, if there is danger of misleading the court, we should either abstain from offering the evidence or, by our own questions, bring out the limitations on its objective demonstrability.

NOTE

1. [*Editor's Note*: Published by New York University School of Law, Arthur T. Vanderbilt Hall, Washington Square, NY, Editorial Staff: The Editors of the *New York University Law Review*, and Isaac Ciechanowicz, Arnold Greenberg, Dorothy L. Killam, Fannie J. Klein, Anna C. Migliore, Diane H. Wojcik. "Jurisprudence," by Edmond Cahn, January 1955: 655–668.]

New York University Law Review: "Jurisprudence," by Edmond Cahn (Excerpts)[1]

In legal philosophy it is a very dangerous thing to comment on happenings that one welcomes and approves. By doing so, an unwary observer may expose himself to the occupational disease of jurisprudence, which in its most virulent form consists in finding the law "the true embodiment of everything that is excellent." When the disease takes hold, its victim gradually loses his early vigor of discontent and passion and reform; by slow stages he subsides into a state of complacency; in course of time, sitting at ease among his memories, he grows to resent the process of change as ardently as he used to welcome it. To him the crop of occurrences seems annually to present more and more of the irremediable, though not necessarily less of the evil, in juristic affairs; and so at last he becomes a recognized sage and elder statesman of the profession. The risk is a dire one. Nevertheless, in the teeth of danger, I shall proceed to comment here on 1954's most important development: the Supreme Court's decisions in the *School Segregation* cases. When the sense of injustice has triumphed on a scale so extensive, comprehension of the meaning of victory may prove useful to it in other conflicts. The decisions have added to the dignity and stature of every American.

Professor Kenneth B. Clark of the psychology department of City College acted as general social science consultant to the NAACP legal staff and served as liaison between the lawyers and the scientists. His endeavors having been long and arduous, perhaps it was natural that he should exaggerate whatever the experts contributed to the case. In an article written while the country was waiting for the Supreme Court's decisions, he asserted, "Proof of the arguments that segregation itself is inequality and that state imposed racial segregation inflicts injuries upon the Negro had to come from the social psychologists and other social scientists."

When Professor Clark wrote this [see Appendix 4, this volume], "Desegregation: An Appraisal of the Evidence," he could not know that Chief Justice Warren's opinions would not mention either the testimony or the expert witnesses or the submitted statement of the thirty-two scientists. The Chief Justice cushioned the blow to some extent by citing certain professional publications of the psychological experts in a footnote, alluding to them graciously as "modern authority" [347 U.S., 483, 484, and n.11, 1954]. In view of their devoted efforts to defeat segregation, this was the kind of gesture a magnanimous judge would feel impelled to make, and we are bound to take satisfaction in the accolade. Yet, once the courtesy has been paid, the Court was not disposed in the least to go farther or base its determination on the expert testimony.

When we come to explain why the statement signed by the thirty-two social scientists went without mention by Chief Justice Warren, I find myself at a disadvantage. Only the reader's assistance can rescue me. I have examined the text of this statement, which has become easy to access by being reprinted in a law review. My personal, subjective reaction is that the text conveys little or no information beyond what is already known in "literary psychology" (by which I mean such psychological observations and insights as one finds continually in the works of poets, novelists, essayists, journalists, and religious prophets). The statement's vocabulary and style would not be called "literary." I refer only to its substance.

Perhaps the main point is that this [doll] test does not purport to demonstrate the effects of *school* segregation, which is what the court was being asked to rejoin. If it disclosed anything about the effects of desegregation on the children, their experiences at school were not differentiated from other causes. Considering the ages of the children, we may conjecture they had not been long at school.

Fortunately, the outcome of the Brown case did not depend on the psychological experts' facing and answering the objections, queries, and doubts I have presented. It is possible that if the questions had been put to Professor Clark, on cross-examination, he would have come forward with convincing answers. But, to all intents and purposes, the questions were not put. The doll test was not analyzed in suitable detail by any of the cross-examiners, probably because they, too, realized that segregation does degrade and injure Negro school children.

As the court's exclusionary rules of evidence tend to relax more and more, the scientists will appear more and more frequently to testify as expert witnesses. How much respect should the judges extend to their testimony? The answer depends in large measure on the scientists. If I have been right in suggestion that their evidence in the desegregation cases seemed persuasive because it happened to coincide with facts of common knowledge, they surely cannot rely on having the same advantage in every future litigation. It is predictable that lawyers and scientists retained by adversary parties will endeavor more aggressively to puncture any vulnerable or extravagant claims. Judges may learn to notice where objective science ends and advocacy begins. At present, it is still possible for the social psychologist to "hoodwink a judge who is not over wise" without intending to do so; but successes of this kind are too costly for science to desire them.

For one thing: Merely translating a proposition of "literary" psychology into terms of technical jargon can scarcely make it a scientific finding. For another: Just because social psychology is in a youthful and somewhat uncertain stage, the utmost rigor should be imposed on its *intermediate* processes.

The point is vital, involving as it does not only social psychology's prestige in the courts but—what is ultimately more valuable—its capacity to evolve and progress as a cumulative body of tested knowledge and approved method. Among the major impediments continually confronting this science are: (1) the recurrent lack of agreement on substantive premises, and (2) the recurrent lack of extrinsic, empirical means for checking and verifying inferred results. As long as these disadvantages remain, and they are likely to remain in some measure for a very long time, social psychology will need, above all things, the use of scrupulous logic in its internal, intermediate processes. If the *premises* must be loose, the *reasoning* from them should be so much tighter; and if the final *results* cannot be validated precisely by eternal tests, then the *methods* of inference should be examined and reexamined all the more critically. It is meticulous standards that bring respect and credence to scientific testimony. When a social psychologist is called to serve as a "friend of the court," he should be able to assume our belief that his best friend, his premier loyalty, is always the *objective truth* [editor's italics].

Some of the consequences—Obviously [the Court's opinions] are susceptible to more than one interpretation. My views do not agree with those of some very able commentators, who consider that the opinions show important marks of the psychologists' influence. Granting this variety of interpretations, does it really matter whether the Supreme Court relies or does not rely on the psychologists' findings? Does it make any practical difference?

I submit it does. In the first place, since the behavioral sciences are so very young, imprecise, and changeful, their findings have an uncertain expectancy of life. Today's sanguine asseveration may be cancelled by tomorrow's new revelation—or new technical fact. It is one thing to use the current scientific findings, however ephemeral they may be, in order to ascertain whether the legislature has acted reasonably in adopting some scheme of social or economic regulation; deference here is shown not so much to the findings as to the legislature. It would be quite another thing to have our fundamental rights rise, fall, or change along with the latest fashions of psychological literature. Today the social psychologists—at least the leaders of the discipline—are liberal egalitarian in basic approach. Suppose, a generation hence, some of their successors were to revert to the ethnic mysticism of the very real recent past; suppose they were to present us with a collection of racist notions and label them "science." What then would be the state of our constitutional rights? Recognizing as we do how sagacious Mr. Justice Holmes was to insist that the Constitution be not tied to the wheels of any economic system whatsoever, we ought to keep it similarly uncommitted in relation to the other social sciences.

When the American people suffered a moral defeat in *Plessy v. Ferguson*, Mr. Justice Harlan's dissent survived on the record. It reminded people of the solemn promises and mutual pledges that had inspired their beginnings as a nation, and appealed from what was narrow and mean in their traditions to what was broad and fraternal. As years went by, Harlan's prophetic phrases were taken up, repeated, and reiterated—until they passed gradually into the popular vocabulary. Clergymen, social scientists, publicists and jurists imagined they were coining novel phrases as they unwittingly borrowed his, which he would have been glad to lend them. By the end of the 1930s, when the Supreme Court began to utter its series of lessons to the states on fair treatments in education, the American people were fully prepared to support their judicial pedagogue. Now the advance has reached its climax, with the principle of equality firmly established. In this struggle, there can be no one to hail as a victor except the whole American people, who alone have the power to insure that the principle becomes a living reality in their public schools. The achievement is theirs. With this, I believe, the lone dissenter of 1896 would agree. Even as the shame of his time belonged to all, so should the vindication of our time; and so too the hope of a more benevolent American community.

NOTE

1. [*Editor's Note*: From Edmond Cahn, "Jurisprudence," *New York University Law Review* 30.1 (1955): 150–169.]

"The Desegregation Cases: Criticism of the Social Scientist's Role," by Kenneth B. Clark (Excerpts)[1]

Basic to the direct and indirect criticisms which have been raised concerning the generally unstated scientists in the school desegregation cases is the generally unstated question of the propriety of social scientists playing any role in this type of legal controversy. It is clear that the public school desegregation cases are crucially related to the delicate and specific problems of the relative status of the Negro and white groups in American culture and the equally delicate and general problem of social change.

Social scientists, like other knowledgeable individuals in our society, must be sensitive to the problems of power and the techniques of social control which are operative in the society in which they work. In spite of the demand for objectivity and integrity in the search for truth, the important determinant of serious scientific work, social scientists are influenced indirectly and sometimes directly, subtly and sometimes crudely, by the prevailing social biases and uncritically accepted frames of reference of their society.

Given this perspective, one can then begin to evaluate the specific criticisms which have been raised against the social scientists who have been involved in these desegregation cases. The implications of any of these criticisms are not restricted to the more academic problems of social science theory, methodology, and the nature of social science evidence. Nor are they limited to the more complex problems of the delicate relationship between the social sciences and the law. These are indeed crucial problems which merit continuous discussion and debate in the relatively young and dynamic social sciences. The full import of a given criticism must be understood in terms of whether it clarifies or distorts the larger social issues;

specifically, the practical reality of the nature, function, and consequences of racial segregation in American life, the stresses and strains inevitably involved in attempts to change institutionalized patterns of social injustices, and the role of the courts for changes in, or maintenance of, the status quo.

Some of the most intense criticisms have come from political leaders of the deep southern states. Men like Senators Eastland and Talmadge, former Governor Byrnes and Governor Faubus have attacked the Supreme Court's decision not only on the grounds that it violated "states rights" but also, significantly for the purpose of this paper, on the grounds that it attempted to substitute psychological and sociological theories for the law. There is a question whether these types of criticisms should be taken seriously by social scientists since they seem motivated largely by political considerations.

Attacks on the role of social scientists in these [school segregation] cases have not been restricted to politicians who object to the Court's decision and the social changes which they fear may result, but have come also from serious students of jurisprudence and more recently from social scientists. One of the most consistent of the legal critics is the distinguished professor of jurisprudence, Edmond Cahn, of New York University Law School. Ernest van den Haag is an example of critics from within the field of social sciences. Professor Cahn has undoubtedly influenced the thinking of other students of jurisprudence and Dr. van den Haag has presented the most specific and intense critical comments that have so far been published by a social scientist.

EDMOND CAHN'S CRITICISMS

The criticisms of Professor Cahn take many forms. Essentially, however, he states that it is incorrect to believe that the *Brown* decision was "caused by the testimony and opinions of the scientists" and that the constitutional rights of Negroes or any other Americans should not "rest on any such flimsy foundation as some of the scientific demonstrations in these records." He contends that the cruelty inherent in racial segregation "is obvious and evident."

Among his other charges are: (1) that this writer exaggerated the contribution of social science experts to these cases; and, (2) that in writing a report of the role of social scientists which was published before May 17, 1954, the writer could not have known that Chief Justice Warren's opinion would not mention either the testimony of the expert witnesses or the statements submitted by the thirty-two social scientists. Professor Cahn added soliticitously:

The Chief Justice cushioned the blow to some extent by citing certain professional publications of the psychological experts in a footnote, alluding to them graciously as "modern authority." In view of their devoted efforts to defeat segregation, this was the kind of gesture a magnanimous judge would feel impelled to make, and we are bound to take satisfaction in the accolade.

In speculating on why the Court did not mention the social scientists' brief in its opinion, Professor Cahn states his personal, subjective reaction that the text of this statement conveyed little or no information beyond what is known as "literary psychology." The fact is, however, that all but one of the references cited by the Court in Footnote 11 of the *Brown* decision were cited as references in the social science brief which had been submitted to the Court. The one reference which had not been listed but cited by the Court was Witmer and Kotkinsky's *Personality in the Making*, the relevant portion of which was a summary of this writer's White House Conference manuscript on the effects of prejudice and discrimination on personality development.

Whatever might be one's degree of agreement or disagreement with Professor Cahn's estimate of the worth of the social scientists' testimony in these cases or the degree of the Court's regard for the social scientists' material presented in the brief or in the trial records, one must take seriously his arguments that the constitutional rights of Negroes or other Americans should not rest on social scientists' testimony alone. If he had concentrated and elaborated on this issue on a high level of academic discourse, he might have made an important contribution to thought in the field in which he is competent. When he leaves the area of law, constitutional rights, and matters of jurisprudence and invades the area of social sciences, making broad and general comments about the validity of social science methods, premises, approaches, findings and conclusions, and when he explicitly or implicitly attacks or suggests that the social scientists who participated in these cases as witnesses and consultants did not do so with the utmost personal and scientific integrity, he gratuitously leaves his field of competence and communicates his personal opinions, biases and misconceptions as if they were facts. His prestige is in a field in which he has been trained thereby disguises his ignorance in a field in which he has no training. For these reasons, it is necessary to answer these charges and generalizations with clarity.

SOME RELEVANT FACTS

Before one enters a general appraisal of the validity of some of the many assumptions, implications, and charges raised by Professor Cahn, it is necessary to clarify certain points of fact which are relevant to opinions about the role of social scientists in these cases:

(1) The social scientists who participated in these cases were invited to do so by the lawyers of the NAACP. It was these lawyers who had the

primary and exclusive responsibility for developing the legal rationale and approach upon which these cases would be tried and appealed. It was they who made the decision to bring the legal attack on the problem of overruling the *Plessy* "separate but equal" doctrine by attempting to demonstrate that state laws which required or permitted segregation in public schools violated the equal protection clause of the fourteenth amendment. It was their decision that the chances of success would be greater if it could be demonstrated that racial segregation, without regard to equality of facilities, damaged Negro children. Furthermore, it was their decision to determine whether they could find acceptable evidence from social psychology and other social sciences which would support their belief that psychological damage resulted from racial segregation. Social scientists were not involved and did not participate in any way in these initial and important policy or legal strategy decisions. Only after these decisions were made by the lawyers of the NAACP were the social scientists approached and invited by the lawyers to participate in these cases. The social scientists were asked whether there were any relevant scientific studies on the psychological effects of racial segregation. Finally, it was the judgment of these lawyers that the studies and evidence offered by the social scientists were relevant and crucial enough to form an integral part of their trial and appellate case.

(2) The studies which were relied upon by the social scientists in arriving at the conclusion that racial segregation damaged the human personality were not studies which were conducted specifically for these legal cases. Systematic research on the psychological aspects of racial prejudice, discrimination, and segregation had been going on for more than fifteen years. The White House Conference manuscript, which was cited by the United States Supreme Court in Footnote 11 in the *Brown* decision, was a compilation of all of the available knowledge of the effects of prejudice and discrimination on personality development in children and was prepared by this writer months before he was aware of the fact that the NAACP intended to bring cases before the federal courts challenging the validity of segregated schools.

(3) The studies cited in this White House Conference manuscript and the joint primary research of this writer and his wife formed the bulk of his testimony in three of these five cases. The primary research studies were conducted ten years before these cases were heard on the trial court level. Professor Cahn's allegation that the writer served in the role of advocate rather than that of an objective scientist in his participation in these cases seems difficult to sustain in the face of testimony given on the basis of research conducted ten years before these cases were heard. One would have to be gifted with the power of a seer in order to prepare himself for the role of advocate in these specific cases ten years in advance.

(4) The use of the "Dolls Test" (actual dolls, not pictures of dolls, were used in this research) on some of the plaintiffs was to determine whether

the general findings from the larger number of Negro children who had been tested years before were true also for the children who were the actual plaintiffs in these cases. The decision to test some of these plaintiffs was a legal one made by the lawyers of the NAACP. It was their assumption as lawyers that general scientific findings would have more weight in a court if it could be demonstrated that they also applied in the specific cases and for the particular plaintiffs before the court. When these plaintiff children were tested and interviewed by this writer, it was his judgment that some of these children showed evidence of the same type of personality damage related to racial prejudice, segregation, and discrimination which was found in the larger number of subjects who were studied in the original, published research. This opinion was presented to the courts in the form of sworn testimony.

(5) The justices of the federal district courts were at all times free to rule that the testimony of the social scientists was irrelevant and immaterial. The United States Supreme Court could have refused to accept the Social Science statement which was submitted to it in the form of an appendix to the legal brief of the appellants. If either of these had been done, there would now be no question of whether the courts did or did not reply on the findings and opinions of social scientists.

It is still a matter of social reality that social scientific findings and opinions are not incorporated into, nor do they determine, policy decisions, legislative action, or judicial decisions except to the extent that those who have the power to make these practical decisions choose to accept or reject the relevant findings of scientists. Whether this should continue to be so is, of course, debatable.

"FIDELITY," "TRUTH," AND ACADEMIC COURTESY

Professor Cahn implies in a chapter on Jurisprudence, *Annual Survey of American Law* [*New York University Law Review* 30.1 (1955): 150–169], that the primary motive of the social psychologists who participated in these cases was not "strictly fidelity to objective truth." This is a serious, grave, and shocking charge. Professor Cahn did not present evidence to support his implication that the social scientists who participated in these cases, and particularly this writer, betrayed their trusts as scientists. He merely makes the assertion that some day judges will be wise and will be able to notice, "where objective science ends and advocacy begins." For the present, however, "it is still possible for the social psychologist to 'hoodwink' a judge who is not overwise. . . ."

It is difficult to take this type of comment seriously. Since it has been published over the signature of an individual who commands the respect of his legal colleagues, it cannot be dismissed. It cannot be waived aside as evidence that Professor Cahn believes himself wiser than the entire legal staff of the NAACP, the battery of lawyers employed by the opposition—including the late John W. Davis, who devoted a considerable amount of space in his Supreme Court brief and his first arguments before the United States Supreme Court to the social science testimony—or the lawyers of the Department of Justice of the United States, and, finally, the Justices of the United States Supreme Court.

This point must be answered by a description of concrete facts in the relationship between the NAACP lawyers and the social scientists who were involved in these cases. The social scientists who testified in these cases or endorsed the Social Science appendix at the invitation of this writer were not the type of human beings who were capable, personally or professionally, of testifying to a fact or stating an opinion which they did not believe to be consistent with the scientific evidence, as they knew it. These men are neither infallible nor all wise; but they are the outstanding experts in this field. What is even more important, they are men of integrity.

When the lawyers of the NAACP in their understandable zeal to develop the strongest possible case asked the social scientists whether it was possible to present evidence showing that *public school segregation*, in itself, damaged the personalities of Negro children, it was pointed out to them that the available studies had so far not isolated this single variable from the total social complexity of racial prejudice, discrimination, and segregation. It was therefore not possible to testify on the psychologically damaging effects of segregated schools alone. Such specific evidence, if available at all, would have to come from educators and educational philosophers. Some of the more insistent lawyers felt that only this type of specific testimony would be of value to them in these cases. It was pointed out to these lawyers that if this were so then their social psychologists and other social scientists could not be of any significant, direct help to them. A careful examination of the testimony of the social scientists, found in the record of these cases and the Social Science appendix submitted to the United States Supreme Court, will show that the social scientists presented testimony, opinions, and information consistent with the available empirical studies, conclusions, and observations. As expert witnesses, they made not a single concession to expediency, to the practical and legal demands of these cases, or even to the moral and humane issues involved as they adhered to their concept of "strict fidelity to objective truth." Certainly, Professor Cahn cannot be the judge of whether his concept of "strict fidelity to objective truth" in the field of social science is more acceptable or valid than theirs.

It must now be stated that one of the responsibilities assigned to this writer in his role of social science consultant to the legal staff of the NAACP was to advise the lawyers not only about those studies and individuals who were scientifically acceptable, but also to advise and warn them away from studies and individuals of questionable scientific repute. At least one well-publicized report on the damaging effects of segregation on the personality of Negroes was not used in these cases because it was in the judgment of this writer, which was communicated to and accepted by the lawyers, that its methodology was scientifically questionable, its selection of subjects and sampling were clearly biased, and that its conclusions bordered on the sensational. In short, it was believed that in spite of the fact that this study purported to present clear evidence in support of the hypothesis that racial oppression damaged the personality of Negroes, its flaws and scientific inadequacy were so clear it could not be defended in court.

It is difficult to determine precisely what Professor Cahn means by "objective truth." According to his article, "most of mankind already acknowledged . . ." that segregation is cruel to Negro children, involves stigma and loss of status, and may ultimately shatter their "spines" and deprive them of self-respect. The "shattering of spines" is Professor Cahn's contribution to the knowledge of the detrimental effects of racial segregation. No social scientist testified to this "fact." Professor Cahn contends, however, that when the scientists attempt to demonstrate these same "well-known facts" through their use of the methods and approaches of science, they "provide a rather bizarre spectacle." What is more, he maintains they exaggerate their role, their methods are questionable, their logic and interpretations weak and fallacious, and they distort their findings as they become advocates who seek to "hoodwink" the judges. A serious question would be: How could the social scientists be so unreliable yet nonetheless come out with a picture of social reality which Professor Cahn and everyone else already knew.

Professor Cahn presents a novel concept of the relationship between common knowledge and scientific knowledge. The logic of his position rests upon the premise that science concerns itself with one order of reality which is distinct from other forms of reality or truth—that a scientific "fact" has different attributes or characteristics than a "fact" of common knowledge. Another related theme which runs through his comments is that a "legal fact" is distinct from both "scientific fact" and a "fact of common knowledge."

Cahn's pluralistic approach to the nature of "facts," while not a novel philosophical position, seems to involve a mystical semantic confusion which is inconsistent with the assumptions imperative for a scientific approach to the understanding of the nature of man, his society, and his environment. . . .

THE BASIC ISSUE

After one has cut through the emotional irrelevancies of Professor Cahn's article, one is confronted with the basic plea that the law and the courts of the land should be isolated in Olympian grandeur from other intellectual and scientific acclivities of man. Specifically, Cahn seems primarily—even if unconsciously—disturbed by the fact that the upstarts of the new social sciences should have been involved at all in these important cases which belonged exclusively to lawyers and students of jurisprudence. It is to be hoped that a decreasing number of lawyers believe that laws and courts are sacred and should be kept antiseptically isolated from the main stream of human progress. Such isolation cannot be and never has been true except in the classrooms of some puristic law school professors.

The law is concerned with society and the regulation of human affairs. Social science, government, philosophy, and religion are also concerned with society, its understanding and regulation. Man's relations with his fellow man involve matters far too grave and crucial to be left to lawyers and judges alone. Respect for the law, intelligently and ethically conceived and executed, is essential for stable government. Intelligence and ethics cannot stem from the laws alone but must be fed to it through ceaseless struggles of scholars, scientists, and others toward truth and understanding. This may be difficult for Professor Cahn to accept. It nonetheless remains a fact.

ERNEST VAN DEN HAAG'S CRITICISM

The most serious and significant forms of criticisms are those which are now beginning to come from social scientists. . . . Ernest van den Haag published a book entitled *The Fabric of Society*. The criticisms by Dr. van den Haag must be seen as distinct from the criticisms of politicians and students of jurisprudence. These are the criticisms of a social scientist who bears the responsibility and must be held to the rules of social science.

In an appendix to chapter 14 of *The Fabric of Society* entitled "Prejudice about Prejudice," Dr. Van den Haag, who is responsible for this section of the book, makes the following statements among others:

Whether humiliation leaves deep and lasting traces and whether it increases the incidence of personality disorders among Negroes, we do not know (nor do we know whether congregation would obviate them).

It (the United States Supreme Court) did not depend on the attempt of the social scientists to detect and prove the psychological injuries by 'scientific' results—which is fortunate for the evidence presented is so flimsy as to discredit the conclusion. . . .

Dr. van den Haag then proceeds to repeat, with some elaborations, Edmond Cahn's criticisms of the role of social scientists in the desegregation cases. According to van den Haag, although the Court "did not depend" upon social scientists, "much weight was given to certain 'generally accepted tests' which Professor Kenneth B. Clark undertook with certain Negro children in a segregated school."

In attempting to answer Dr. van den Haag's criticism of the wisdom of the May 17, 1954, decision of the United States Supreme Court and his criticism of the social science testimony which was presented in the federal courts at the trial level of these cases, one is confronted with a difficult task. To those students who are familiar with the facts of the Supreme Court's decision and the limited role of social scientists in the cases which led to this decision, it will be apparent that Dr. van den Haag's criticisms of this decision and the role of the social scientists are not based upon his direct knowledge of the facts. Either Dr. van den Haag did not read or did not understand the basic documents which are relevant to a scholarly discussion or criticism of these problems.

In reference to his [Dr. van den Haag's] attack on the role of the social scientists and particularly the role of the writer in these cases, it is equally clear that Dr. van den Haag relied upon secondary sources for his "facts" and published his critical analysis without reading the original reports of these research studies and without reading the Appendix to the Appellant's Briefs written by three social scientists and endorsed by thirty-two outstanding research workers in the field of race relations in America.

This writer's testimony in these cases was not based exclusively on his own research findings but on the literature or his evaluation of the weight of evidence from other investigations of this problem. The record states:

I have reached the conclusion from the examination of my own results and from an examination of the literature in the entire field that discrimination, prejudice, and segregation have definitely detrimental effects on the personality development of the Negro child.

Dr. van den Haag's criticism of the "flimsy" nature of the scientific evidence would have to be taken more seriously if he had examined carefully the nearly sixty references which were used as the basis of the social science brief which was submitted to the United States Supreme Court. If this were too arduous a task, then he could have examined the seven references cited by the United States Supreme Court in footnote 11 of the *Brown* decision.

Probably the most disturbing and revealing aspect of Dr. van den Haag's criticism is the fact that an examination of other portions of his book demonstrates that he maintains a double standard of what he considers scientific objectivity and acceptable evidence. On the one hand, he contends that the writer's work and findings were unscientific and based on the number of cases that would be "too small to test the reaction to a new soap," and on the other hand, he accepts and presents the sweeping conclusions

... based on unstated total number of children. . . . The question remains whether the following conclusions drawn by van den Haag are justified:

The infant reaching the outside world after a dreadful travail, must be made to feel at home if he is to stay. Even the greatest maternal comfort cannot replace what he had left behind.

. . . It seems entirely possible that lack of maternal affection in the first few years of life deals a blow which cannot be mended later. . . .

Dr. van den Haag seems to have one set of standards for the scientific acceptability of findings concerning the effects of hospitalism and maternal deprivation on infants and another set of standards for findings concerning the effects of a total pattern of racial prejudice, discrimination, and segregation on the personality development of children. Nowhere does he reveal the basis for his judgment that the evidence in the latter case is flimsy while the evidence in support of the former can be accepted uncritically as he presents it.

CONCLUSIONS

Those who attempt to use the methods of social science in dealing with problems which threaten the status quo must realistically expect retaliatory attacks, direct or oblique, and must be prepared to accept the risks this role inevitably involves. Attacks motivated by understandable political opposition or the criticisms which reflect the vested interests or limitations of other disciplines must be expected.

Differences of opinion and interpretation concerning the relative weight given to the available evidence must, of course, be expected among conscientious social scientists. In this latter instance, however, certain fundamental rules of social scholarship, consistency and logic must prevail if the controversy is to be intellectually constructive and socially beneficial.

It is a fact that the collaboration between psychologists and other social scientists which culminated in the *Brown* decision will continue in spite of criticism. Those who question the propriety of this collaboration will probably increase the intensity of their criticism—particularly as social controversy and conflict increase. Nevertheless, some social scientists will continue to play a role in this aspect of the legal and judicial process because as scientists they cannot do otherwise. They are obligated by temperament, moral commitment and their concept of the role and demands of science. They will continue to inspire criticism or threats. They will do so because they see the valid goals of the law, government, social institutions, religion and science as identical; namely, to secure for man personal fulfillment in a just, stable, and viable society.

NOTE

1. [*Editor's Note*: From Kenneth B. Clark, "The Desegregation Cases: Criticism of the Social Scientist's Role," *Villanova Law Review* 5.2 (Winter 1959–1960): 226–228.]

Selected Bibliography

Adolf, Arnold. *Black on Black: Commentaries by Negro Americans*. New York: Macmillan, 1968.

Ahmann, Mathew A., ed. *The New Negro*. Notre Dame, IN: Fides Publishers, 1961.

Allport, Gordon W. *The Nature of Prejudice*. Boston: Perseus Publishing, 1979.

Bond, Julian, Kenneth B. Clark, and Richard G. Hatcher. *The Black Man in American Politics: Three Views*. New York: Metropolitan Applied Research Center, 1969.

Bowen, William, and Derek Bok. *The Shape of the River: Long Term Consequences of Considering Race in Colleges and Universities*. Princeton, NJ: Princeton University Press, 1998.

Branch, Taylor. *Parting the Waters: America in the King Years, 1954–1963*. New York: Simon & Schuster, 1988.

Brink, William, and Louis Harris. *Black and White: A Study of U.S. Racial Attitudes Today*. New York: Simon & Schuster, 1966.

Brown v. Board of Education, 347 U.S. 483 (1954): Argued December 9, 1952; Reargued December 8, 1953; Decided May 17, 1954, U.S. Supreme Court.

Cheek, Donald K. *Assertive Black . . . Puzzled White*. San Luis Obispo, CA: Impact Publishers, 1976.

Clark, Kenneth B., and Mamie P. Clark. "Segregation as a Factor in Racial Identification in Negro Pre-school Children: A Preliminary Report." *Journal of Experimental Education* 8 (1939): 161–163.

Clark, Kenneth B. "Some Factors Affecting the Remembering of Meaningful Phrase Material." *Archives of Psychology* no. 253 (1940): 1–73.

Clark, Kenneth B. "Morale among Negroes." In G. Watson, ed., *Civilian Morale*. Boston: Houghton Mifflin, 1942.

Clark, Kenneth B. "Morale of the Negro on the Home Front: World Wars I and II." *Journal of Negro Education* 12.3 (1943): 417–428.

Clark, Kenneth B. "A Brown Girl in a Speckled World." *Journal of Social Issues* 1 (1945): 10–15.

Clark, Kenneth B. "Candor about Negro-Jewish Relations." *Commentary* 8 (1945): 8–14.

Clark, Kenneth B., with G.A. Seward. "Race, Sex, and Democratic Living: Two Questions with Answers." In G. Murphy, ed., *Human Nature and Enduring Peace*. Boston: Houghton Mifflin, 1945.

Clark, Kenneth B. "Some Factors Influencing a Group Estimation of the Intelligence and Personality Wholesomeness of Negro Subjects." *Journal of Psychology* 19 (1945): 73–75.

Clark, Kenneth B. "The Zoot Effect in Personality: A Race Riot Participant." *Journal of Social and Abnormal Psychology* 40 (1945): 143–148.

Clark, Kenneth B., with M.P. Clark. "Racial Identification and Preferences in Negro Children." In E. Maccoby, T.M. Newcomb, and E. H. Hartley, eds., *Readings in Social Psychology*. New York: Holt, Rinehart & Winston, 1947.

Clark, Kenneth B. "Social Science and Social Tensions." *Mental Hygiene* 32 (1948): 15–26.

Clark, Kenneth B. 1st Draft: "The Effects of Prejudice and Discrimination on Personality Development." Fact-Finding Report, Mid-Century White House Conference on Children and Youth, Children's Bureau. Federal Security Agency, 1950. Mimeographed. "Kenneth Bancroft Clark: A Register of His Papers in the Library of Congress," Professional File, Box 104, January 25, 1950. The Library of Congress, Manuscript Division, Washington, DC.

Clark, Kenneth B., with M.P. Clark. "Emotional Factors in Racial Identification and Preference in Negro Children." *Journal of Negro Education* 19 (1950): 506–513.

Clark, Kenneth B. "Racial Prejudice among American Minorities." *International Social Science Bulletin* 2 (Winter 1950): 4–5.

Clark, Kenneth B. "How to Protect Children against Prejudice." *Child Study* 26 (1951): 4–5, 9–11, 24–26.

Clark, Kenneth B. "Appendix to Appellant's Briefs—The Effects of Segregation and the Consequences of Desegregation: A Social Science Statement." Library of Congress, Clark Archives, Hastings-on-Hudson, NY, 1952.

Clark, Kenneth B. "Desegregation: An Appraisal of the Evidence." *Journal of Social Issues* 9 (1953): 1–77.

Clark, Kenneth B. "Racial Attitudes: Words versus Deeds." *Today's Speech* 1 (1953): 20–22.

Clark, Kenneth B. "The Social Scientist as an Expert Witness in Civil Rights Litigation." *Social Problems* 1.1 (1953): 9.

Clark, Kenneth B. "Current Trends in Desegregation." *American Child* 36 (1954): 1, 4.

Clark, Kenneth B. "Some Principles Related to the Problem of Desegregation." *Journal of Negro Education* 23 (1954): 339–347.

Clark, Kenneth B. "Desegregation of the American Public Schools." In *Current Problems and Issues in Human Relations Education*. New York: A publication of the Anti-Defamation League, 1955.

Clark, Kenneth B. *Prejudice and Your Child.* Boston: Beacon Press, 1955.

Clark, Kenneth B. "The Most Valuable Hidden Resource." *College Board Review* 29 (1956): 23–26.

Clark, Kenneth B. *Report to the Unitarian Service Committee, Inc.* Boston: Community Service-USA, 1956.

Clark, Kenneth B. "A Struggle for Complete Human Dignity." *The Christian Register* (Massachusetts Christian Universalist Association) (July 1956): 15.

Clark, Kenneth B. *Minority Status, Social Power and Some Problems of Psychotherapy.* Hanover, NH: University Press of New England, 1957.

Clark, Kenneth B. "The Desegregation Cases: Criticism of the Social Scientist's Role." *Villanova Law Review* 5.2 (Winter 1959–1960): 226–228.

Clark, Kenneth B. "Discrimination and the Education of the Disadvantaged." *College Board Review* 40 (1960): 5–10.

Clark, Kenneth B. "The Psychodynamic Implications of Prejudice toward Children from Minority Groups." In Monroe G. Gottsegen and Gloria B. Gottsegen, eds., *Professional School Psychology.* New York: Grune & Stratton, 1960.

Clark, Kenneth B. "The Role of the Social Sciences." *Teachers College Record* (1960): 1.

Clark, Kenneth B. "Creative Discipline." In E. Ginzberg, ed., *Values and Ideas of American Youth.* New York: Columbia University Press, 1961.

Clark, Kenneth B. "Liberalism and the Negro." *Commentary* (American Jewish Committee, New York) (March 1961).

Clark, Kenneth B. "The Negro in the North." In Mathew A. Ahmann, ed., *The New Negro.* Notre Dame, IN: Fides Publishers, 1961.

Clark, Kenneth B. "Policy and Implementation—Problems of Race in the Protestant Episcopal Church." Report of the Advisory Committee on Intergroup Relations, Department of Christian Relations, The National Council, October 9, 1962.

Clark, Kenneth B. "Black Power and Basic Power: An Examination of Black Nationalism, White Withdrawal." *Congress Bi-Weekly,* July 8, 1963.

Clark, Kenneth B. "Emotional Stimulation of Racially Disadvantaged Children." In A.H. Passow, ed., *Education in Depressed Areas.* New York: Teachers College Press, 1963.

Clark, Kenneth B., with L. Plotkin. *The Negro Student at Integrated Colleges.* New York: National Scholarship Service and Fund for Negro Students, 1963.

Clark, Kenneth B. "Clash of Cultures in the Classrooms." In M. Weinberg, ed., *Learning Together: A Book on Integrated Education.* Chicago: Integrated Education Association, 1964.

Clark, Kenneth B. "The Management of the Civil Rights Struggle." In A. Weston, ed., *Freedom Now! The Civil Rights Struggle in America.* New York: Basic Books, 1964.

Clark, Kenneth B. "The Negro in Turmoil." In E. Ginzberg, ed., *The Negro Challenge to the Business Community.* New York: McGraw-Hill, 1964.

Clark, Kenneth B. *Youth in the Ghetto: A Study of the Consequences of Powerlessness and a Blueprint for Change.* New York: Harlem Youth Opportunities Unlimited, Inc., 1964.

Clark, Kenneth B. *Dark Ghetto: Dilemmas of Social Power*. New York: Harper & Row, 1965.

Clark, Kenneth B., "Education: My Way of Life." *Boys' Life* (November 1965): 12.

Clark, Kenneth B. "HARYOU: An Experiment." In J.H. Clarke, ed., *Harlem: A Community in Transition*. New York: Citadel Press, 1965.

Clark, Kenneth B. "Civil Rights Movement: Momentum and Organization." *Daedalus* 95 (1966): 239–267.

Clark, Kenneth B. "Intelligence, the University and Society." *American Scholar* 36 (1966): 23–32.

Clark, Kenneth B. Introduction, "The Civil Rights Movement: Momentum and Organization." In Talcott Parsons and Kenneth B. Clark, eds. *The Negro American*. Boston: Beacon Press, 1966.

Clark, Kenneth B. Introduction, "The Dilemma of Power." In Talcott Parsons and Kenneth B. Clark, eds., *The Negro American*. Boston: Beacon Press, 1966.

Clark, Kenneth B. "The Negro Students at Northern Inter-Racial Colleges: An Overview." *The Black Student* 1 (1966): 1.

Clark, Kenneth B. Report, "The Disadvantaged Poor, Education and Employment," Chamber of Commerce of the United States, Washington, DC, 1966.

Clark, Kenneth B. *The Civil Rights Reader: Basic Documents of the Civil Rights Movement*. New York: Walker, 1967.

Clark, Kenneth B. "Contemporary Educational Emergency in America." *Journal of the Association of Deans and Administrators of Student Affairs* 5 (1967): 111–115.

Clark, Kenneth B. "Explosion in the Ghetto." *Psychology Today* (September 1967): 34–38, 62–64.

Clark, Kenneth B. "Higher Education for Negroes: Challenges and Prospects." *Journal of Negro Education* 36 (1967): 196–203.

Clark, Kenneth B. "Implications of Adlerian Theory for an Understanding of Civil Rights Problems and Actions." *Journal of Individual Psychology* 23 (1967): 181–190.

Clark, Kenneth B. "Sex, Status, and Underemployment of the Negro Male." In Arthur M. Ross and Herbert Hill, eds., *Employment, Race, and Poverty: A Critical Study of the Disadvantaged Status of Negro Workers from 1865 to 1965*. New York: Harcourt, Brace & World, 1967.

Clark, Kenneth B. "American Education Today." In M. Weinberg, ed., *Integrated Education*. Beverly Hills, CA: Glencoe Press, 1968.

Clark, Kenneth B. "Black Power and Basic Power: An Examination of Black Nationalism, White Withdrawal and Negro-Jewish Relationships." *Congress Bi-Weekly* 35 (1968): 6–10.

Clark, Kenneth B. "The Crises: Attitudes and Behavior." In E. Ginzberg, ed., *Business Leadership and the Negro Crisis*. New York: McGraw-Hill, 1968.

Clark, Kenneth B. "The Negro in the Urban Crisis." In K. Gordon, ed., *Agenda for the Nation*. Washington, DC: Brookings Institution, 1968.

Clark, Kenneth B. "No Gimmicks, Please, Whitey." Address at the National Conference on the Effective Utilization by Industry of the Hard-Core Unemployed, Chicago, March 20, 1968.

Clark, Kenneth B. "Where It's At: Civil Rights." *Vogue*, April 1, 1968, 178.

Clark, Kenneth B. "The Wonder Is There Have Been So Few Riots." In S. Endleman, ed., *Violence in the Streets*. Chicago: Quadrangle Books, 1968.

Clark, Kenneth B. "Alternative Public School Systems." In B. Gross and R. Gross, eds., *Radical School Reform*. New York: Simon & Schuster, 1969.

Clark, Kenneth B. "A Charade of Power: Black Students at White Colleges." *Antioch Review* 39 (1969): 145–148.

Clark, Kenneth B. "Efficiency as a Prod to Social Action." *Monthly Labor Review* 92 (1969): 54–56.

Clark, Kenneth B. "Fantasy Barrier." In N.A. Ford and W. Turpin, eds., *Extending Horizons: Selected Readings for Cultural Enrichment*. New York: Random House, 1969.

Clark, Kenneth B. Introduction. In Louis Friedman, ed., *The History-Making Decision That Sparked the Civil Rights Revolution in the United States. Argument: The Complete Oral Argument before the Supreme Court in Brown v. Board of Education of Topeka, 1952–1955*. New York: Chelsea House Publishers, 1969.

Clark, Kenneth B. "Learning Obstacles among Children." In A Roaden, ed., *Problems of School Met in Depressed Urban Centers*. Columbus: Ohio State University Press, 1969.

Clark, Kenneth B. "The Negro Elected Official in the Changing American Scene." *Black Politician: A Journal of Current Political Thought* 1 (1969): 8–12.

Clark, Kenneth B. "The Present Dilemma and Challenges of Negro Elected Officials." New York: Metropolitan Applied Research Center, December 1969.

Clark, Kenneth B. "Q. & A. with Dr. Kenneth B. Clark." *This Week Magazine* (New York), 1969.

Clark, Kenneth B., with Jeanette Hopkins. *A Relevant War Against Poverty: A Study of Commodity Action Programs and Observable Social Change*. New York: Harper & Row, 1969.

Clark, Kenneth B. "Social Conflict and the Problems of Mental Health." *Journal of Religion and Health* 8 (1969): 217–225.

Clark, Kenneth B. "Crisis in Urban Education." Address given at Middlebury College, Middlebury, VT, January 28, 1971.

Clark, Kenneth B. *Racism in American Education: A Dialogue and Agenda for Action*. New York: Harper & Row, 1971.

Clark, Kenneth B. "The Educationally Deprived: The Potential for Change." New York: Metropolitan Applied Research Center, 1972.

Clark, Kenneth B. "A Possible Reality: A Design for the Attainment of High Academic Achievement for the Students of the Public Elementary and Junior High Schools of Washington, D.C." New York: Metropolitan Applied Research Center, 1972.

Clark, Kenneth B. "Why Some Choose Not to Adopt Through Agencies." MARC Monograph no. 1, April 1972.

Clark, Kenneth B. "School Desegregation in the North: The Current Battlefront." New York: Metropolitan Applied Research Center, October 24, 1973.

Clark, Kenneth B. Introduction to "Corporal Punishment and School Suspension: A Case Study." MARC Monograph no. 2, November 1974.

Clark, Kenneth B. *Pathos of Power*. New York: Harper & Row, 1974.

Clark, Kenneth B. "The Costs of Discrimination." *Challenge* (May–June 1977): 33–39.

Clark, Kenneth B. Excerpt of text of Clark introduction of Dr. Martin Luther King on December 21, 1956, to the National Committee for the Rural Schools in New York. In *Tech Talk* (MIT News Office) 25.21 (January 12, 1981): 2.

Clark, Kenneth B. Excerpt from a statement to the U.S. Commission on Civil Rights, March 10, 1981.

Clark, Kenneth B., and John Hope Franklin. *The Nineteen Eighties: Prologues and Prospect*. Washington, DC: Joint Center for Political Studies, 1981.

Clark, Kenneth B. *King, Malcolm, Baldwin: Three Interviews*. Middletown, CT: Wesleyan University Press, 1985.

Clark, Kenneth B. Introduction and design. In *African Roots* by Jerry Silverman. New York: Chelsea House Publishers, 1993.

Clark, Kenneth B. "Racial Progress and Retreat: A Personal Memoir." In Herbert Hill and James E. Jones, Jr., eds., *Race in America: The Struggle for Equality*. Madison: University of Wisconsin Press, 1993, 3–18.

Clark, Kenneth B. "In Pursuit of a Dream Deferred: Linking Housing and Education, Beyond *Brown v. Board of Education*, Housing and Education in the Year 2000." *Minnesota Law Review* 80.4 (April 1996): 745–748.

Clarke, John Henrik. *Malcolm X: The Man and the Times*. New York: Macmillan, 1969.

Commager, Henry Steele. *The Struggle for Racial Equality*. New York: Harper & Row, 1967.

Des Verney Sinnette, Elinor. *Arthur Alfonso Schomburg: Black Bibliophile & Collector, A Biography*. New York and Detroit, MI: New York Public Library and Wayne State University, 1989.

De Tocqueville, Alexis. *Democracy in America*. New York: Harper & Row, 1966.

Dunbar, Leslie W., ed., *Minority Report: What Has Happened to Blacks, Hispanics, American Indians, & Other Minorities in the Eighties*. New York: Pantheon Books, 1984.

Evans, Richard, ed. *The Making of Social Psychology: Discussions with Creative Contributors*. New York: Gardner Press, 1980.

Fairclough, Adam. *Better Day Coming*. New York: Viking Press, 2001.

Franklin, John Hope, and Eleanor Holmes, Norton. Introduction to *Black Initiative and Government Responsibility*. Washington, DC: Committee on Policy for Racial Justice, 1987.

Frazier, Franklin E. *Black Bourgeoisie: The Rise of the New Middle Class in the U.S.* New York: Free Press, 1957.

Friedman, Louis, ed. *The Civil Rights Reader: Basic Documents of the Civil Rights Movement*. Introduction by Kenneth B. Clark. New York: Walker and Company, 1967.

Gates, Henry Louis, Jr. *What's in a Name? Some Meanings of Blackness*. New York: Oxford University Press, 1992.

"Ghetto Education: New Directions." *Harvard Educational Review* (1973): 117–118.

Ginzberg, Eli, ed. *Values and Ideals of American Youth.* New York: Columbia University Press, 1961.

Ginzberg, Eli, ed. *Business Leadership and the Negro Crisis.* New York: McGraw-Hill, 1968.

Goodman, Mary Ellen. *Race Awareness in Young Children.* Introduction by Kenneth B. Clark. London: Collier Books, 1964.

Goodman, Walter C. *Junior History of the American Negro.* Vol. 2: *The Civil War and the Civil Rights War.* New York: Fleet Press, 1970.

Gordon, Elinor, ed. *Racism and American Education: A Dialogue and Agenda for Action.* New York: Harper & Row, 1970.

Gottehrer, Barry, and the Staff of the *New York Herald-Tribune. New York City in Crisis.* New York: WCC Books/Pocketbooks, Inc., and David McKay and Company, 1965.

Gottsegen, Monroe G., and Gloria B. Gottsegen. "The Psychological Implications of Prejudice toward Children from Minority Groups." In Monroe G. Gottsegen and Gloria B. Gottsegen, eds., *Professional School Psychology.* New York: Grune & Stratton, 1960.

Gross, Beatrice, and Ronald Gross, eds. *Radical School Reform.* New York: Simon & Schuster, 1969.

Hacker, Andrew. *Two Nations, Black and White, Separate, Hostile, Unequal.* New York: Scribner's, 1993.

Harvard Educational Review (1973).

Hentoff, Nat. *The Nat Hentoff Reader.* Cambridge, MA: DaCapo Press, Perseus Books Group, 2001.

Hickey, Neil, and Ed Edwin. *Adam Clayton Powell and the Politics of Race.* New York: Fleet Publishing Corporation, 1965.

Hill, Herbert. *Black Labor and the American Legal System.* Madison: University of Wisconsin Press, 1983.

Hill, Herbert, and James E. Jones, Jr., eds. *Race in America: The Struggle for Equality.* Madison: University of Wisconsin Press, 1993.

Hopson, Darlene Powell, and Derek S. Hopson. *Different and Wonderful: Raising Black Children in a Race-Conscious Society.* New York: Prentice-Hall, 1990.

Jordan, Vernon E., Jr., with Annette Gordon-Reed. *Vernon Can Read!* New York: Public Affairs of Perseus Books Group, 2001.

Keppel, Ben. *The Work of Democracy: Ralph Bunche, Kenneth B. Clark, Lorraine Hansberry and the Cultural Politics of Race.* Cambridge, MA: Harvard University Press, 1995.

King, Anita, comp. and ed. *Quotations in Black.* Westport, CT: Greenwood Press, 1997.

Kluger, Richard. *Simple Justice: The History of* Brown v. Board of Education *and Black America's Struggle for Equality.* New York: Alfred A. Knopf, 1976.

Lasch, Christopher. *The Culture of Narcissism: American Life in an Age of Diminishing Expectations.* New York: W.W. Norton, 1978.

Lewis, Anthony, and *New York Times. Portrait of a Decade: The Second American Revolution.* New York: Random House, 1953.

The Library Journal 9.12 (June 15, 1966): 3085.

Lomax, Louis E. *The Negro Revolt*. New York: Harper & Row, 1971.

Margolis, John D. *The Campus in the Modern World*. New York: Macmillan, 1969.

Myrdal, Gunnar. *An American Dilemma*. New York: Harper & Row, 1944.

Negro Heritage Library: A Martin Luther King Treasury. New York: Educational Heritage, Inc., and Harper & Row, 1964.

"The Negro Student in Northern Inter-Racial Colleges." *The Black Student*, journal of the Student Afro-American Society of Columbia University (Spring 1966): 7.

Orfield, Gary, with Erika Frankenberg and Chungmei Lee. "A Multiracial Society with Segregated Schools: Are We Losing the Dream?" Study by the Civil Rights Project at Harvard University, 2003.

Papers of the First Eight Chief Executives of the University of Chicago from 1891–1975. Chicago: University of Chicago Press, 1976.

Passow, Harry, ed. *Education in Depressed Areas*. New York: Teachers College Press, 1963.

Patterson, James T. *Brown v. Board of Education, a Civil Rights Milestone and Its Troubled Legacy*. New York: Oxford University Press, 2001.

Plimpton, George, ed. *American Journey: The Times of Robert F. Kennedy*. New York: Harcourt Brace, 1970.

Polsgrove, Carol. *Divided Minds: Intellectuals and the Civil Rights Movement*. New York: W.W. Norton, 2001.

"A Psychologist Looks at Discrimination Patterns." *mba Magazine* 6.4 (January 1972): 33–34.

Report of the National Advisory Commission on Civil Disorders. Washington, DC: GPO, 1968.

Rose, Peter I., ed. *The Study of Society: An Integrated Anthology*. New York: Random House, 1967.

Ross, Arthur M., and Herbert Hill, eds. *Employment, Race, and Poverty: A Critical Study of the Disadvantaged Status of Negro Workers from 1865 to 1965*. New York: Harcourt, Brace & World, 1967.

Saturday Review (1969), 963.

Schlesinger, Arthur M., Jr. *A Thousand Days: John F. Kennedy in the White House*. Boston: Houghton Mifflin, 1965.

Sowell, Thomas. *The Economics and Politics of Race: An International Perspective*. New York: Quill, 1983.

Terkel, Studs. *RACE: How Blacks & Whites Think & Feel about the American Obsession*. New York: The New Press, 1992.

Thomas, Alexander, and Samuel Sillen. *Racism and Psychiatry*. New York: Brunner/Mazel, 1972.

Wade, Richard. *Negroes in American Life*. New York: Houghton Mifflin, 1970.

Washington, Joseph R., Jr., ed. *The Declining Significance of Race? A Dialogue among Black and White Social Scientists*. New York: Pantheon Books, 1979.

Westin, Alan F., ed. *Freedom Now! The Civil Rights Struggle in America*. New York: Basic Books, 1964.

"What Negroes Think about Jews." *Anti-Defamation League Bulletin* (New York) (December 1957): 15–16.

Wilkinson, J. Harvie III. *From Brown to Bakke: The Supreme Court and School Integration, 1954–1978.* London: Oxford University Press, 1979.

Wilson, William Julius. *The Declining Significance of Race: Blacks and Changing Institutions.* Chicago: University of Chicago Press, 1978.

Worthy, William. *The Rape of Our Neighborhoods.* New York: William Morrow, 1976.

Index

About the Editor and Contributors

WOODY KLEIN, an award-winning author and journalist, has written about race relations since he was a newspaper reporter in the 1960s. He is the author of three previous books: *Let in the Sun* (1964), *Lindsay's Promise* (1970), and *Westport, Connecticut: The Story of a New England Town's Rise to Prominence*, with foreword by Joanne Woodward, sponsored by the Westport Historical Society (2000). He has contributed numerous articles to magazines and newspapers, including the *New York Times*. In addition, he served as editor of *Think* magazine, IBM's employee publication, and as editor of the *Westport News* in Westport, CT. He has been an adjunct professor of journalism at New York University, Fairfield University, and Iona College, and taught a course in civil rights and the media at The New School University.

CLIFFORD L. ALEXANDER, JR., is president of Alexander & Associates, Inc., a private consulting firm that provides advice on workforce inclusiveness for corporate directors and executives. He was Secretary of the Army from 1977 to 1981 and served as chairman of the federal Equal Employment Opportunities Commission from 1967 to 1969, while also working as special consultant on civil rights for President Lyndon Johnson. In 1963, President John Kennedy named him Foreign Affairs Officer of the National Security Council. From 1959 to 1961, he served as assistant district attorney for New York County, then as executive director of Harlem Youth Opportunities Unlimited (HARYOU). He earned a B.A. degree cum laude from Harvard University in 1955 and an L.L.B. degree from Yale University Law School in 1958.

BILL BRADLEY, a former U.S. senator (1979–1997), is a Democrat who is known for his interest in race relations. Prior to his Senate career, he was a Visiting Professor at Stanford University, the University of Notre Dame, and the University of Maryland, (1997–1998); a professional basketball player with the New York Knickerbockers (1967–1977); and a member of the Air Force Reserve (1967–1978). He was a Rhodes Scholar at Oxford University (1965–1968) and earned a B.A. with Honors (American history) at Princeton University (1965). In 2000, he ran unsuccessfully for the Democratic nomination for president. His books include *Life on the Run* (1976), *Time Present, Time Past: A Memoir* (1996), *Values of the Game* (1998), and *The Journey from Here* (2000).

CALVIN O. BUTTS III, pastor of the Abyssinian Baptist Church in Harlem, NY, is also president of the State University of New York College, Old Westbury, Long Island. He has a B.A. in philosophy from Morehouse College, a Master of Divinity Degree in Church History from Union Theological Seminary, and a Doctor of Ministry in Church and Public Policy from Drew University. In 1972 Butts became associated with the church he now serves. He succeeded Adam Clayton Powell and Dr. Samuel D. Proctor as minister.

ROBERT L. CARTER has been a U.S. District Court judge for the Southern District of New York since 1972. He served as counsel for the NAACP from 1944 to 1968 and won twenty-two cases in the U.S. Supreme Court, including *Brown v. Board of Education*. He was responsible for the pivotal involvement of social scientists who provided evidence on segregation's devastating effects on the psyches of black children. He is a graduate of Lincoln University (A.B., magna cum laude) and received his law degree from the Howard University Law School (magna cum laude). Among his honors, in 1995 he was awarded the Federal Bar Council's Emory Bucknor Medal for Outstanding Public Service.

HILTON B. CLARK, a graduate of Columbia College, where he majored in political science, was elected to serve on the New York City Council from 1986 to 1990. He has worked with his father, Kenneth B. Clark, for three decades. He attended the Kent School in Connecticut and the Columbia Law School. He grew up in Hastings-on-Hudson, New York, where his father still resides.

JOHNNETTA B. COLE, president of Bennett College in Greensboro, North Carolina, is also president emerita of Spelman College and professor emerita of Emory University. She received her undergraduate degree from Oberlin College and earned a master's and Ph.D. in anthropology from Northwestern University. Her first teaching position was at Washington

State University; then she went to the University of Massachusetts at Amherst as Professor of Anthropology and Afro-American Studies. In 1984 she joined the faculty of Hunter College as Professor of Anthropology and Director of the Latin American and Caribbean Studies Program, while serving on the graduate faculty of the City University of New York. Her most recent book, *Conversations*, was published in 1993. Dr. Cole returned to teaching at Emory University in 1998 as Presidential Distinguished Professor of Anthropology, Women's Studies, and African-American Studies.

MARIAN WRIGHT EDELMAN is founder and president of the Children's Defense Fund. A graduate of Spelman College and Yale Law School, she was the first black woman admitted to the Mississippi bar, and she directed the NAACP Legal Defense and Educational Fund office in Jackson. She has received many awards, including the Albert Schweitzer Humanitarian Prize; the Presidential Medal of Freedom, the nation's highest civilian award; and the Robert F. Kennedy Lifetime Achievement Award for her writings, which include six books: *Families in Peril: An Agenda for Social Change* (1987), *The Measure of Our Success: A Letter to My Children and Yours* (1993), *Guide My Feet: Meditations and Prayers on Loving and Working for Children* (1995), a children's book titled *Stand for Children* (1996), and most recently, *Lanterns: A Memoir of Mentors* (1999) and *I'm Your Child, God: Prayers for Our Children* (2002).

PAUL FINKELMAN is Chapman Distinguished Professor of Law at the University of Tulsa College of Law. Prior to joining the College of Law faculty in 1999, Finkelman was the John F. Seiberling Professor of Law at the University of Akron Law School. In addition, he previously taught at Cleveland Marshall School of Law, Hamline Law School, the University of Miami, Chicago-Kent College of Law, Brooklyn College, and the University of Texas at Austin. Finkelman is the author or editor of numerous articles and books, including *Baseball and the American Legal Mind* (1995), *American Legal History: Cases and Materials* (1996), *Slavery and the Founders: Race and Liberty in the Age of Jefferson* (2001), *A March of Liberty: A Constitutional History of the United States* (2002), and *Landmark Decisions of the United States Supreme Court*, with Melvin I. Urovsky (2003). He was a Fellow in Law and the Humanities at Harvard Law School and received his Ph.D. and M.A. from the University of Chicago. Finkelman teaches constructional law and American legal history.

JOHN HOPE FRANKLIN, one of America's most distinguished historians, is James B. Duke Professor of History Emeritus and former Professor of Legal History at Duke University's Law School. In 1997, he was appointed by President Bill Clinton as chairman of the Advisory Board of "The President's Initiative on Race," which published a study, *One America in the*

21st Century, in 1998. Franklin is a graduate of Fisk University, receiving his M.A. and Ph.D. degrees in history from Harvard University. He taught at many institutions including Fisk, North Carolina Central and Howard Universities, and at Brooklyn College. He is perhaps best known for his study *From Slavery to Freedom: A History of African-Americans* (1947). Franklin's other works include *The Militant South 1800–1860* (1956), *Reconstruction after the Civil War* (1961), *The Emancipation Proclamation* (1963), *A Southern Odyssey: Travelers in the Antebellum North* (1976), *Racial Equality in America* (1976), *George Washington Williams: A Biography* (1985), *Race and History: Selected Essays 1935–1988* (1990), *The Color Line: Legacy for the 21st Century* (1993), and *Runaway Slaves: Rebels on the Plantation* (1999), coauthored with former student Loren Schweninger. In November 2001, he was honored with The National Conference for Community Justice's "Charles Evans Hughes Award." In 2000, Franklin was the recipient of the Joint Center for Political and Economic Studies' Racial Reconciliation Award. He also received the Presidential Medal of Freedom Award (1995) and the NAACP Spingarn Medal (1995). In 2000, Duke University celebrated the opening of the John Hope Franklin Center for Interdisciplinary and International Studies.

HENRY LOUIS GATES, JR., graduated summa cum laude with a degree in history from Yale University in 1973. He was given tenure at Cornell University at the age of thirty-three, earned his master's and doctorate in English literature from Clare College at Cambridge University, and was the first African American to receive a Ph.D. from Cambridge. He taught English literature and Afro-American studies at Yale and Cornell before joining Harvard in 1991. Gates now serves as the W.E.B. Du Bois Professor of the Humanities at Harvard and director of the W.E.B. Du Bois Institute for Afro-American Research. Among his awards is the 1998 National Humanities Medal conferred by President Bill Clinton. In 1997, he was voted one of *Time* magazine's "25 Most Influential Americans." He has authored many books including *Figures in Black: Words, Signs and the "Racial" Self* (1987), *The Signifying Monkey: Towards a Theory of Afro-American Literary Criticism* (1988), *Loose Canons: Notes on the Culture Wars* (1992), *Colored People: A Memoir* (1994), *Speaking of Race, Speaking of Sex: Hate Speech, Civil Rights, and Civil Liberties* (1995), *The Future of the Race* (with Cornel West, 1996), *Thirteen Ways of Looking at a Black Man* (1997), and *Wonders of the African World* (1999).

HERBERT HILL served as labor director of the National Association for the Advancement of Colored People (NAACP). He attended New York University and joined the NAACP in 1948, leading the movement to pressure the AFL-CIO to eliminate discrimination in labor unions and the mass media. His articles have appeared in *Commentary, The New Leader, Dis-*

sent, and other publications. He has also authored many books, including *Employment, Race, and Poverty: A Critical Study of the Disadvantaged Status of Negro Workers from 1865 to 1965* (1971), which he edited with Arthur M. Ross. It includes a chapter by Dr. Kenneth B. Clark. Hill is currently Evju-Bascom Professor Emeritus of African-American Studies and Professor of Industrial Relations at the University of Wisconsin, Madison.

ROY INNIS attended the City College of New York, joined the Congress of Racial Equality (CORE) Harlem chapter in 1963, and led CORE's fight for an independent Police Review Board to address cases of police brutality. In 1965, he was elected chairman of Harlem CORE. Innis was appointed the first resident fellow at the Metropolitan Applied Research Center (MARC), headed by Dr. Kenneth Clark. In the summer of 1967, he was elected second national vice chairman of CORE. In the 1993 New York City mayoral primary, Innis unsuccessfully challenged incumbent David Dinkins.

VERNON E. JORDAN, JR., former president and chief executive officer of the National Urban League, is a senior managing director of Lazard Frères & Co. LLC in New York. Prior to joining Lazard, Mr. Jordan was a senior executive partner with the law firm of Akin, Gump, Strauss, Hauer & Feld, L.L.P., where he remains of counsel. He has also served as executive director of the United Negro College Fund, Inc.; director of the Voter Education Project of the Southern Regional Council; attorney-consultant, U.S. Office of Economic Opportunity; assistant to the executive director of the Southern Regional Council; Georgia field director of the NAACP; and an attorney in private practice in Arkansas and Georgia. Jordan has served on a number of panels and boards for the White House, and in 1991, he was chairman of the Clinton Presidential Transition Team and remained a close friend and adviser during Clinton's two terms in office. Jordan's book *Vernon Can Read!*, an autobiography, was published in 2001.

NICHOLAS deB. KATZENBACH, best known to the public for his confrontation of Alabama Governor George Wallace in the "school house door" in 1963, served first as deputy U.S. attorney general under President John F. Kennedy, then as U.S. attorney general (1964–1966), and then as undersecretary of state under President Lyndon B. Johnson. From then until retirement he served as general counsel to IBM. Mr. Katzenbach served in the U.S. Air Force from 1941 to 1945. He received a B.A. from Princeton University in 1945 and an L.L.B. from Yale in 1947, followed by a Rhodes scholarship in Oxford, England. He practiced law in New Jersey and New York and taught law first at Yale Law School and then at the University of Chicago Law School.

DAVID LEVERING LEWIS is Martin Luther King Jr. and University Professor of History of Rutgers University. He holds a B.A. from Fisk University, an M.A. from Columbia University, and a Ph.D. from the London School of Economics. He is author of *King: A Biography* (1970, 1979), *Prisoners of Honor: The Dreyfus Affair* (1973, 1994), *District of Columbia: A Bicentennial History* (1976), *When Harlem Was in Vogue* (1980, 1994); *The Race to Fashoda: European Colonialism and African Resistance in the Scramble for Africa* (1987, 1994), *W.E.B. Du Bois: Biography of a Race, 1868–1919* (1993), *The Portable Harlem Renaissance Reader* (1994), *W.E.B. Du Bois: A Reader* (1995), and *W.E.B. Du Bois: The Fight for Equality and the American Century, 1919–1963* (2000).

JOHN LEWIS (D–GA), the recipient of the "Profiles in Courage Award" from the John F. Kennedy Library in 2001, was first elected to Congress in 1986 from Georgia's 5th District. Previously, he served as chairman of the Student Nonviolent Coordinating Committee (SNCC). Lewis began his career as a civil rights activist in 1961, participating in the Freedom Rides and challenging segregation at interstate bus terminals across the South. He helped plan the 1963 March on Washington led by the Rev. Dr. Martin Luther King, Jr., and was a leader in the protest march from Selma to Montgomery, Alabama, in 1965. He is a chief Democratic whip in Congress and also serves on the Congressional Black Caucus. Together with writer Michael D'Orso, Lewis authored *Walking with the Wind: A Memoir of the Movement* (1998). He earned a B.A. in religion and philosophy from Fisk University; and he is a graduate of the American Baptist Theological Seminary in Nashville, Tennessee.

BURKE MARSHALL, who served as assistant attorney general for civil rights under Attorney General Robert F. Kennedy, played a key role in ensuring the constitutional grounding of the Kennedy administration's civil rights bill, which was enacted in 1964. As assistant attorney general, he directed the federal government's action against voting discrimination and served as a troubleshooter in racial disturbances in Mississippi, Alabama, and other areas of the South. In 1965, Marshall returned to private law practice and was named that year as vice president and general counsel of International Business Machines (IBM) Corporation. After his retirement from IBM, he continued his law practice and taught at Yale Law School. He received his B.A. degree from Yale University in 1943 and graduated from Yale Law School in 1951. During World War II he served as an officer in the Intelligence Corps. Mr. Marshall died in 2003.

KWEISI MFUME (pronounced Kwah-EE-see Oom-FOO-may), whose West African name means "conquering son of kings," won a seat on the Baltimore City Council in 1979 and was elected to the congressional seat representing Maryland's 7th Congressional District in 1986. Mfume served on the Banking and Financial Services Committee and held the ranking seat on the General Oversight and Investigations Subcommittee. He also served as a member of the Committee on Education and as a senior member of the Small Business Committee. Mfume also served as chairman of the Congressional Black Caucus. In 1996, Mfume became president and chief executive officer of the National Association for the Advancement of Colored People (NAACP). His autobiography is titled *No Free Ride* (1996). Mfume graduated magna cum laude from Morgan State University. In 1984, he earned a master's degree in liberal arts, with a concentration in international studies, from Johns Hopkins University.

GUNNAR MYRDAL, the Nobel Prize–winning Swedish economist and lawyer, is best known for his seminal work on race relations in the United States, *An American Dilemma: The Negro Problem and Modern Democracy*, which was commissioned by the Carnegie Corporation of New York in 1938 and published in 1944. Dr. Kenneth B. Clark was the research psychologist on his study team. From 1945 to 1947, he was Sweden's minister of commerce, then served as executive secretary of the United Nations Economic Commission for Europe. In 1957, Myrdal left this post to direct a comprehensive study of economic trends and policies in South Asian countries for the Twentieth Century Fund. From 1961, he was in Sweden as professor of international economics at Stockholm University. During the academic year 1973–1974, he was visiting Research Fellow at the Center for the Study of Democratic Institutions in Santa Barbara, California, and during 1974–1975, he served as Distinguished Visiting Professor at New York University. He died in 1987 at the age of eighty-nine.

ELEANOR HOLMES NORTON, a native of Washington, DC, has represented the District in the House of Representatives since 1990. She served as executive assistant to New York Mayor John V. Lindsay, chair of the New York City Commission on Human Rights, and was appointed by President Jimmy Carter as the first woman to chair the federal Equal Employment Opportunity Commission from 1977 to 1981. She has also been a professor of law at George Washington University and a Visiting Fellow at the John F. Kennedy School of Government and served on the board of the Martin Luther King, Jr., Center for Social Change and Environmental Law Institute. Norton has served as the Democratic chair of the Women's Caucus. Ms. Norton is a tenured professor of law at Georgetown University. After receiving her B.A. from Antioch College in Ohio, she simultaneously earned her law degree as well as a master's degree in American Studies from Yale Law School and was awarded the Citation of Merit as an Outstanding Alumna of that school.

GARY ORFIELD is Professor of Education and Social Policy at the Harvard Graduate School of Education. He is also the director of the Harvard Project on School Desegregation and codirector of the Harvard Civil Rights Project. Orfield has been a court-appointed expert in school desegregation cases in a number of large cities and has testified in civil rights suits by the U.S. Department of Justice and civil rights, legal services, and educational organizations. In 1997, Orfield was awarded the American Political Science Association's Charles Merriam Award for his "contribution to the art of government through the application of social science research." He holds a Ph.D. from the University of Chicago. His published works include *Dismantling Desegregation: The Quiet Repeal of Brown v. Board of Education* (with S. Eaton, 1996), *Chilling Admissions: The Affirmative Action Crisis and the Search for Alternatives* (with E. Miller, 1998), *Religion, Race and Justice in a Changing America* (with H. Lebowitz, 1999), *Diversity Challenged: Evidence on the Impact of Affirmative Action* (with M. Kurlaender, 2001), and *Raising Standards or Raising Barriers* (with M. Kornhaber, 2001).

CLARENCE PAGE is a two-time Pulitzer Prize–winning syndicated columnist and editorial board member of the *Chicago Tribune* based in Washington, DC. He became a foreign correspondent in Africa in 1976, an assistant city editor, and an investigative task force reporter in 1979. In 1980, he joined WBBM-TV, a CBS-owned station, as director of the Community Affairs Department. At various times, he was a documentary producer, reporter, and planning editor. He returned to the *Tribune* in 1984. In 1989, his column won that year's Pulitzer Prize for Commentary. He has been published in *Chicago* magazine, the *Chicago Reader*, *Washington Monthly*, *New Republic*, the *Wall Street Journal*, *New York Newsday*, and *Emerge*. His first book, *Showing My Color: Impolite Essays on Race and Identity*, was published in 1996. He is a regular contributor of essays to *The NewsHour* with Jim Lehrer, the Public Broadcasting Station, and a host of documentaries on the Public Broadcasting System. He is also a regular panelist on Black Entertainment Television's weekly *Lead Story* program and an occasional commentator on National Public Radio's *Weekend Edition Sunday*. Page graduated in 1965 from Middletown High School in Ohio, and he earned a bachelor of science degree in journalism in 1969 from Ohio University.

LAWRENCE PLOTKIN, a close colleague of Dr. Clark's who has co-authored several important articles with him, is Professor Emeritus in the Department of Psychology, City College of New York.

ALVIN F. POUSSAINT, M.D., is a clinical professor of psychiatry at the Harvard Medical School, where he has taught since 1969. He is on the staff at Boston's Children's Hospital and is the director of the Media Center for Children at the Judge Baker Children's Center in Boston. Prior to joining the Harvard faculty, he was director of the psychiatric program from 1967 to 1969 in a low-income housing project at the Tufts University Medical School. Poussaint received a bachelor's degree in 1956 from Columbia University, a medical degree in 1960 from Cornell University, and a master's of science degree in 1964 from the University of California, Los Angeles (UCLA). He then served as chief resident in psychiatry from 1964 to 1965 at UCLA's Neuropsychiatric Institute. From 1965 to 1967 he was southern field director of the Medical Committee for Human Rights in Jackson, Mississippi. Poussaint is the author of *Why Blacks Kill Blacks* (1972) and *Black Children: Coping in a Racist Society* (1987). He also has coauthored two books with psychiatrist James Comer—*Black Child Care: How to Bring Up a Healthy Black Child in America* (1976) and *Raising Black Children* (1992).

HUGH PRICE served as president of the National Urban League from 1994 to 2003. He launched the Campaign for African-American Achievement, started the "Achievement Matters" public service campaign, and revived *Opportunity*, the publication of the National Urban League. Before that, Price was a senior officer at the Rockefeller Foundation, where he managed domestic initiatives in education for at-risk youth. He began his career as a neighborhood attorney in New Haven after he graduated from Yale Law School. Price also worked at an urban affairs consulting firm and as human resources administrator for the City of New Haven. Price then changed career paths and moved into journalism, writing editorials for the *New York Times* in the late 1970s and later for WNET/Thirteen, America's largest public television station.

A. PHILIP RANDOLPH attended City College at night and, in 1925, founded the Brotherhood of Sleeping Car Porters. As president, Randolph organized black workers and, at a time when half the affiliates of the American Federation of Labor (AFL) barred blacks from membership, took his union into the AFL. The brotherhood won its first major contract with the Pullman Company in 1937. Opposed to federal hiring practices, he warned President Franklin D. Roosevelt that he would lead thousands of blacks in a protest march on Washington, DC. Roosevelt responded on June 25, 1941, with an Executive Order barring discrimination in defense industries and federal bureaus and creating the Fair Employment Practices Committee. After World War II, Randolph founded the League for Nonviolent Civil Disobedience Against Military Segregation, resulting in the issue by President Harry S. Truman on July 26, 1948, of an Executive Order banning segregation in the armed forces. When the AFL merged with the Congress of Industrial Organizations (CIO) in 1955, Randolph became a vice president. In 1963, he served as director of the August 28 March on Washington. He resigned as president from the Brotherhood of Sleeping Car Porters in 1968 and retired from public life. He died on May 16, 1979.

CHARLES B. RANGEL (D–NY) has been the representative from the 15th Congressional District since 1970, is the Ranking Member of the Committee on Ways and Means, Deputy Democratic Whip in the House of Representatives, and chairman of the Democratic Congressional Campaign Committee. Rangel is a member of the Trade Subcommittee of the Committee on Ways and Means, which has jurisdiction over all international trade agreements. Rangel is the principal author of the $5 billion Federal Empowerment Zone demonstration project to revitalize urban neighborhoods throughout America. He is a founding member and former chairman of the Congressional Black Caucus; he was also chairman of the New York State Council of Black Elected Democrats. Rangel served in the U.S. Army in Korea in 1948–1952, and was awarded the Purple Heart and Bronze Star. A graduate of New York University and St. John's University School of Law, Rangel has spent his career in public service, first as an assistant U.S. attorney for the Southern District of New York and later in the New York State Assembly.

PAUL ROBESON, JR., son of the late singer, actor, scholar, and human rights advocate, is a freelance journalist, translator, and lecturer on American and Russian history. He served as a personal aide to his father for over twenty years and has been a civil rights activist since the 1940s. He is the owner and archivist of the Paul Robeson and Eslanda Robeson Collection.

NADINE STROSSEN, Professor of Law at New York Law School, has written, lectured, and practiced extensively in the areas of constitutional law, civil liberties, and international human rights. Since 1991, she has served as president of the American Civil Liberties Union, the first woman to head the nation's largest civil liberties organization. *The National Law Journal* has twice named Strossen one of "The 100 Most Influential Lawyers in America." She graduated Phi Beta Kappa from Harvard College and magna cum laude from the Harvard Law School, and was editor of the *Harvard Law Review*. She is the author of *Defending Pornography: Free Speech, Sex, and the Fight for Women's Rights* (1995).

FRANKLIN A. THOMAS, born in the Bedford-Stuyvesant section of Brooklyn in 1934, graduated from Columbia University in 1956. In 1960, he received his law degree from Columbia University's Law School and worked as a legal adviser to the Federal Housing and Home Finance Agency. In 1964 he was appointed assistant district attorney for the Southern District of New York, then deputy police commissioner of New York in charge of legal matters. In 1967, he was named by Attorney General Robert F. Kennedy to be chief executive officer of the experimental Bedford-Stuyvesant Restoration Corporation. In his ten years at the helm, the corporation rejuvenated the community. In 1977 Thomas was named a trustee of the Ford Foundation, resumed his law practice, and served as president of the John Hay Whitney Foundation; when McGeorge Bundy, a former national security adviser to Presidents John Kennedy and Lyndon Johnson, retired from his post as head of the Ford Foundation, Thomas was named to succeed him. In 1979, Thomas—who had visited South Africa with Vernon E. Jordan, Jr.—became chairman of the eleven-member Study Commission on United States Policy toward Southern Africa. It urged the United States to eliminate apartheid. In 1996, he left the Ford Foundation and resumed his law practice and is serving on the boards of several international corporations and practicing law in New York City.

CORNEL WEST, one of America's most prominent black intellectuals, is the Class of 1943 University Professor of Religion at Princeton University. Prior to his appointment at Princeton, he was the Alphonse Fletcher, Jr., University Professor at Harvard University from 1994 to 2002, teaching Afro-American Studies and Philosophy of Religion. He received his A.B. magna cum laude in three years from Harvard University and his M.A. and Ph.D. from Princeton University. He taught at Yale, Union Theological Seminary, and Princeton University, where he was Chair of the Department of Afro-American Studies. His first scholarly book was *Prophesy Deliverance! An Afro-American Revolutionary Christianity* (1982). Among his other twelve books are *Beyond Eurocentrism and Multiculturalism* (1993), *Keeping Faith* (1993), *Race Matters* (1993), and *Jews and Blacks: Let the Healing Begin* (1995).

ROGER WILKINS, journalist, educator, and lawyer, is Clarence J. Robinson Professor of History and American Culture at George Mason University. Wilkins attended the University of Michigan, receiving his B.A. in 1953 and his J.D. in 1956. During the Johnson administration, Wilkins served as assistant attorney general. He later served as an officer of the Ford Foundation before making the transition, in 1972, to journalism as a member of the editorial staff of the *Washington Post*. His editorials on the Watergate scandal won him a Pulitzer Prize in 1973. He then moved to the *New York Times*, where he served as the first African American on its editorial board as well as a columnist. Subsequently, Wilkins worked for the Institute for Policy Studies, and appeared on National Public Radio and CBS Radio. He is the author of several books including *A Man's Life* (1982), *Quiet Riots* (1988) with Fred Harris, and most recently, *Jefferson's Pillow: The Founding Fathers and the Dilemma of Black Patriotism* (2001).

In addition, Wilkins is the publisher of the NAACP's journal *Crisis*, a title that his uncle, Roy Wilkins, head of the NAACP, once held.

GREGORY H. WILLIAMS, president of the City College of New York, holds a doctorate in political science and a law degree and has held senior administrative and academic positions at the Ohio State University, the University of Iowa, and the George Washington University. Williams served as dean of the College of Law, the Ohio State University, from 1993 to 2001. In 1999 he was elected president of the Association of American Law Schools and selected "Dean of the Year" by the National Association of Public Interest Law. Williams graduated from Ball State University in 1966. He earned a master's degree in government and politics from the University of Maryland and a master's degree, a law degree, and a doctorate in political science from George Washington University. Williams served as assistant director of the Division of Experimental Programs of the George Washington University. Williams spent sixteen years at the University of Iowa and served as associate vice president for Academic Affairs. In 1995, Williams authored *Life on the Color Line: The True Story of a White Boy Who Discovered He Was Black*, an autobiography.